Praise for *Teaching Digital Natives: Partnering for Real Learning*

By Marc Prensky

For years, Marc Prensky analyzed and came to understand digital natives (our kids) and digital immigrants (our teachers/educational system). Now he assimilates teaching, learning, and technology into a brilliant how-to for 21st-century teachers and students—a model of what he calls a "partnering pedagogy." *Teaching Digital Natives* proposes that educators focus on verbs (essential skills) and nouns (tools to learn skills). Teachers own the verbs; students own the nouns. Holy cow—it's content agnostic (all content fits) and metacognitive (help kids *think* about how they are learning)! This book will set the educational preparation world on its heels with a compelling argument for positive change.

—**Lawrence L. Smith, PhD**
Professor of Elementary Education, Ball State University

Great book—really fabulous! What sets Marc Prensky's new book uniquely apart from just about any educational book I have read in the past few years is his consistent focus on students and learning, not just technology. This book is a must-read for any educator who wants to effectively work with the digital generation because it is so practical and filled with numerous fantastic and easy-to-implement ideas designed to engage students in 21st-century learning environments. Bravo—this is the book that I would have liked to have written.

—**Ian Jukes**
Author, Speaker, Writer, Consultant, 21st Century Fluency Group

Marc's understanding of how our school-age digital natives learn underpins his prescient "pedagogy of partnering." As always, he looks to the learner as the first consideration in the educational equation. The insightful advice and gentle guidance Marc provides classroom teachers in this book will directly assist them in moving powerful digital tools into the right hands: their students! Marc's understanding that the pedagogy of partnering is built on a relationship of colearning is fundamental to the 21st-century classroom. This book looks to the future with an urgent spirit of possibility and promise!

—**David Engle**
North Platte Public School District, North Platte, NE

Prensky offers us real hope for a school-based Digital Enlightenment that will transform teachers and teaching. The book is a must-read for anyone interested in school reform and 21st-century learning.

—**James Paul Gee, PhD**
Fulton Presidential Professor of Literacy Studies
Division of Curriculum and Instruction, Arizona State University

Loving the screening copy of Prensky's new book. So many delicious nuggets. I'll be sharing some and buying lots of copies for NYC educators.

—**Lisa Nielsen**
Educator, Speaker, Author, "The Innovative Educator Blog"

Prensky's introduction of the partnering concept for teaching and learning is brilliant in its simplicity. Crossing the paradigm from telling to a more student-centered approach is difficult absent a simple but powerful new model. Prensky has provided that model, with partnering as the common thread. And the real power here is that he has carefully defined and redefined roles of teachers, learners, parents, etc.—not just as prose, but also with concrete examples and practical hints. I found myself reading toward each Practical Tips box with expectation and excitement that *finally* someone has written a book for teachers that goes beyond pedagogy and philosophy, and gives teachers something they can use on Monday morning!

—**Sandy Fivecoat**
Founder and CEO, We Are Teachers

Loved loved loved it! I've now read it through twice, just to be as thorough as possible, and I wanted to see how much I would retain, it being such an easy read and all. I highly enjoyed it and look forward to directing my staff development training now toward the verbs rather than the nouns.

—**Amber Teamann**
Title I Technology Facilitator,
Garland Independent School District, Garland, TX

Now is the time to rethink schools. Now is the time not to teach as we were taught. Today's world, today's schools, today's students are not what they were before 1992. Every industry has embraced technology except education. Now is the time to change education before it is too late for America. Marc Prensky has always been aware of this, as his previous books have shown. *Teaching Digital Natives* is a must-read book for those of us who use technology, for those needing more details about why we must use technology in our teaching, and for all teachers of teachers to use as a crucial text in their classes. It is more than a paradox that schools in America are so far behind in the use of technology in our schools; it borders on irresponsible. Today's students aren't just consumers of information, they are producers, and Prensky provides evidence of this and methods to continue to foster this new kind of pedagogy in the 21st century.

—**Ted Nellen**
New York City Teacher of the Year
Edward A. Reynolds West Side High School, New York, NY

This book is an outstanding guide to new learning. It explores, explains, helps us evaluate, and gives us ways to show the exchanges and entries into new practices that will excite digital natives. I very much appreciate the job that Marc has done. Being a visionary is one thing; translating the practice of those who get it into real words, action items, and ways to transform so that others can seize the skills is another thing entirely. Marc defines and gives us ideational scaffolding and multiple ways to meet the goals of the future, and he leapfrogs ideas to the next level: how do you do this, what is the framework, how do you customize with different pedagogical strategies? You really have to read *Teaching Digital Natives* to see the beauty of the way in which he shares complex practices in teaching in simple ways, easy for anyone to understand. This book can be a passport to change for educators of all kinds.

—**Bonnie Bracey Sutton**
Teacher and Researcher

Prensky explains the often-perceived daunting task of marshalling 21st-century technologies for classroom instruction in a way that teachers can easily understand and apply immediately. The concept of partnering and allowing both teachers and students to capitalize on their strengths clarifies the issues for educators. The good news: teachers don't have to be masters of technology to master the 21st-century classroom. Prensky has developed a new map for a new era of teaching and learning that educators will find a breeze to navigate and well worth the trip!

—**Jonathan Ben-Asher**
Principal, Henry and Wrightstown Elementary Schools, Tucson, AZ

A truly great and inspiring book. *Teaching Digital Natives* provides innovative, realistic, and clearly explained techniques that increase student engagement and learning. My students are a testament that partnering, as laid out in this book, does work. Prensky's ideas around "nouns" and "verbs" are groundbreaking and immediately effective in the classroom. In addition, the expansive list of "nouns" is helpful for educators at all levels of technology experience. *Teaching Digital Natives* is a must-read for every educator that truly wants to reach out and engage students in the classroom.

—**Randon Ruggles**
Teacher, FAIR School, Minneapolis, MN

Marc Prensky has expertly captured the sense of urgency needed in education today. 21st-century skills, needed core curriculum, rigor, and methodology are outlined in a way all educators can appreciate and implement. The important roles of teachers, parents, and learners are outlined in easy-to-follow strategies that make perfect sense. His "pedagogical partnering" with students to facilitate a new way to teach is invaluable for educators working to better meet the needs of all learners. *Teaching Digital Natives* is a must-read for all educators who strive to meet the emerging demands of our profession. Needless to say, we will be purchasing many copies.

—**Jere Vyverberg**
Superintendent, Waverly-Shell Rock Community Schools, Waverly, IA

Teaching

DIGITAL NATIVES

PARTNERING FOR REAL LEARNING

MARC PRENSKY

FOREWORD BY STEPHEN HEPPELL

CORWIN
A SAGE Company

For information:

Corwin
A SAGE Company
2455 Teller Road
Thousand Oaks, California 91320
(800) 233-9936
Fax: (800) 417-2466
www.corwin.com

SAGE Ltd.
1 Oliver's Yard
55 City Road
London EC1Y 1SP
United Kingdom

SAGE India Pvt. Ltd.
B 1/I 1 Mohan Cooperative
   Industrial Area
Mathura Road, New Delhi 110 044
India

SAGE Asia-Pacific Pte. Ltd.
33 Pekin Street #02-01
Far East Square
Singapore 048763

Printed in the United States of America

Library of Congress Cataloging-in-Publication Data

Prensky, Marc.
Teaching digital natives: partnering for real learning/Marc Prensky; foreword by Stephen Heppell.
       p. cm.
Includes bibliographical references and index.
ISBN 978-1-4129-7541-4 (pbk.)

   1. Active learning. 2. Effective teaching. 3. Teacher-student relationships. 4. Educational change. I. Title.

LB1027.23.P74 2010
371.39—dc22   2010001676

This book is printed on acid-free paper.

11   12   13   14   10   9   8   7   6   5   4

Acquisitions Editor:	Debra Stollenwerk
Associate Editor:	Julie McNall
Editorial Assistant:	Allison Scott
Production Editor:	Amy Schroller
Copy Editor:	Sarah J. Duffy
Typesetter:	C&M Digitals (P) Ltd.
Proofreader:	Gail Fay
Indexer:	Sylvia Coates
Cover Designer:	Scott Van Atta

Brief Table of Contents

To Jim Gee, for his wisdom, ideas, and generosity of spirit
To my wife, Rie, for her love and support
and to
Sky, and children everywhere, with the hope for a worthwhile 21st century education

Contents

What we want is to see the child in pursuit of knowledge,
and not knowledge in pursuit of the child.

—George Bernard Shaw

Foreword

What a remarkable century this is already turning out to be for learning. All around the world, teachers, schools, families, and even policy makers are waking up to the view that building learning in the 21st century using the structures and strictures of the 20th century is a wild and reckless gamble that all too often fails. But sadly, for so many of them, exploring and testing new ideas within their own context leaves them feeling lonely, brave, and rather exposed. Curiously, and rather reassuringly, in isolation many have arrived at very similar conclusions about just what effective 21st century learning strategies and practices might look like. Think what progress they might make together!

Marc Prensky has been a pivotal contributor to building that togetherness. Through previous writing and contributions, Marc has already done a remarkable job of steering the world toward a new shared vocabulary, one that helps us all see the fresh opportunities this century offers to its young citizens. That shared vocabulary has given lonely, brave, and exposed innovators some collegiality, camaraderie even. Suddenly, they are part of something big, something consensual.

And now once again, in this new book, Marc comes along with just the right contribution at just the right time. His stout and unanswerable defense of the need to move learning forward is clearly and accessibly articulated. So much in this book will feed winning lines into debates at schools or in policy forums.

Marc has added to this a treasure chest of heartwarmingly effective practice. The palpable sense of a bottom-up revolution in learning—built by children, teachers, and communities who really care about it—comes over as loud, clear, and comforting. The ability to rapidly browse the book for proven, effective, attainable ideas will ensure a well-thumbed copy in every staff room.

Lately, the United States has seemed reawakened by a new president who has done a remarkable job of reengaging younger and disinterested voters. There is something in the words "Yes we can" that reached out to a new generation, and well beyond the United States, to convey a new optimism. We need that optimism focused very firmly on learning. Our forebears began a revolution with medicine, changing the lives of whole continents and transforming the potential life chances of generations. They didn't stay content with the apparent certainties of their own forebears, but pushed ahead to create a modern medical revolution and in doing so changed their world.

Today the world is in quite a mess, and many of us have seen the impact that learning might have on repairing that mess. We've seen children inoculated against poverty through great learning, seen the disengaged reengaged, seen community rifts healed, seen that insurmountable problems can be breached and bridged with ingenuity, seen that children who learn together joyfully are simply less likely to grow to want to kill each other. Our generation can have a remarkable and enduring impact, too, through learning. Our contribution can be a modern learning revolution.

"Yes we can" indeed. And what Marc has done here is to show precisely why and how we can. I'm just adding in this foreword that, given all the opportunities that we now have to make a local and global difference through learning, and given the world's needs, then surely "Yes we jolly well should."

This book will help us, and help us to help each other.

—Professor Stephen Heppell
Centre for Excellence in Media Practice,
Bournemouth University

Précis

This book unites three strands of current educational discussion that have rarely been considered together:

First, that the students in our classrooms are changing—largely as a result of their outside-of-school experiences with technology—and are no longer satisfied with an education that doesn't immediately address the real world in which they live.

Second, that the "telling and testing" pedagogy we have, for the most part, been using in our schools has become less and less effective with today's students. A better pedagogy is needed, and the good news is that it's available and usable today.

Third, that the digital technology now coming, more or less rapidly, into our classrooms—if used properly—can help make our students' learning real, engaging, and useful for their future.

Ironically, it is the generation raised on the expectation of interactivity that is finally ripe for the skill-based and "doing-based" teaching methods that past experts have always suggested are the best for learning, but that were largely rejected by the education establishment as being too hard to implement.

The happy thread tying the three strands together is that the same digital technology which caused the changes in our students also provides the tools to finally implement the most effective, real ways of learning.

Acknowledgments

There have been many contributors both to the formulation of my ideas and specifically to this book. People who have been influential in my thinking include (in alphabetical order and with apologies for any omissions) Mark Anderson, Jessica Braithwait, Milton Chen, Chris Dede, David Engle, Howard Gardner, James Paul Gee, Lynnette Guastaferro, Stephen Heppell, Ian Jukes, Liz Kolb, Juliette LaMontagne, Kip Leland, Nicholas Negroponte, Lisa Nielsen, Alan November, Will Richardson, Phil Schlechty, David Warlick, Tom Welch, the countless audience members of my presentations, and many e-mail correspondents, who have graciously offered their feedback.

The original thought for this book came from my editor, Deb Stollenwerk, who, throughout the book's writing process, graciously suggested, gently pushed, and shaped the book into what it is. Also of enormous benefit was the major sculpting of the original version done by Dan Richcreek, also of Corwin.

People who read and commented on early versions of the book include Jessica Braithwait, Chris Dede, Jim Gee, Lynnette Guastaferro, and Stephen Heppell.

Although I take final and sole responsibility for what is written here, it is important for readers to understand that many of the ideas I espouse are shared among a growing number of forward-thinking teachers, supervisors, board members, speakers, and consultants. In fact, it is their growing consensus, as I perceive it, that prompted the writing of this book.

Thank you all, and may your good ideas gain increased acceptance!

Publisher's Acknowledgments

Corwin thanks the following reviewers:

Jim Anderson
Principal
Andersen Jr. High School
Chandler Unified School District
Chandler, Arizona

Stephen Bartlett
Teacher
Los Angeles, CA

Regina Brinker
Science Teacher
Christensen Middle School
Livermore, CA

Jennifer Caputo
Media Specialist
Sparta Middle School
Sparta, NJ

Gerard A. Dery
Principal
Nessacus Regional Middle School
Dalton, MA

James Paul Gee
Mary Lou Fulton Presidential Professor
    of Literacy Studies
Arizona State University
Phoenix, AZ

Sally Koczan
Grade 6 Science Teacher
Wydown Middle School
Clayton, MO

Inez Liftig
Grade 8 Science Teacher
Fairfield Woods Middle School
Fairfield, CT

Beth Madison
Principal
George Middle School
Portland, OR

Cheryl Oakes
Collaborative Content Coach for
    Technology
Wells Ogunquit Community
    School District
Wells, ME

Jessica Purcell
High School Science Teacher
Fargo South High School
Fargo, ND

Marilyn Steneken
Life Science Teacher
Sparta Middle School
Sparta, NJ

Jason Thompson
Teacher
Cobleskill-Richmondville Central
    School District
Cobleskill, NY

About the Author

Marc Prensky is an internationally acclaimed speaker, writer, consultant, futurist, visionary, and inventor in the critical areas of education and learning. He is the author of several critically acclaimed books and over 60 articles on education and learning, including multiple articles in *Educational Leadership, Educause, Edutopia,* and *Educational Technology.* More information about his ideas, writing, and publications can be found at www.marcprensky.com/writing.

Marc's presentations around the world challenge and inspire audiences by opening up their minds to new ideas and approaches to education. One of his critically important perspectives is to look at education through the eyes of the students—during his talks, he interviews hundreds of students every year.

Marc's professional focus has been on reinventing the learning process, combining the motivation of student passion, technology, games, and other highly engaging activities with the driest content of formal education. He is the founder of two companies: *Games2train,* an e-learning company whose clients include IBM, Bank of America, Microsoft, Pfizer, the U.S. Department of Defense, and Florida's and Los Angeles's Virtual Schools; and Spree Learning, an online educational games company.

Marc is one of the world's leading experts on the connection between games and learning, and was called by *Strategy+Business* magazine "that rare visionary who implements." He has designed and built over 50 software games in his career, including worldwide, multiuser games and simulations that run on all platforms, from the Internet to cell phones. *MoneyU* (www.moneyu.com), his latest project, is an innovative, engaging, and effective game for teaching financial literacy to high school and college students. Marc is also the creator of www.spreelearninggames.com and www.socialimpactgames.com. His products and ideas are innovative, provocative, and challenging, and they clearly show the way of the future.

The New York Times, The Wall Street Journal, Newsweek, TIME, Fortune, and the *Economist* have all recognized Marc's work. He has appeared on FOX News, MSNBC, CNBC, PBS's *Computer Currents,* the Canadian and Australian Broadcasting Corporations, and the BBC. Marc also writes a column for *Educational Technology.* He was named as one of training's top "New Breed of Visionaries" by *Training* magazine and was cited as a "guiding star of the new parenting movement" by *Parental Intelligence Newsletter.*

Marc's background includes master's degrees from Yale, Middlebury, and Harvard Business School (with distinction). He has taught at all levels, from elementary to college. He is a concert musician and has acted on Broadway. He spent six years as a corporate strategist and product development director with the Boston Consulting Group and worked in human resources and technology on Wall Street.

Marc is a native of New York City, where he lives with his wife, Rie—a Japanese writer—and their five-year-old son, Sky.

Introduction: Our Changing World

Technology and Global Society

Guiding Questions

1. Are today's students different? Are they attention deficient? What do they want?

2. How can we motivate and engage today's students?

3. Is there a better way to help today's students learn? How can we get there?

In the 21st century, so many of our old assumptions and strongly held ideas have been turned around—and so many more upheavals are on the way—that it is clearly a different place in which our kids are growing up. Two-thirds of the people on the planet have a cell phone. A new virtual (i.e., online) world has emerged out of the ether and become the focus of many of our kids' attention. Engineers are putting a trillion transistors on a single computer chip. Scientists are manipulating individual atoms to make nano-scale machines that we can't even see. The world's volume of information will soon be doubling every few hours. No longer do TV game shows put you in an isolation booth to prove no one is helping you; they encourage you to phone a friend or poll the audience.

It is inevitable, in such an environment, that change would finally come to our young peoples' education as well, and it has. But there is a huge paradox for educators: the place where the biggest educational changes have come is not our schools; it is everywhere else *but* our schools. The same young people who we see bored and resistant in our schools are often hard at work learning *afterschool* (a term I use to encompass informal learning through peers, the Internet, YouTube, television, games, cell phones, and lots of other emerging opportunities, as

1

well as through organized programs such as FIRST Robotics). It is in the afterschool world, rather than in schools, that many of our kids are teaching themselves and each other all kinds of important and truly useful things about their real present and future. A host of powerful tools are available to them for this purpose, and those tools—and our kids through using them—are growing more and more powerful each day. After school, no one tells kids what to learn or do. They follow their interests and passions, often becoming quite expert in the process.

ATTENTION?

Despite what you may hear, or even observe, today's students don't have short attention spans or the inability to concentrate that they are often accused of having. Many of the same students who don't concentrate in school will sit for hours, for example, totally focused on movies or video games. So, it is not our students' attention capabilities that have changed, but rather their tolerance and needs. Today's young people must continuously choose among a plethora of very expensively produced demands on their attention—music, movies, commercials, TV, Internet, and more. They have learned to focus only on what interests them and on things that treat them as individuals rather than as part of a group or class (as we so often do in school). In an increasingly populated and crowded world, choice, differentiation, personalization, and individualization have become, for today's young people, not only a reality, but a necessity.

More and more young people are now deeply and permanently technologically enhanced, connected to their peers and the world in ways no generation has ever been before. Streams of information come at them 24/7. More and more of what they want and need is available in their pocket on demand. "If I lose my cell phone, I lose half my brain," comments one student.

Do such kids need school? More and more of them (almost a third nationally and half in the cities) think not, and drop out. But we adults, especially educators, know that this is a huge mistake—there is so much today's young people can and should learn from us. The problem is, though (again in the words of a student), "There's so much difference between how students think and how teachers think." Increasingly, we're failing to deliver what students need in the ways that they need it. What today's kids *do* have a short attention span for are our old ways of teaching.

WHAT TODAY'S STUDENTS WANT

So what do these students want from school? Based on interviews of almost a thousand of today's students from all economic, social, intellectual, and age strata, all over the world, I have found that what they say is remarkably consistent:

- They do not want to be lectured to.
- They want to be respected, to be trusted, and to have their opinions valued and count.
- They want to follow their own interests and passions.
- They want to create, using the tools of their time.

- They want to work with their peers on group work and projects (and prevent slackers from getting a free ride).
- They want to make decisions and share control.
- They want to connect with their peers to express and share their opinions, in class and around the world.
- They want to cooperate and compete with each other.
- They want an education that is not just relevant, but *real*.

It is possible, of course, to view this list as a narcissistic or unrealistic set of expectations on the part of students. But to do so would be a big mistake. Or one might find this set of expectations incompatible with teaching the required curriculum or with getting better results on standardized tests. But that would be a wrong conclusion as well.

Today's students want to learn differently than in the past. They want ways of learning that are meaningful to them, ways that make them see—immediately—that the time they are spending on their formal education is valuable, and ways that make good use of the technology they know is their birthright.

Our students see a new world coming—their world—a world in which what they think should be important actually is. The world they are headed for is different and important to them, and they already know more about some aspects of it than we do. But the world they came from is also important to them, and we know more about that than they do. We need to teach kids to respect the past but to live in the future.

And that is why we need to partner. The key change and challenge for all 21st century teachers is to become comfortable not with the details of new technology, but rather with a different and better kind of pedagogy: partnering.

PARTNERING AND 21ST CENTURY TECHNOLOGY

All teachers today know that digital technology is becoming an important part of students' education. But just how to use it in school is not yet completely clear, and most educators are at some stage of figuring out (or worrying about) how to use technology meaningfully for teaching. And these teachers are right to be concerned, since depending on how it is used, technology can either help or hinder the educational process.

Concerned teachers are continually requesting more training and additional professional development about using technology. But again, there is a paradox, because to be the most successful at using technology in their classrooms, teachers do not need to learn to use it themselves (although they can if they want to). What teachers do need to know is just how technology can and should be used by students to enhance their own learning.

In a partnering pedagogy, using technology is the students' job. The teachers' job is to coach and guide the use of technology for effective learning. To do this, teachers need to focus on, and become even more expert at, things that are already part of their job, including asking good questions, providing context, ensuring rigor, and evaluating the quality of students' work.

REAL, NOT JUST RELEVANT

An important result of the introduction of technology into our children's education is a much shorter span today between learning and meaningful action. Today's students know that when they learn something after school, they can immediately apply it to something real. When they learn to play a game, they can collaborate and compete with others around the globe. When they learn to download, text, and tweet, they can immediately participate in profound social revolutions, such as changing the music business and influencing government policies. As they learn to post their creations and ideas online, they become aware that even as young people they can truly influence and change the world. This gives new urgency and meaning to the "Why should I learn this?" question that our students eternally ask, and demands that we have a better answer than "Someday you'll need it." Today's students expect the same thing from their formal education as from the rest of their lives—that it be not just relevant, but *real*.

MOTIVATION THROUGH PASSION

Teachers have always known that engagement and motivation are what causes students to put in the effort necessary to learn well. And that effort is not trivial. Both scholars, such as Howard Gardner (in *Five Minds for the Future*), and popular writers, such as Malcolm Gladwell (in *Outliers*), point to a large body of research showing that it takes roughly 10,000 hours (some say 10 years) to become really expert at something, anything at all. Today's teachers, of course, often can't get their students to do one hour of homework. One reason is that, in the 21st century, the road to engagement has changed.

Education's approach to motivating students has traditionally been the stick, that is, discipline. The stick has long been used both literally and figuratively (as demerits, detention, and downgrades). In some circles, discipline is even making a comeback as a remedy for our often-failing system.

But educational experts and teachers who really know kids are increasingly pointing to a better approach to student motivation, one that works much more effectively in both the short and long term. That better way is to motivate each student to learn through his or her passion. Passion drives people to learn (and perform) far beyond their, and our, expectations. And whatever is learned through the motivation of passion is rarely if ever forgotten.

As we shall see, in addition to opening students' minds to new ideas, today's teachers need to be sure to seek out and understand the passion that each student already has for some particular thing, subject, or idea (or will have if he or she hasn't found it already). Those passions are, or can be, the key to students' learning almost anything. If a teacher truly encourages each student to discover his or her passion and understands deeply what each student's passion is, that teacher can provide a learning path for each student that is maximally beneficial and can enable each student to achieve and go as far as he or she is capable.

And that, as far as I can tell, is our goal as educators.

TEACHING FOR THE FUTURE

Today's students will not live in a world where things change relatively slowly (as many of us did) but rather one in which things change extremely rapidly—daily and exponentially. So today's teachers need to be sure that, no matter what subject they are teaching, they are teaching it with that future in mind. While there is much about that future that we don't know, we know enough to understand that today's English students must be posting, publishing, and communicating with the world in the multiple media of today and tomorrow; that today's science students must study what is happening on the cutting edge—not just of the disciplines, but of their interstices, which is where all the really interesting work is going on; that today's math students must truly understand orders of magnitude, estimation of unknown quantities, and the math behind all the polling and statistics that are thrown around in our political lives; and that today's social studies students must be learning to deal with, and effect change in, an increasingly crowded, chaotic, and dangerous world.

We know we must respect and learn from the past. But if the future isn't getting equal time in our education, we are selling our students terribly short.

SO HOW DO WE DEAL WITH THIS?

If you are an experienced teacher, you almost certainly have students filling up your classes who are, in many ways, different from those in the past. You probably feel a need, or some pressure, (and may have even started) to do something different for them. You likely also feel pressure to raise the students' test scores and make or exceed adequate yearly progress. Yet many of the teaching techniques you once used successfully do not seem to be working with today's students. You have probably wondered about, and perhaps already begun, making changes to the ways you previously taught.

If you are new to the profession, a teacher just starting out, you may have arrived on your first day with lots of fresh ideas about how to teach and reach students who are still fairly close to your age. But you may have experienced pressure from administrators to do things the old, traditional way in order to keep test scores up and to not rock the boat.

If you are a new teacher switching in from another profession, as many are these days, you may not know much about teaching at all, except how you yourself were taught and what you've picked up from a brief training program. As a result, you may have a very traditional idea of what teaching is. But you may be looking for more effective ways to teach this new generation—particularly after you meet the kids.

And if you are an education student, thinking about or preparing for teaching while still in school, you may be wondering what you will do, either because you are excited about the possibilities for doing things in new ways, or because some of the old ideas you are hearing about teaching conflict with your past or current experiences as a 21st century student.

Whatever your background, you are not alone. There are a great many teachers today who feel the need to teach differently and are looking for specific guidance in making that shift.

A NEW APPROACH

How This Book Will Work for You

This is a book for teachers and school leaders in which the primary focus is on pedagogy: a pedagogy of partnering that addresses the needs of 21st century learners. Of course, the book incorporates 21st century technology, and the key role technology plays in the partnering pedagogy as well. Because many teachers are concerned about what it takes to use up-to-date technology in their teaching, this book offers specific information about the technology and ways to allay the fears about technology that many teachers have. The book offers ways to deal with whatever level of technology is, or isn't, available in your school and classroom, and discusses when and how teachers should and shouldn't be using technology themselves. Finally, the book emphasizes how maximizing the use of technology *by students* will benefit students most.

Additionally, the book addresses the important question often asked by educators about how to preserve what is important from the past—and in education generally—while embracing the tools of the future. I make the helpful distinction between "verbs" and "nouns," where verbs are the skills students should know (such as understanding and communicating), which change little or not at all, and nouns are the tools we use to learn, practice, and use these skills (such as PowerPoint, e-mail, Wikipedia, YouTube, etc.), which change with increasing rapidity. I encourage teachers to think of verbs as the part that is fundamental and nouns as something that will continue to evolve continually in our lifetimes.

The pedagogical changes discussed in this book are already well under way around the world. Thousands of teachers, both new and experienced, are already using the partnering pedagogy in one form or another. This is your opportunity to join this positive worldwide wave—a movement that will benefit both you and your students. This book will show you the path to making the changes required to get from being a lecturer who tightly controls students' learning through discipline and testing to being a coach, partner, and guide to students who, driven by their own passion, are teaching themselves and learning on their own with your help.

Because an overwhelming majority of teachers love and want to help the kids they teach, most have the courage required to feel the real fear associated with making these changes, and yet make them anyway. All change takes courage, courage to begin and, perhaps more important, courage to continue even when things don't always go as expected. Wherever that courage comes from—whether from teachers' desire to help their kids, from teachers' own self-respect and desire to do the best possible job, or, preferably, from both—it is crucial to succeeding.

THE ROAD TO A PEDAGOGY OF PARTNERING

This book provides a roadmap for educators who would like to begin (or continue) partnering with their students, to prepare their students for living and working in the 21st century.

The approach I advocate actually goes by many names. I prefer (for reasons I will explain in the course of the book) *partnering*. But the name you use is less important than the steps you take.

In this book you will find strategies, steps, ideas, and examples for how to make the transition to partnering. There are suggestions on how to think about teaching differently. There are examples and suggestions for finding other examples that may be better for you. There are instructions on how to partner, both with colleagues and with students, to create and share good examples of your own. Because not everyone is a beginner at this, there are ways to assess where you currently are along the road to the new pedagogy. And there is help in going further.

I very much hope this book proves useful to you. I hope it sparks in you a new round of energy and creative force with which to approach your demanding but potentially wonderful job.

I welcome your feedback on your successes at marcprensky@gmail.com.

ORGANIZATION

The book is structured to take you logically from a deeper understanding of the problem (Why are so many of today's kids not engaged?) to a solution that works (partnering) to the daily implementation of that solution in your classroom.

Chapter 1 begins by offering a new, more positive way to look at 21st century students and then describes the partnering pedagogy, including the new roles of the teacher, the students, and all the other players. Chapter 2 introduces more detail on how to move to and implement the partnering pedagogy, including setting up your classroom differently, leaving the stage, choosing the best type of partnering for you and your students, understanding the verb/noun distinction, and connecting partnering to the current curriculum. Chapters 3–6 are devoted to key partnering issues. Chapter 3 is about using students' own passions to motivate them to learn. Chapter 4 is about making students' learning real, not just relevant. Chapter 5 discusses translating content into guiding questions and emphasizing verbs, or skills. Chapter 6 focuses on how to use technology in partnering. Chapter 7 is an annotated list of more than 130 of the technologies available for students to use today. Chapter 8 emphasizes student creation. Chapter 9 discusses continuous improvement, particularly through sharing. Chapter 10 takes up the issue of assessment in partnering. In the Conclusion I look ahead to ways in which we can improve digital natives' education even further.

In addition to these discussions, throughout the book there are special features designed to help you and serve as references. These include the following:

- Many practical suggestions, labeled "partnering tips" and set off in boxes
- A number of strategies and choices for making partnering more successful in your particular environment
- Numerous comments from the almost 1,000 students whom I have interviewed
- A chart of more than 50 learning verbs

- An annotated list of more than 130 nouns (tools) that your students can use while partnering, along with the verbs for which they are appropriate (Note that Chapter 7 is set off with shaded edges to make it easier to find it as a reference.)

I hope you will take advantage of, enjoy using, and return to these tools and features.

Finally, to make it easier to use this book as a study guide, I have followed my own advice with regard to guiding questions, and have placed a set of these questions at the head of each chapter. They are intended to provide context and to help you reflect as you read. I hope they prove useful.

Partnering

A Pedagogy for the New Educational Landscape

Guiding Questions

1. What works in the classroom today? What needs changing?

2. Can we see students differently? Can we achieve mutual respect?

3. What is partnering? What are the teachers' and the students' roles?

Consciously or not, all of today's teachers are preparing their students not only for the world they will face the day they leave school (a world we know), but also for a future in which, within the students' working lifetimes, technology will become over one trillion times more powerful (a world we can hardly imagine). Every year of these students' lives, the world's information will explode anew: Tools will get smaller, faster, better, and cheaper; people will have access to more of these tools (and will change their behavior because of them); and schools and teachers will no doubt struggle to keep up. Given all these changes, and the new realities of students' out-of-school environment, how can teachers best prepare students for their long-term future—as well as for tomorrow—while at the same time preserving the important legacy of the past? This is not an easy question.

But the consensus among experts is clear.[1] The way for us to succeed under such conditions is not to focus only on the changing technology, but rather to conceptualize learning in a new way, with adults and young people each taking on new and different roles from the past.

Young people (students) need to focus on using new tools, finding information, making meaning, and creating. Adults (teachers) must focus on questioning, coaching and guiding, providing context, ensuring rigor and meaning, and ensuring quality results.

This 21st century way of working together to produce and ensure student learning is what I call *partnering*. Learning to do it is the subject of this book.

MOVING AHEAD

Today's overwhelming (and, to various extents, outmoded) educational division of labor is for teachers to lecture, talk, and explain, and for students to listen, take notes, read the text, and memorize. This is often known as *direct instruction*. Unfortunately, direct instruction is becoming increasingly ineffective; that too many of their teachers just talk and talk and talk is today's students' number-one complaint. And unfortunately, the students' response is almost always to tune out.

So the era in which this type of teaching—lecturing, presenting, explaining to all, or telling—worked has pretty much come to an end. To the extent that teachers are a tool for learning, those who teach mainly by telling are becoming a less effective tool in the 21st century.

Yet most teachers were trained to tell. Most of them learned (and learned well) by being lectured to. Many teachers like explaining and think they are good at it. And they may, in fact, be good at it. But this method is no longer relevant, because students are no longer listening. I often liken this to Federal Express: you can have the best delivery system in the world, but if no one is home to receive the package, it doesn't much matter. Too often, today's students are not there to receive what their teachers are delivering. They are off somewhere else, often in the electronic world of 21st century music, socializing, or exploring. The goal of this book is to help teachers bring them back.

What Is Working

Most students recognize and applaud their creative, energetic teachers—especially the ones who respect them and care about their opinions. But when I ask students "What in your entire school experience has engaged you the most?" the most frequent answer I get is "School trips." While trips have always been popular, I think this answer reflects the urgency that today's students feel to connect to the real world. Why? Because another frequent answer is "Connecting with other kids our age in other places electronically" (e.g., through a secure e-mail service such as ePals).

Inside their classrooms, what students say they find most engaging is group work (except when slackers are allowed to get away with not contributing), discussions, sharing their own ideas, and hearing the ideas of their classmates (and of the teacher when expressed as the ideas of an equal).

While they typically say they enjoy using technology, the single thing most valued by students is being respected by their teachers as individuals and not treated as kids who don't know much and thus have to learn. "We're not stupid" is a universal lament.

Seeing Students Differently

Some teachers bemoan current students' capabilities, compared to students of the past. But there is another way to see students, a better, more positive way for the 21st century. We too often treat kids as if they were still (using a 19th century metaphor) trains on a track when actually today's kids are a lot more like rockets (a much more up-to-date metaphor).

Which, by the way, makes educators (again metaphorically) rocket scientists! (Who knew?)

Why should we think of today's kids as rockets? At first blush, it's their speed; they operate faster than any generation that has come before. Although little may have changed in the rate kids grow up emotionally, there has been enormous change in what today's kids learn and know at early ages, and therefore, many think, in the rate they grow up intellectually.[2] Many kids are on the Internet by the age of two or three. I recently found that a NASA moon simulation I used in graduate school works just as well with fourth graders. Although today's parents and educators struggle with getting kids to learn in the old sense, the fuel they offer kids (i.e., the curriculum and materials) is often way behind what today's kids need. "Age appropriate" has totally outrun us. Even students of Piaget suggest it is time for a new look.[3] While some want kids to slow down and "just be kids," like before, speed is clearly a reality for young people in the 21st century.

But Wait . . . There's More

What makes today's kids rockets is not just this increased speed. They are headed to faraway destinations, places that those who launch them often can't even see. They have been designed by their 21st century upbringing—especially by the Internet and the complex games many play—to explore and find out for themselves what works. Like rockets, they often cannot be controlled at every moment, but are initially aimed, as far as possible, in the right direction, with mid-course corrections to be made as necessary. And because both kids and rockets are difficult to repair in flight, they must be made as self-sufficient as possible.

As with all rockets, kids' fuel mix is volatile. Some go faster and farther than others. Some lose their guidance or their ability to follow direction. Some go off course or stop functioning unexpectedly. Some even blow up. But as we get better at making them, many more hit their mark, and it is our job as rocket scientists to help them do so.

Huge Potential

Perhaps most important, today's rockets—and kids—can potentially go much farther and do things far beyond what any such voyager could do in the past. With the arrival of widely distributed and easy-to-use digital tools, kids already, on a daily basis, accomplish things that still seem like far-off science fiction to many of us adults. They communicate instantaneously with, play complex games with, and learn from peers around the globe; ePals, a secure electronic interchange site for kids, reaches every country and territory. Kids regularly make videos and post them for the world to see and comment on. They organize themselves socially and politically across the planet.

Educators as Rocket Scientists

So what does this metaphor imply for those whose job is to educate today's young people? It tells us that we must conceive of what educators do in a new way—not just as teachers, but as rocket designers, building and sending off the best rockets we possibly can. This includes not filling students with the educational fuel of the past, because that fuel just doesn't make today's kids go. We need new fuel, new designs, new boosters, and new payloads. Rocket scientists understand that their rockets will likely encounter many unforeseen events and trials, so they work hard to build into the rockets enough intelligence to get the job done with minimum outside help. They build into the rockets the ability to self-monitor, self-assess, and self-correct as much as possible. They create the ability for their rockets to use whatever devices and instrumentation are available to regularly gather data and then analyze it, even as they are speeding along. They perform rigid quality control, not of what the rockets' brains know— that's updatable on the fly—but of what they can do with the information they encounter. And while they may preprogram a target, they know that the target will likely change midcourse and that there are likely to be other changes during the course of the rocket's life.

A Useful Perspective

Seeing our students and ourselves in this new way encourages educators to set the bar for student achievement extremely high, far higher than we typically do currently. I have often heard educators say they are "blown away" by what their students have accomplished. We should not be blown away by our students; we should be expecting even more from them.

Of course, rockets are high maintenance and often require more of designers' effort and skills to build and keep up. They are also useless on the ground, so that is not where we should be preparing them to stay (many of the "ground skills" have been taken over by machines and are no longer needed).

Exploration or Destruction?

Depending on the payload installed at the beginning of the journey, students (like real rockets) can be powerful forces for exploration and change or potential weapons of destruction. Educators, along with parents and peers, install the payload. Then we send them off to fly into the future, hoping we have prepared them well for what they will meet. To make the payload positive, installing ethical behavior—the ability to figure out the right thing to do and how to get it done—ought to be our number-one concern. We need to best configure students' brains so they can constantly learn, create, program, adopt, adapt, and relate positively to whatever and whomever they meet, and in whatever way they meet them, which increasingly means through technology.

Conceptual, Not Technical Changes

It is with this positive view of 21st century students in mind that we turn to partnering. We want young people, like rockets, to "boldly go where no one has gone before,"[4] and partnering offers the best prospects for getting them there. Surprisingly, perhaps, the most important changes required of educators are not technological, but rather conceptual—thinking of themselves less as guardians of the past and more as partners, guiding their living, breathing rockets toward the future. No one advocates throwing away the past completely. But unless we start preparing our students to fly much further than before and land safely, we won't be doing them much good. If we don't soon start putting some new and different fuel and payload into the rockets that are in our charge, then they will never get off the ground.

HOW PARTNERING WORKS

The term *partnering* can mean different things to different people. After all, a teacher's talking while the students take notes is a kind of partnership. But that's not at all the type of partnership I am talking about here. Let me specify precisely what partnering means in this book's context: letting students focus on the part of the learning process that they can do best, and letting teachers focus on the part of the learning process that they can do best.

Letting the students do what they can do best means giving students primary responsibility for the following:

- Finding and following their passion
- Using whatever technology is available
- Researching and finding information
- Answering questions and sharing their thoughts and opinions
- Practicing, when properly motivated (e.g., through games)
- Creating presentations in text and multimedia

Letting teachers do what they can do best means giving teachers primary responsibility for the following:

- Creating and asking the right questions
- Giving students guidance
- Putting material in context
- Explaining one-on-one
- Creating rigor
- Ensuring quality

Partnering is the very opposite of teaching by telling. In fact, in the partnering pedagogy, the teacher's goal is to do no telling at all (at least to the whole class). Rather than lecture, or even explain, the teacher needs only give students, in a variety of interesting ways, questions to be answered and, in certain cases, suggestions of possible tools and places to start and proceed. In partnering the onus is then completely on the students (alone or in groups) to search, make hypotheses, find answers, and create presentations, which are then reviewed by the teacher and the class and vetted for their correctness, context, rigor, and quality. The required curriculum gets covered because the questions the students answer are the ones they need to know. And as we will see, there exist levels of partnering to fit different types of students, different situations, and different backgrounds.

PARTNERING TIP

How you can eliminate telling, or direct instruction (and what to replace it with), is a great topic for you to discuss with your class, in a specific time that you set aside. Ask your class if they think you talk too much, or more than you need to. Then ask them for suggestions on how you could reduce the amount of time you tell. You will likely be surprised by their answers.

Such a major shift in pedagogy—from telling to partnering—is clearly not a change that either teachers or students will make overnight. It is, in reality, a gradual shift that can take years to perfect. But as thousands of teachers will attest, it can happen. And it must happen for 21st century students to get the education they need and deserve. The good news is that there are now a great many teachers—in every subject and at every level—happily and effectively partnering with their students every day, and you can use them as models.

Partnering Basics: A Simple Example

The best example of partnering that I have ever heard came from a teacher during one of my student panels. The teacher asked the students on the panel this question: "Suppose there are three causes of something that you, the students, have to learn about. Which of the following would you prefer: that I say, "There were three causes of [whatever]. I will now lecture and tell you what they were—please take notes," or that I say, "There were three main causes of [whatever]. You all have 15 minutes to find out what they were, and then we'll discuss what you've found."

To nobody's great surprise, whenever students are asked this question they almost universally prefer the second alternative. Most of today's students, no matter what their age or grade level, prefer to take an active role and find things out for themselves, rather than be told them by the teacher.

Do Some Things Require Lectures?

Yet whenever I say, "No lectures," I get people who push back with "Some things require lectures." So please take a minute right now to reflect on what, in your subject area, you think might not be possible to teach without lecturing, telling, or explaining in front of the class. Now ask yourself this question: "Could I reframe this topic or information instead as answers to a series of questions, questions that I might ask, say, on a test to see if the students understood the topic or material?"

At its simplest, partnering is just giving the students those questions to research, explore, and find answers to, and then for the class to discuss and review. I believe partnering can be done in any subject with any material. But it does require a new perspective.

Is Partnering New?

At this point you may be saying to yourself, "Partnering is nothing new. It's just what used to be called [put your answer here]." If so, you are absolutely right. To a great extent, partnering falls into the great pedagogical tradition known, variously, as

- student-centered learning,
- problem-based learning,
- project-based learning,
- case-based learning,
- inquiry-based learning,
- active learning,
- constructivism, or co-constructing
- learning by doing.

John Dewey famously espoused this form of pedagogy in the early 20th century,[5] and it has probably been used, in one form or another, since Socrates. (One early reader of this book pointed out nicely the lineage from Pestalozzi to Frances Parker to Dewey to Bruner.) Other names for this pedagogy exist as well. The Massachusetts Institute of Technology calls its version technology-enhanced active learning (TEAL). A teacher recently wrote me about process-oriented guided inquiry learning (POGIL). Challenge-based learning is another variation from Apple that was recently described in a report from the New Media Consortium.[6] Quest-based learning is being tried in a New York City experimental school. All of these are continually being revised and updated.[7]

But while each of these pedagogies has its own proponents, principles, and peculiarities, they are all, at their core, very similar. In a sense, they are merely brands, if you will, of the same general type of learning. The common thread is that students learn on their own, alone or in groups, by answering questions and solving problems with their teacher's help, coaching, and guidance.

I prefer the term *partnering* to any of the others because it emphasizes that the roles of each group, teachers and students, are different, but equal. Partnering underscores that each party must draw on its own particular strengths to improve the learning process as a whole. I also like what partnering has to say about the role of technology: that it is the job of the students, and not the teacher, to use it, and the job of the teacher to assess the quality of that use. But this last term may only reflect that digital technology didn't exist when some of these other brands were established—I think it really applies to all.

Again, what matters is not the name or brand of partnering you choose—that will depend on you, your students, and your context, such as the school, or state, you teach in. What does matter is that you move in the partnering direction. Figure 1.1 points out some of the different ways that work in the partnering pedagogy is split between the students and the teacher.

Partnering and the Curriculum

One concern frequently raised by teachers is that they are constrained by a mandated curriculum, which somehow conflicts with partnering. Certainly, at least in public schools, there is for every subject and level a required set of (increasingly skills-based) standards to be taught. But remember that those standards specify only *what* to teach, not how to do it.

Partnering can, and does, work with today's required curricula. But it demands a rethinking of those curricula on the part of teachers from the "this is the material to be learned" approach of textbooks to an approach of "guiding questions to which students need to find answers." Interestingly, textbooks—most of which reflect the old, telling pedagogy—have gotten things completely backward from the point of view of partnering (and, generally, student interest). Textbooks put the answers (i.e., the content) up front and the questions in the back. Partnering reverses this, putting the questions first, which, as it turns out, is far more motivating to students. Asking "Why?" upfront (Why do we have seasons? Why do opposites attract? Why does English have so many nonstandard past tenses? Why do we forget, or make bad decisions? Why did people from Europe come to America?) is far more likely to make kids think than are lectures on seasonality, polarity, irregular verbs, psychology, or discovery and immigration.

But what students have to know (and what they will, of course, be tested on in the standardized tests), remains the same regardless of the pedagogy. Partnering teachers find that the process of students actively answering the questions leads almost universally to higher engagement (I've never heard a partnering teacher say that his or her students were *less* engaged.) The increased engagement, in turn, typically produces better retention of material and higher test scores, as in the case of the primary school teacher who saw his students' descriptive writing scores go up an entire testing level.[8] Many teachers describe similar phenomena.

Figure 1.1   How Partnering Work Is Shared

Teacher	Student
Doesn't tell, *asks*!	Doesn't take notes, *finds out*!
Suggests topics and tools	Researches and creates output
Learns about technology from students	Learns about quality and rigor from teacher
Evaluates students' output for rigor and quality; supplies context	Refines and improves output, adding rigor, context, and quality

Technology in Partnering: The Enabler and Personalizer

And what, in the partnering pedagogy, is the role of technology? Technology's role is to support the partnering pedagogy and to enable each student to personalize his or her learning process. All students and teachers know that students get the greatest reward for their efforts when things are individualized and customized for each student. What's always been needed in our classrooms is a way to deal with each student individually or, at the most, in extremely small groups in a way that is truly implementable and effective. Up until now, though, the combination of large class sizes and few resources outside of textbooks, outdated reference books, and limited library and teacher time have made total individualization and differentiation difficult, if not impossible, for most teachers to pull off.

The greatest single boon of the arrival—albeit slowly and unevenly—of digital technology in our schools is that it will, in the long run, enable teachers and students to partner in this much more personal and individual way, that is, for each student to learn on his or her own, with the teachers' coaching and guidance. It will permit students not just to "learn at their own pace," as is often heard, but to learn more or less in whatever ways they prefer, as long as they are in pursuit of the necessary and required goals.

Just adding technology, however, will not make this happen. In fact, in some cases, laptops have already been added *and* removed for having "failed."[9] But the failure in those cases was neither of the students nor of the technology, but rather of the pedagogy. In order for technology to be used successfully in classrooms, it *must* be combined with a new type of pedagogy—partnering. Partnering works with technology because it allows technology to be used, especially by students, to its fullest extent.

Rather than teachers interrupting their lecture for a technology "exercise," partnering enables students to be engaged, from the start of every class, in discovering on their own (and sharing with each other) what the material is and how it works, in finding examples in multiple media, in creating and sharing their own examples, and in communicating with peers and writers around the globe.

ESTABLISHING ROLES AND MUTUAL RESPECT

For any type of partnering to succeed, however, it is key that mutual respect between students and teachers be established. To some readers this may sound obvious, or like something that is already there, but that is not always the case. My discussions with both students and teachers have taught me that there is not nearly enough respect in our schools and in teaching. And it goes both ways—students' respect for teachers and vice versa. Respect is, of course, a key element of any teaching and learning, but it is especially important for teaching and learning via partnering.

The key requirement for respect in a partnering context is that it be mutual; each partner must truly respect the other. I'm quite sure that all teachers want and expect their students to respect them, and all teachers would say, if asked, that they respect their students. But that is often not what happens in reality. Frustrated teachers say (or think) things like "My students can't concentrate" or "My kids have the attention span of a gnat"—things that are just not true overall. (Although these things may be true in the context of school, most students concentrate just fine on topics and activities that interest them.)

I've heard many teachers comment (mostly when students are not around) about their students' lack of caring, interest, motivation, even ability. When students overhear teachers saying these things (and other things that, outside of the school context, are similarly untrue), they feel disrespected—and rightfully so. And in reaction they often turn around and disrespect their teachers right back, frequently by pointing out the teachers' technological illiteracy.

Such mutual *dis*respect almost entirely prevents effective learning and partnering. For learning to take place, disrespect must be rooted out wherever it exists, on both sides of the teacher's desk. For successful partnering, teachers and students alike must realize and accept that we have entered an era in which both students and teachers have something of equal importance to contribute to the learning process. Each side must respect and learn from what the other has to offer.

Some teachers have used the strategy of putting up a large sign in the classroom that says, "We are all learners, we are all teachers," and some schools have even gone so far as to adopt this as their official motto. These words can be reinforced and internalized by giving students the chance, whenever appropriate, to teach the teacher (for example, about technology) and by the teacher being a willing and eager learner.

Student Roles in Partnering

The metaphor I introduced earlier of students as rockets, needing to be properly fueled by teachers, programmed with self-directing capabilities, and sent to new and distant places is far more respectful of students than the old pedagogy's view of students as empty vessels to be filled with knowledge (or blank slates to be written upon). Making students more active and equal participants in the learning process is a sign of respect—respect that students everywhere are looking for. But what, specifically, are the students' roles in partnering?

Student as Researcher

One important role is that of researcher. When we adopt the partnering pedagogy of no longer telling students what they need to know, but instead requiring them to find it out for themselves (and then to share it with their peers and with the teacher for evaluation), that immediately puts students in this new and very different role. One bonus of doing this is that the role of researcher, being a professional one, carries with it a level of respect not always accorded to mere "students." For this reason, some schools have actually chosen to officially rename their students as "researchers." Consider the case of a student in Texas, a former dropout, who commented, "That is almost all I do—look things up on the computer." She was quite happy to spend most of her school day in this way.

Take a minute to picture yourself working in such a school. It might be more akin to working at a magazine or a library, where you expect a very professional job from all your partners or colleagues. Obviously, if you get less than you expect from someone, you would give that person feedback, but preferably in a way that would help him improve next time. The atmosphere would be much more equal and collegial, which is exactly the goal in the partnering pedagogy.

Student as Technology User and Expert

A second key role for students in the partnering pedagogy is that of the technology user and expert. Students typically love this role and use as many technologies as they are given access to. I have watched different groups of students in a class simultaneously using video, audio podcasts, games, blogs, and other social networking tools to answer the same guiding question posed by the teacher. Such guiding questions (which I discuss much more in Chapter 5) could range from "How would you like your teachers to use technology in class?" to "How do people persuade each other?" to "What is the evidence for evolution?"

Obviously, no student knows everything there is to know about technology. Some know a lot, and some know surprisingly little. (That doesn't, by the way, make them any less digital natives, a distinction which is more about attitude than knowledge.) Many teachers, of course, are extremely technology savvy. But whether students or teachers know a lot or a little, in partnering it is key for teachers to reserve the role of using the technology for students. Even when some (or even most) students in a class do not know about the technology, teachers should never use technology *for* them. Rather, teachers should only suggest what students might use (and solicit students' suggestions) and then get them to use it for themselves and teach each other (possibly modeling some examples of effective use up front). This is true whether we are talking about interactive white boards, computers, podcasts, blogs, or any other technology.

In the partnering view, even when teachers know a lot about technology and like it, they should not make things for students; they should rather help and supervise students in using technology to make things for themselves (and, in some cases, for the teachers to use). In fact, many partnering teachers have designated the most tech-savvy students in their classes as technology assistants to create things that are needed and to deal immediately with any problems with equipment or with lack of knowledge on the part of the teacher or other students.

Student as Thinker and Sense Maker

Another key role for students in the partnering pedagogy is thinker and sense maker. Most teachers would probably say students are supposed to have that role today, but it's often not clear to the students that they do, or what this entails. When partnering, the role of thinker and sense maker needs to be made much more explicit.

Our students do think, of course. To say they don't (or can't) is to disrespect them. But the way they think, and what they think about, is often not what teachers would prefer. It is important in all teaching, and especially in partnering, to let students know frequently that thinking more logically and more critically is one of their primary roles. That is one reason that peer-to-peer communication, both orally and in writing, is so important to the partnering pedagogy; it lets students see and evaluate just how logically and critically they and their peers think. Teachers with students writing for publicly available blogs have reported an immediate improvement in both writing and thinking quality on the part of students once they know their work will be seen by others.[10] To emphasize this thinking role, Ted Nellen, a New York City Teacher of the Year, calls all of his students "scholars."

Student as World Changer

The fourth student role relates to learning being *real*, and not just relevant. Real learning (as I discussed in the Introduction and will do in more detail in Chapter 4) involves students immediately using what they learn to do something and/or change something in the world. It is crucial that students be made aware that using what they learn to effect positive change in the world, large or small, is one of their important roles in school. For example, some middle school students outside Atlanta, Georgia, made a video on genetically modified food that changed their parents' shopping habits. Another group in the same school used what they learned to raise money to help cure malaria in Africa.[11] Many schools also use what students learn to help their local communities.

Student as Self-Teacher

The fifth role of the student (and the role that is perhaps most different in the partnering pedagogy) is that of self-teacher. That students can teach themselves might sound strange at first. But consider how you would learn about something new—say, a disease that someone in your family had suddenly contracted. While you could opt to go to a class and have someone tell you, most likely you would choose to learn on our own. You would do research in books or on the Internet, ask friends and colleagues for information and guidance, and consult experts when possible. It is really important that students learn these same skills and become self-reliant when it comes to learning, rather than depending on a teacher or anyone else. The best way for them to do so is to be expected to do it repeatedly, with feedback, until they get really good at it. For this reason, the role of self-teacher might be the most important student role of all. One student who learned that his grandmother had cancer was able to find online, by himself, using skills he had learned, not only the best hospital for her to go to, but the name of the doctor with the best success rate in dealing with the particular cancer she had.

It is extremely important to understand, however, that students learning to teach themselves doesn't mean that the teacher's role goes away, or even that it gets diminished. On the contrary. In the partnering pedagogy, the teacher's job retains its importance, but its roles change dramatically. We will look at the teacher's many roles in the partnering pedagogy in the next section. Perhaps unexpectedly, it turns out that these new roles for the teacher are far more important and useful to students than the old role of teller.

Other Student Roles

Some additional roles for students in partnering include, from time to time, journalist, writer, scientist, engineer, and politician. They also include being the "doer" of the many verbs I will discuss later. I will have more practical things to say about all of these roles in Chapter 3.

Teacher Roles in Partnering

Some of the many roles a teacher plays in partnering will be comfortable and familiar to almost any teacher. Others, though, may be new and will require some learning and practice.

Teacher as Coach and Guide

In the roles of coach and guide, the partnering teacher sets daily and longer-term goals for the class as a whole and then sets each student free (within appropriate limits) to reach those goals in his or her own way, providing assistance when requested or clearly needed. The role of guide implies taking students on a journey; the role of coach implies each student having an individual helper. Neither coach nor guide is a new role for teachers, but each is one that, in the partnering pedagogy, they can spend much more time on. And these roles allow teachers to provide a much more personalized, or differentiated, education for their students.

In general, today's students much prefer getting there on their own to being micromanaged. But not all students can find their way with equal ease. Some find it more difficult than others to work by themselves. This is especially true when confronting partnering for the first time: it is new for students as well as teachers. Part of the coach's role is to monitor each student's work and progress, and to give assistance where it is needed—not by reverting to telling in the old style, but by gently nudging students back on track with useful questions and suggestions for how to proceed (and never doing it for them). For example, a coach might refer a student having trouble to a web site, a YouTube video, an online animation, or even a game, if available.

Some educators, particularly those working in difficult inner-city schools, say, "I'm sure this would work in the suburbs, but our kids need much more structure." No doubt they do. And teachers do need to be able to scaffold the new way of learning for all kids. But as many teachers have demonstrated (mostly in charter schools), *all* kids can learn to partner and take on the responsibilities involved in their part of the learning process. Depending on where students start, guiding some of them into partnering can be a long and complex process. But as with everything in partnering, it is done student by student, rather than with classes as a whole.

Teacher as Goal Setter and Questioner

In the partnering pedagogy, freed from telling and preparing and giving lectures, the teacher has a number of other important roles to play. One is setting goals for students' learning. These goals are almost always best expressed as guiding questions for students to answer, which are typically open-ended and include both overarching questions and more detailed ones. The larger questions are followed more specifically by the kinds of questions that students would or might be asked on a test. Many teachers now hand out or post their guiding questions as they start a term or unit. The premise is that if the students can answer all those questions, they ought to do pretty well on any exam.

Questioner is a truly important role for the teacher in the partnering pedagogy. Despite teacher training and the professionally developed questions created for standardized tests by Educational Testing Service and other organizations, the art of good questioning has to a large extent fallen into disuse in schools. An important lesson for partnering students is that four-answer multiple-choice questions do not reflect the real questions in the world. The art of Socratic questioning (i.e., asking challenging questions designed to get people to reflect and reconsider their point of view) is an important skill for partnering teachers to relearn and practice.

Much of the work in the problem-based learning variation of partnering has been to develop rich questions that can serve as the basis for extended projects. Some districts and states (such as West Virginia) have been leaders in collecting these questions and connecting them to standards. But although many predesigned questions are now available online and in books, turning any content into good guiding questions is a skill that each partnering teacher needs to perfect over time. I consider this skill in more detail in Chapter 5.

Teacher as Learning Designer

Another important role for the teacher in the partnering pedagogy is as designer of original learning-creating experiences. No one wants class days that are repetitive; teachers as well as students are hungry for variety and frequent, positive change. In the role of designer, starting from where he or she wants students to wind up in their understanding, the partnering teacher crafts the questions, problems, and suggested activities that will lead students to understanding.

Designing is a role that should not be unfamiliar to most teachers, as it is somewhat akin to lesson planning. But in the partnering pedagogy designing takes on very different forms. For example, there are no presentations or worksheets to design. Rather than all students following the teacher on the same designed path, partnering students need to be coached and guided toward the goal along a variety of individual paths. This makes the learning designer role of the partnering teacher one of increased complexity and importance. When planning, a teacher needs to reflect on and prepare for various ways in which students might come to an understanding of what is being taught, particularly in view of students' individual passions. So a teacher focusing on the Gettysburg Address, for example, might think up ways to approach it from many student perspectives such as conciseness (comparison to Twitter), politics (comparison to recent speeches), arts (comparison to Oscar acceptance speeches), music (comparison to memorable lyrics), visual images (what pictures does it evoke?), oral interpretations and readings, and so on. There is even a web site that illustrates what the address might have looked like as a PowerPoint (http://norvig.com/Gettysburg/).

Abandoning Total Control for Controlled Activity

An important thing for teachers to know and understand about partnering is that it generally involves activity and movement on the part of students. To a casual observer, a partnering class may not seem controlled or disciplined in the traditional sense. A partnering class looks and feels different from a traditional class. For example, one typically does not see students sitting in rows listening to a lecture or filling in worksheets. Rather, one is likely to see desks and chairs arranged in a variety of configurations, students working in groups of different sizes, and groups and individuals using all the technology that is available.

Given the increased level of student movement and conversation in a partnering classroom, it is important to underscore that partnering does not mean chaos in the classroom—that is never acceptable—but rather controlled activity, where each student's movement around the room has a learning purpose. In a partnering class students might be all over the place, some working at their desks or computers, some working or discussing in groups, some at the library or shooting a video. (For this to be allowed, administrators, too, must become comfortable with partnering, and more and more of them are. I have heard principals welcome the idea of having students in the halls, or even outside, shooting videos—just as long as their activity has a clear connection to their learning.)

> **Check It Out!**
>
> For an example of a useful (and fun) student project done in the halls, see the student-made video about not videoing other students and posting it on YouTube, found at www.youtube.com/watch?v=kJEnVzMXK1E.

For teachers new to partnering, who have been taught that control is crucial and lack of order is a sign of students not learning, a higher level of classroom activity may take some getting used to. But when done right, this increased activity is good because it directs students' often high energies in a positive learning direction. While at first it might be hard for a teacher (or administrator) to learn to tolerate this, I recommend having faith and patience, because the end result is worth it.

One high school teacher told me an illustrative story of how she let her class of girls use her room in an "off" period to design their senior class project while the teacher worked at her desk.

> The girls were off the walls, yelling, talking, running in and out of the room. But by the end of the hour, they had designed a fantastic senior project. Still, when I thought about it, I realized that if that had been my class I couldn't have tolerated that level of chaos in the classroom, even if I were sure that the end result would be great.

This insight led the teacher to begin to change the level of what she could tolerate in class.

At every level, kids today do not want to—and in many cases cannot—sit quietly in neat little rows. They need to be much freer, and they often do their best work when free to relate in ways that are much "wilder" than in the past. More and more teachers and parents are realizing that they benefit from tolerating more of this. Teachers often get better results by taking a much more flexible view of control (while still being sure that students are always learning and on track and that a class does not devolve into actual chaos).

What most allows this increased classroom flexibility to happen, and to happen without chaos, is mutual respect, with teachers respecting students' need for freedom in how they work and students respecting their teachers' need for real learning to take place. Achieving this ideal state and balance for each partnering classroom is not something that happens automatically; it is a teaching skill that must be learned and practiced. Remember, though, that it is possible to have an animated, even noisy, classroom and still be in control.

PARTNERING TIP

If the concept of a less tightly controlled class is a tough one for you, you might try it first with a single partnering project, first talking with your students to mutually set rules and parameters, and afterward assessing the results. You can then expand from there as you and the students become more comfortable with the process. As a group, you might decide, for example, that no permission from you is needed for students to use technology in the classroom or talk to each other when working in groups, but that non-work-related comments or disturbing the work of others is inappropriate and will cause a student to lose group or technology privileges.

Teacher as Context Provider

Yet another important role of the partnering teacher is context provider. While students in their role as researchers are often good at finding content, they are often less capable of putting that content in the proper context. My favorite example of the importance of context is the following test answer by a student:

While most of us laugh at this response, it is important to realize that, in a searching context, it would be perfectly correct. It is wrong (and funny) because we know it is in a math context. Every subject has a context from which individual facts and ideas derive their true meaning. Whether helping students understand the role of Wikipedia in a research context or the existence of hate mongering in a free speech context, providing context is a key role of the partnering teacher. As with most things in partnering, this role is best accomplished through asking (e.g., through Socratic questioning) rather than through explaining or telling. Students can be asked what things are right or acceptable in some contexts but not in others. This would be a great lead-in, for example, to an English class discussion of types of writing and speech, and their contextual appropriateness.

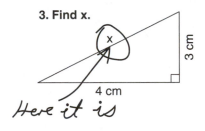

Teacher as Rigor Provider and Quality Assurer

The last two major roles of the teacher in the partnering pedagogy are rigor provider and quality assurer, which are closely related although not precisely the same. What they have in common is setting the bar really high for student accomplishment. I strongly believe that, in general, we set the bar far too low for students and that they are capable of (and want to do) much, much more than we generally ask or require of them.

The place where I first truly learned the meaning of rigor was in my freshman literature class in college. I had not done much writing of literature papers in my public high school career, so I was very much at sea in writing my first required paper. I ended up handing in only a single, difficultly produced page. When the instructor handed back the papers the following week, I kept my eyes lowered, fully expecting an F. The instructor stopped at my desk. "Prensky," I still remember him saying to me, "I'm not even going to grade this. You go out and learn how to write a literature paper and then turn it in, and then I'll grade it." Somehow I did, and I learned that there is a minimum floor that work must rise above in order to be considered acceptable.

Rigor is that floor. In partnering, when you give students a task to do, you don't give those who are below the level of acceptability an F—you just don't accept anything less than that floor.

Quality, on the other hand, is something else. Quality is what separates a merely acceptable effort from a really good one. Of course, we have a system of As, Bs, Cs, and Ds (or 0–100) for administrative purposes, but for partnering students those grades alone are not good enough. Letter or number grades exist only in school, not in life. A boss or supervisor will rarely if ever give you a letter or number grade, but will certainly have a minimum standard and will almost always reward you for high-quality work. So students need to have a good understanding of what high-quality work is. Therefore, for partnering teachers, assessing quality—not just by assigning letter grades but by explaining to students why something they do is or isn't high quality and helping (and requiring) them to iterate until it is—is perhaps the most important part of the job.

Of course, doing that—and not just giving a letter grade—is a very time-consuming and intensive task, especially with large class sizes. That is why a successful implementation of partnering pedagogy needs to include a large amount of peer-to-peer teaching, learning, and evaluation, as we shall see in the next section.

An important issue arises when assessing quality in student projects done in media that are unfamiliar to a teacher. How do you judge what is a high-quality machinima, game, or mashup? I have occasionally had teachers show me, with great pride, student work that most kids would totally dismiss as unworthy of even a D. In such cases you will need to rely on your student partners to teach and guide you. Between their knowledge of the media and your own experience, you should be able to arrive at fair quality assessments no matter what the medium.

Peer Roles in Partnering

Many of today's students, given a choice, would prefer to learn not from their teachers but from their peers. I have been told this by hundreds of kids. Some people might find it upsetting that today's kids often trust their peers' opinions (and even abilities) more than those of their teachers. But this is not necessarily a bad thing, particularly if monitored by the teacher. Although a teacher's contextual framework is likely to be much deeper than a friend's, one's friends share the same references, the same generation of TV, movies, songs, and so on. In students' terms, they all speak the same language.

If it is used to the teachers' (and students') advantage and if monitored well, peer-to-peer teaching and learning can be a great ally to partnering teachers. It is a tool that teachers could benefit from much more than they currently do. Not only do students enjoy learning from their peers, but a great many students really like it when teachers give them the opportunity to teach other students. One strategy that has worked well for some partnering teachers is to directly teach only a few kids in a class and make those kids responsible for teaching the rest, in whatever ways they all want. Giving students this opportunity is yet another way of showing respect. For these reasons, peer-to-peer learning is an important part of the partnering pedagogy.

A striking example of the power of peer-to-peer learning in action is the phenomenal music teaching program from Venezuela known as *El Systema*. In this program, poor kids from all over Venezuela—often street kids—are trained to be truly fine classical musicians in local, regional, and national orchestras, mostly through peer-to-peer teaching and learning.

> **Check It Out!**
>
> You can learn more about El Systema and see it in action—along with its amazing results—by watching the videos on the program at www.ted.com.

One of El Systema's major principles is that as soon as kids learn something, they have to teach it to someone else. This is not all that different from the surgeon's model of "watch one, do one, teach one."

There are many ways of using the power of peer-to-peer learning in partnering, and partnering teachers are constantly figuring out new ones. For example, peer-to-peer is an excellent (and possibly the best) way to spread the knowledge and use of technology among students and bridge any digital divide that may exist in your classroom. Also, because of the power of peer-to-peer learning, for some partnering tasks, such as understanding or evaluating a particular text or finding a solution to a problem, putting two or three students in front of a single computer may be as good as, or even better than, having each student work individually.

The School Principal as Leader, Facilitator, and Partner

The participation of the school principal (and the school administration) in the partnering pedagogy is crucial, in the multiple roles of leader, facilitator, and yet another partner. Although it is not impossible for partnering to survive and flourish without strong administrative support, it is difficult.

Many teachers have told me that they have wanted to try, or even did try, to use some or all of the partnering pedagogy described in this book, but were frustrated by the lack of support from the administration in their school. Yet I hear just as often from principals who are frustrated and often have trouble when attempting to get their teachers to try these new methods.

Clearly, to be most successful, teachers and administrators must work in partnership. In the long run, teachers must be supported by their administration in order to succeed in partnering with their students. An administrator who formally observes or just walks into a class where the teacher is coaching and not telling, where students are teaching themselves and each other with various amounts of controlled activity going on, and where students are presenting and critiquing in a truly vigorous give-and-take manner needs to understand that all of this is producing learning that is as good as or better than that which results from traditional direct instruction.

Things will go much more smoothly if principals and other administrators do understand and accept this new approach and are willing to support their teachers in transition and guide them to the new partnering pedagogy. But a principal or administrator who believes in partnering can and should do more than just support and encourage. He or she should be evaluating teachers on where they currently are along the continuum from telling to partnering (see Figure 9.1) and providing assistance to those who are moving more slowly, or not at all. Such assistance can come in the form of pairing teachers who are further along the continuum with those who are less advanced, pairing teachers with advanced students, and offering teachers professional development. But—and this is crucial—administrators should make sure that any professional development or training offered focuses not (at least at first) on using various technologies, but rather on shifting teachers' thinking and actions to the partnership mentality and pedagogy. Unless and until this is done, the technology training is unlikely to prove fruitful.

Parents as Partners

There is one more group that is key to the success of the partnering pedagogy, and that is parents. Unless they are properly initiated and engaged in the partnering process, parents can often be a point of resistance to the changes it brings. In particular, many parents expect (or at least say they expect) their students to be taught as they were, that is, by telling. Unless their understanding of the partnering process is complete, parents may view what they hear their children are doing, or what they see them doing if they come to class, as a reason to complain.

In most cases, though, this distrust goes away with time, as kids arrive home much more excited about school than in the past and talk positively about their accomplishments. "[Now] when we sit down to dinner," says one parent, "the kids talk nonstop for twenty minutes, telling us what they did and what they saw. This is literally every day!"[12] It also helps when the kids' grades and attendance rise accordingly.

Most parents know instinctively that the 21st century is different; they see the changes all around them. What they really want is to be assured that their children are being well prepared for their future lives and jobs. Partnering teachers need to help parents understand that colleges and employers are also changing their expectations. Teachers need to let parents know that the teaching is changing to keep up with these new expectations, emphasizing what students can do as much as what they know and giving young people many more future-oriented capabilities and skills than just listening and taking notes. It is terribly important that parents understand this, not just for the partnering pedagogy, but especially for students. Having this dialogue with parents is the responsibility of the entire school, faculty, and administration.

In that dialogue, parents should be encouraged, just as educators should, to respect their kids as users of technology, even when that technology baffles or alarms them (as is often the case with video and computer games). Like teachers, parents need to be encouraged to talk with their kids frequently, to ask them about what they are doing, both school-related and not, and to praise them for their creative accomplishments, both in and out of school.

It helps enormously when a school or district employs technology as a means to reach out to parents. Wi-Fi coverage of students' homes, as well as dedicated web sites for parents (with feedback from them), is now, with judicious use of grants, within almost every district's financial reach. For a great example of what can be done with relatively little, look at Lemon Grove, an economically below-average school district in Southern California (www.lemongroveschools1.net). Its Wi-Fi system to schools and homes, created entirely with government grants, is so robust that the district was able to pass along some of the upkeep costs to the local police and fire departments, who use it as a backup.

GETTING MOTIVATED TO PARTNER WITH YOUR STUDENTS

Hopefully, you have already begun the move to partnering. But if not, how can you, as a teacher, get motivated to make big changes? And, even more important, how do you stay motivated to continue changing and not fall back to old, familiar ways at the first sign of trouble? The best way, I think, is not to make the changes in secret, but to be as open as possible—with your students, your administrators, and your colleagues—about what you are trying to do. After all, the goal is to improve your students' experience, your own experience, and the test scores.

The easiest and most effective way of doing this is to enlist the help of those who have gone before you and succeeded. These can be colleagues you know, and hopefully there are at least a few where you teach. But help can also come from people you don't know, people whom you will meet online by joining support groups, such as Listservs, blogs, and Ning groups (see Chapter 7) and by searching YouTube and TeacherTube. Many teachers, several quite experienced, have e-mailed me to say how much these partnering ideas have reinspired them and brought them back to the original level of excitement they felt when they started teaching.

It is also crucial to enlist your supervisors, your students, and their parents in your own personal change process. Often, when they understand your goals, they will be quite supportive.

Have Courage, but Also Have Fun

For most people, doing anything for the first time elicits some fear. You probably felt fear the first time you stood in front of a class as a student or first-time teacher. When you feel such fear and need the courage to proceed anyway, it often helps to remember the lion in *The Wizard of Oz*—you don't need the medal, because the courage is inside you all the time.

But also keep in mind that change is not all fear and pain. In fact, it can be quite invigorating and exciting to rethink your job from a new perspective. Thinking not in terms of material or content but in terms of the questions the material answers is often liberating to long-time teachers.

And do not think that teaching in this new way will necessarily make your job harder. A very important lesson I have learned from the partnering I do regularly in workshops with students and teachers is that there are times when the best thing I can do to enhance everyone's learning is actually nothing at all. After I offer guiding questions and the teams or individuals get to work, I ask frequently if anyone needs my help. But I often get no requests for assistance from the busy learners. So I walk around watching, asking what people are doing, and usually they are right on track. In those moments of teaching when no one "needs" me, I have learned to smile to myself and think, "What a nice job I have."

My hope is that, as you change your pedagogy, this same thought will occur, more and more often, to you as well.

In the remainder of the book, I'll discuss how to apply partnering step by step. I will do this not by presenting you with preset lessons and plans, but rather by considering general principles of partnering and providing numerous examples and practical suggestions. That is the equivalent of teaching you to fish—you'll eat for a lifetime.

2

Moving to the Partnering Pedagogy

Guiding Questions

1. What can teachers and students do to facilitate partnering?

2. How do I choose the level of partnering that's right for my students?

3. How should I think about technology and connect it to the curriculum?

Switching to partnering can be a thrilling, rejuvenating experience. It can take you into new realms of teaching and bring you closer to both your students and your professional roots. It will transform you into more of a tutor and coach for your students, and give you much more time and ability to differentiate instruction to meet individual student needs and passions.

To partner well, however, both you and your students will need to learn some new (and, most would agree, fun and intellectually challenging) skills. Let's begin with your students. How ready are they to partner? Ask yourself the following:

1. Do your students often seem bored and restless?

2. Do they have trouble paying attention when you are talking?

3. Are they often active in distracting ways?

4. Are they doing less well than you would like?

Believe it or not, these are all positive signs—signs that students are ready for a more active, challenging approach to learning. Even if all your students are happy, well motivated, pay attention in class, and achieve way above average on exams, partnering will still greatly benefit them in the long run by making them better, more independent learners.

Now, how ready are you to partner? Ask yourself the following:

1. Do I (or could I) think of my students as partners with different skill sets, and do I (or can I) talk to them directly about how they want to learn?

2. Do I (or could I) know each of my students' passions, and can I use these to facilitate their learning?

3. Do I (or could I) see alternatives to lecturing, telling, and explaining to all? Am I ready to "leave the stage"?

4. Do I (or could I) know what level of partnering is appropriate for my students and me?

5. Do I (or could I) make learning *real* and not just relevant?

6. Do I know how (or could I learn) to translate content into guiding questions?

7. Do I (or could I) understand learning and technology in terms of verbs and nouns?

Hopefully, you already do, or think you can do, many of these things. This chapter and the remaining chapters in the book are designed to help you answer each of the above questions with a resounding yes!

SEEING YOUR STUDENTS DIFFERENTLY

To be successful, partnering teachers a must see their students as partners in the learning process—with different but equal skill sets than their own. This is a massive change from the way the roles are set up in a traditional classroom, where teachers are expert with all the skills and information and students are the less capable receivers of the teachers' knowledge.

Of course, this does not mean that there is no longer an adult-student distinction in the learning process, or that kids should have the run of the school or the classroom. It does, however, mean treating students with respect and trust, giving them less direction and more guidance and expecting them to change their behavior as a result.

As a partnering teacher, it is your job to promote learning in a way that is meaningful and challenging to all your students. It is the students' job in partnering to accept and live up to the challenges you provide. In partnering, the challenges offered to students will be somewhat different from those in the traditional "telling" classroom. They will require more hands-on doing, more independent thinking, and more creating on the part of students. While some students may take time getting there, most that I talk with are willing and eager to take on this new and more challenging role.

PARTNERING TIP

Reserve some class time, such as a full day at the start of the semester or one period a month, for class discussions on pedagogy and methodology. Ask your students questions such as these: "What could we do to make your learning more challenging and interesting? What things relating to learning do you do well that you would like to do more of? What are some good experiences that you have had in other classes or with other teachers that you think we could use here?"

You may have to do this more than once (and actually put some of their suggestions into practice to let them know you are listening) before the ideas really start flowing. Making your students partners in the learning design process will pay off many times throughout the year.

Leaving the Stage

Corporate trainers, as well as many educational reformers, have long described the change we are talking about for teachers as a move from being the "sage on the stage" to the "guide on the side." But if you have been used to the stage for a long time, even if you have the best of intentions—and high motivation—to make the change, leaving it is not easy. Many teachers feel instinctively that they have not covered or taught material unless every word they want students to know has come out of their mouths at some point. It is important to realize that learning and mastering the art of *not* doing this, and gaining confidence that students will still learn (or learn better), will take time, perhaps even years.

I recently visited a brand-new charter school, set up to do things differently and better, and trying hard to do so. The administrators at the school had certainly thought a great deal about how to employ the latest partnering pedagogy. They had hired the very best teachers they could find, choosing among hundreds of applicants. Yet when I asked the principal, "How much do your teachers 'tell'?" her answer was immediate: "Too much." And she was right. I entered three classrooms to observe, and in each the teachers were telling (with the students in various degrees of listening or not). It was striking to me how much telling had carried over and just how much the teachers, who were trying hard to do something different, still carried over from their previous lives.

On the other hand, I have observed classrooms that worked quite differently. I have seen classes where the students just come in, sit down, and start working (sometimes with computers, sometimes without). Their tasks are obtained from a specified place, on paper or online. Not a minute is wasted with the need to tell any of them to "pay attention." For, as we all know, another big problem with telling is that it is often interrupted by misbehaving students. I once saw on YouTube a student-made video showing an advanced algebra teacher sitting at his desk going through a detailed explanation while writing on an overhead projector, while the students did whatever they pleased (including recording that video). Had this teacher been using the partnering pedagogy, he might have done some or all the following (using peer-to-peer instruction and choosing a different role for himself):

1. Made sure that the top five students in class fully understood the proof (which could have been done as homework or online)

2. Divided the class into groups, each with a student leader whose job was to ensure everyone in his or her group all learned as quickly as possible

3. Set up, in conjunction with some or all of the students, a fun competition between the teams whereby each student's competence, as well as the team's, was assessed by the class

4. Spent class time walking around, making sure learning was happening as planned and offering individual help when needed

PARTNERING TIP

Reflect on the classes you taught recently. How much telling did you do? What percentage of the students do you think you reached? Could you have done less and still helped those students (or even more students) understand the material? How?

Questioning and Discussing

Even though we want partnering teachers to avoid telling, and even though there are times when it is best for teachers to be totally quiet and listen respectfully to students, a teacher in a partnering classroom can still have plenty to say—just not at the front of the room, lecturing while the students sit and listen. A teacher using the partnering pedagogy can and should do many things verbally. These include asking questions (particularly Socratic ones), moderating discussions with students, offering an opinion as part of that discussion, and giving students feedback on projects (in conjunction with other students' feedback).

The distinction between telling (i.e., direct instruction) and other kinds of talking, such as questioning and discussion, is an important one, one that partnering teachers should always bear in mind so that they can monitor their own behavior.

PARTNERING TIP

Most teachers would be surprised if they found out how much telling they actually do. Ways to check this include videotaping your classes (on a regular basis so that you forget the camera is there and don't "perform" for it) and having a student make an audio recording with an MP3 player or computer. As a follow-up, you and the students can analyze the recording to see how much telling is being done (including giving directions). Doing this over time will allow you and your students chart and follow your progress in doing less telling. Be sure to celebrate good results, particularly as test scores improve.

Setting Up Your Classroom to Facilitate Partnering

The way a classroom is physically set up strongly influences how well the partnering pedagogy can work. One thing that can help considerably is setting up your classroom in a way that facilitates partnering (and changing that setup as often as needed).

In too many of our classrooms, the preferred setup is still parallel rows of desks or seats. This setup, often referred to as a theater or auditorium setup, is designed to facilitate telling, not partnering. In the past, this row-based structure was built in to the physical plant. When I taught in a high school in New York City in the late 1960s, all the classrooms had rows of screwed-down desks with attached, fold-down seats. (The desks even had inkwell holes!) I spent an entire spring break one year (with permission) unscrewing, by hand, an entire roomful of desks in order to be able to arrange the furniture differently.

It is ironic that, now that we almost all have the flexibility to move the furniture around, we often don't take advantage of this (except, typically, in the elementary grades). High school and college classrooms that have individual, moveable chairs are still often set up in rows.

The following paragraphs and Figures 2.1–2.5 offer some suggestions for making any classroom more friendly to partnering. None of these setups should be considered permanent; the arrangement should change according to the needs of different activities (plus, frequent change helps maintain interest). It is also important to consult the students (i.e., your partners) on how they would like the furniture to be arranged in order to facilitate their learning.

Particularly when students have their own computers (or if there is a computer to share for every two or three students), it is useful to arrange the desks or tables next to each other going around three sides of the room in a horseshoe shape (as in Figure 2.4). Then, instead of the students sitting on the outside of the horseshoe (as in many meetings), they sit on the inside. With this configuration, when students are working on their own or in groups at the computers, they face the walls and their screens. The teacher, standing in the middle, has an excellent view of what is happening on each screen and an unobstructed path to any student's side to offer him or her help. Whenever the teacher is holding a discussion, however, the students turn their chairs around toward the center of the room, focusing on the teacher and each other and avoiding the distraction of the computers. (Note: If for some reason you are stuck with an "outside the horseshoe" seating arrangement, and you are told that it is extremely difficult or impossible to change, it can be very effective to cover the walls with mirrors so that you can still see the screens from the center of the room. You do not have to use expensive and breakable glass for this; reflective Mylar in yardwide rolls is available inexpensively and can be cut into long strips and easily taped to the walls.)

You can also use a mixed setup, with different places for groups of two, four, six, or eight students to work comfortably. Another part of the room might be configured as a smaller inside horseshoe, accommodating a third or half the class at once. Such a mixed setup is often found in the many computer gaming centers found in Asia.

PARTNERING TIP

To avoid losing time, have your class practice changing furniture configurations rapidly. Time the changes, and have students get it down to seconds, as racing crews do in pit stops.

Figure 2.1   Teacher's Desk in Middle of Room (Deliberately Not Near the Board) With Students Arranged Around It Individually or in Groups

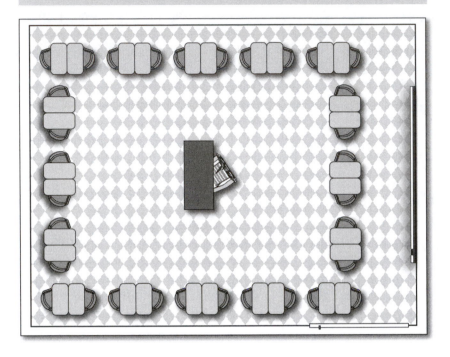

Figure 2.2   Desks in Small Groups to Facilitate Team Interaction

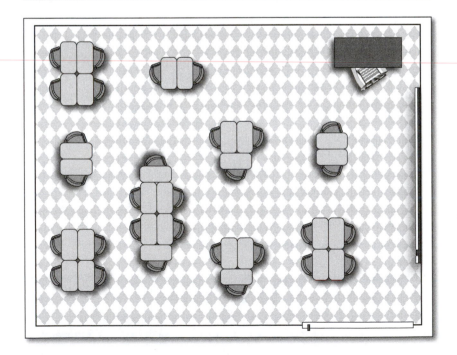

Figure 2.3   Chairs in a Circle for Discussion (Often Cited by Students as a Positive and Equalizing Arrangement)

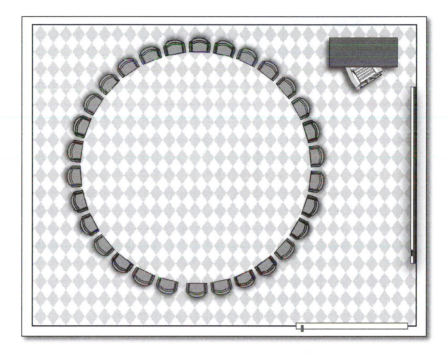

Figure 2.4   Inside Horseshoe Arrangement

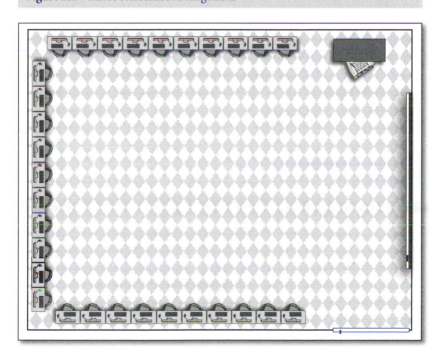

Figure 2.5   Mixed Setup: A Variety of Configurations Throughout the Classroom

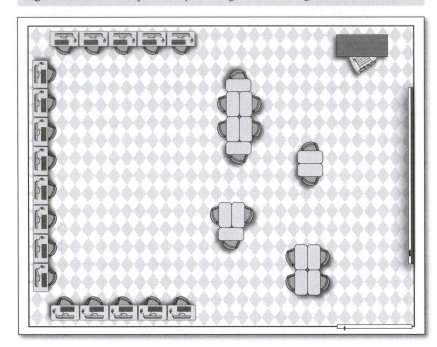

CHOOSING YOUR PARTNERING LEVEL

As with most things, there is no one-size-fits-all partnering that covers all students and all situations. Because in the United States we teach everyone, our districts and schools serve a wide variety of classes and students varying greatly in their abilities, preparation, motivation, home environment, and other factors. How can teachers best set up situations in which all of these students can partner, that is, teach themselves with our guidance?

To illustrate how partnering can be made to fit multiple situations, I will discuss three variations, or levels, of partnering: basic, guided, and advanced (problem, project, or case based). Basic partnering is what I suggest most teachers start with. Guided partnering is good for students that have particular trouble working on their own or performing certain tasks. Advanced partnering is for teachers and students who are ready to branch out from the textbook-ordered curriculum into longer and more complex learning projects.

Before I describe each of these partnering levels in detail, let me introduce two general principles that are true across all levels:

1. All aspects of partnering, from planning to doing to evaluating, must be done as much as possible with students as participants. Otherwise we're not partnering. Structures must be set up to do this, either via class discussions, student planning assistants, or both.

2. It is crucial that partnering students know at all times (or can find out on their own) what they are supposed to do, without the teacher telling them—even if they ask. This can be

done via a posted or written set of required questions, suggested (or sometimes required) activities, and clear outputs and timelines. These should all be available somewhere, offline and/or online, for students to consult.

> **PARTNERING TIP**
>
> The best response from a teacher to a student who says, "I don't know what to do," is "I don't either—check the . . . ." Students will soon learn to stop asking and find out for themselves.

Basic Partnering

Basic partnering, at its simplest, is giving students guiding questions and letting them work on their own, individually or in groups, to answer them (followed by discussion and summation). This is often called *inquiry-based learning*. An example would be, instead of lecturing about lightning and why it happens, you ask students, "Why do we have lightning?" and let them find the answers and present them on their own.

To do this, the content—of any lesson, in any subject that can be taught through the old telling pedagogy—can and should be turned by the partnering teacher into a set of one or more guiding questions, typically one or two open-ended, high-level questions and several detailed questions. Thus a lecture on the use of the comma becomes "Why do we pause when we speak?" followed by "How do we show this in writing?" A lesson on the subjunctive becomes "How do we talk about things that might or might not happen?" followed by "How do we indicate this in English?" and "Can you find five examples in literature?"

The basic criterion for whether the guiding questions are the right ones is simple: if students can answer the questions correctly (and intelligently), they know the material in question. Since guiding questions do not necessarily have right or wrong answers, we are typically looking for well-thought-out and well-supported (i.e., "intelligent") responses. As the teacher, of course, you are the judge of the quality and rigor of the students' answers. Since you haven't given them answers, you are never judging their ability to just parrot those answers back.

> **PARTNERING TIP**
>
> Sometimes, for certain topics, it makes sense to elicit some (or all) of the guiding questions from students. You might ask them, for example, "What would the guiding questions be for studying someone's life or for a historical issue such as women's suffrage or civil rights?" Formulating the questions can sometimes be as valuable to students as answering them.

Basic partnering is, essentially, posting the guiding questions for students and having them find, present, and discuss the answers in a specified time frame. That frame may be a single class or it may be longer, depending on the questions. Some educators make a distinction between project-based learning and problem-based learning (PBL), with the former taking only days and the latter weeks or even months. I classify PBL as advanced partnering and discuss it in detail later in the chapter.

In all levels of partnering, the inquiry and projects are tied to the curriculum through the guiding questions. In addition to the questions coming before the answers, what is distinctive about basic partnering is that how students find the answers to the guiding questions is typically up to them, using whatever tools—from technology to texts to the library—they have at their disposal.

Depending on the particular questions, students may work individually or in groups of different sizes. A question such as "What is your family's cultural heritage?" might be explored individually, while "What is culture?" might be explored in groups. Teachers can provide guidance about appropriate tools to use and decisions to make, but these recommendations are often made to individuals or small groups rather than to the class as a whole. Teachers can also specify and/or alternate student groupings, or even allow them to be based on student preference and choice, which many students prefer.

Providing Variety

Obviously, if a teacher did the exact same version of basic partnering every day, it would become as boring as just telling, so one of the teacher's important roles in partnering is to design interesting variations. Such variation can come in forms such as these:

- Virtually including in groups students (or adults) who are physically in other locations or classes, based on the topics, areas, or languages that are being studied
- Students not always using the same methods and tools to find the answers to the questions, but trying and learning to use a variety of tools (geography questions, for example, can be approached with tools ranging from atlases to GPS to Google Earth)
- Approaching topics through whole-class games or simulations
- Having students design real solutions to real problems
- Going outside the classroom on physical or virtual visits, whenever possible

Sharing Results

In basic partnering students share their findings with the class and the teacher using methods and tools of their own choosing: text, audio, video, animation, multimedia, and even game designs. Because there may be many students or groups of students presenting, short, concise presentations (one or two minutes long) are encouraged. This ability to create and give brief and informative presentations is a useful skill in itself and gets easier with practice.

PARTNERING TIP

The so-called elevator presentation (i.e., If you happen to find yourself in an elevator with an important person whom you want to influence or persuade, what would you say during the one-minute trip?) has become an important tool in business. It is worth limiting your student presentations to one minute (or two at most), which forces them to be concise, to the point, and persuasive. Presentations can be student- and teacher-rated for their effectiveness in meeting these criteria. In partnering, all student presentations should be recorded by students either in audio or (preferably) video, critiqued by students and the teacher, and saved for portfolios and evaluation.

All partnering students should be required to meet a minimum proficiency level in several presentation media, including writing, based on whatever standards your school adopts.

Frequent discussions about the guiding questions and their answers, as well as about how students are working and how it is going, are held in a partnering classroom. As many of these discussions as possible should be led, and recorded, by students. In some classrooms all the critiques are done by students, following a model provided by the teacher that is improved on over time.

Check It Out!

The International Society for Technology in Education's National Educational Technology Standards are available at http://www.iste.org/AM/Template.cfm?Section=NETS.

Basic partnering can get you through any curriculum, but it requires that your students be (or, if you are just starting, that your students learn to be) strongly self-directed. Self-direction is an excellent skill for students to learn and master.

Check It Out!

For an excellent example of a student-led critique, see http://tinyurl.com/yck7ewa.

Most students, no matter what their background, can do and thrive on basic partnering work. I have seen it used in public schools, private schools, religious schools, and charter schools. But nothing works for all classes and all students (particularly at first), and that is why there are alternatives. An important alternative to consider is what I call guided partnering.

Check It Out!

For an article describing partnering in use in West Virginia, visit http://wvde.state.wv.us/news/1716.

Guided Partnering

The open-endedness and freedom for students to choose their own way that characterize basic partnering may not work in all contexts, particularly in classes that are partnering for the first time. Some students, for example, may have trouble working on their own, working in groups, researching, or even reading. For such students there exists a more directed, or guided, version of partnering, which retains the same ideas and ideals as the basic version. Guided partnering still begins with guiding questions and still has students answer those questions by working more or less on their own, individually or in groups, and making presentations. The difference is that the choices for how students work are far more structured, and the kinds of presentations students do are more highly specified as well. Using pedagogical jargon, this level might be called scaffolded partnering.

Guided, structured, or scaffolded partnering is practiced by many teachers who do project- or inquiry-based learning with students considered to be at risk. One group that helps many teachers do guided partnering is a New York City organization called Teaching Matters (www.teachingmatters.org). They offer packaged solutions in the form of fully designed partnering projects on a variety of topics. Their designs include not only guiding questions, but also activities for the students to do in order to answer those questions. They also scaffold carefully the role of the teacher. An example is a partnering project on civil rights (see http://rights.teachingmatters.org). The project takes students from a guiding question, asking them to define "civil rights," through the following five steps: Understand Injustice, Study Methods of Action, Describe a Movement, Create a Campaign, and Make a Difference. Specific links to resources, people timelines, and plans of action are provided.

Check It Out!

Other organizations offering similar services to those provided by Teaching Matters (www.teachingmatters.org) include the Buck Institute for Education (http://www.bie.org), the New Media Consortium (http://www.nmc.org.), and AUSSIE Consultants (http://www.aussiepd.com/about/aussie-consultants).

PARTNERING TIP

Some districts and organizations, as well a few states, have created elaborate partnering examples tied directly to state curricula. Ask your administrators if this is the case in your location.

Advanced Partnering

A third approach to partnering (and the one I think will help all students most in the long run) is advanced partnering. You may have heard of some of these formats, such as case-based learning (often used in medical and business schools), project-based learning, and, as we've already discussed in this book, problem-based learning (PBL). These are more advanced brands, or formats, of the basic partnering idea. One difference is that they are typically longer-term units in which a large number of curricular standards—as well as many elements of content from the textbook curriculum—are integrated and learned through the students solving an overarching problem, or case. Examples of PBL units/guiding questions include the following:

Grade/Subject	Problem
K–Early Elementary	How can we build a "wolf-proof" house? Who stole the cookies? How can we prepare for a storm? Why did the pumpkins rot? Why do teeth hurt? How do you build a good pet home?
Grades 2–3	How can we help someone with leukemia? How can we best explain an Indian culture through a museum exhibit? How can we help rid a neighborhood of caterpillars without doing ecological damge? How can we design the best playground for $10,000?
Grades 4–6	How can we build a great patio for a specific house and price? How should we set up the rules for moon basketball? How can you calculate the cost of space trips? How can you decide whether to preserve or move a landmark?
Grades 7–8	How can we learn about a family disease and help the family members? How can we use existing sports data to pick the best team? How can we design better currency?
High School Math	How can we build roads using the least amount of pavement? How can we build fences using the least amount of fencing?
High School English	How can you write a winning book proposal on _____? How can you market a new product?
High School Science	How can you escape from/navigate through various parts of the human body? How can you diagnose and treat a medical problem from a distance?
High School Social Studies	How can you, as secretary of state, recommend a course of action to the president?

SOURCE: *Problem-Based Learning in K–8 classrooms,* by Ann Lambros (Corwin); *Problem-Based Learning in Middle and High School Classrooms,* by Ann Lambros (Corwin).

Advanced partnering based on such cases or problems is often considered more true-to-life learning than a more logically laid out, topic-by-topic curriculum. It is often used in medical and business schools, where a student might use a case about a patient with certain symptoms or a story of a company having problems to learn about a disease or a business issue, rather than learning about the disease or problem in isolation.

For students using advanced partnering, advantages are that they get to deal with more complex issues and problems than can be dealt with in a single class period, make real-life-type decisions, and do so in a real-world time frame (in which certain information, for example, might become available only later in the process, if and when it is found).

PBL has become popular in many schools in the United States and other countries (e.g., Singapore), and there is a wealth of information available on the Internet and in books about how to do it, including various problems (or guiding questions) one can use and suggested resources.

> **Check It Out!**
>
> An online search for "problem-based learning" will reveal the latest sources.

One caveat regarding PBL is that, to ensure complete coverage of the standards and the curriculum, a teacher must keep careful track of what is and isn't covered by each of the various problems the students take on. Also, because the problems need to be carefully crafted to include many different curricular elements and standards, they can sometimes be less immediately connected to individual students' reality or interests, and this must be monitored by the teacher.

Other Types of Advanced Partnering

A number of groups have created their own variations on partnering, including these:

- Process-oriented guided inquiry learning (POGIL) for general, organic, and physical chemistry, funded by the National Science Foundation
- Challenge-based learning (involving topics such as cultural identity, apathy, war, and sustainability of food, resources, and energy), created by Apple
- Technology-enhanced active learning (TEAL) for introductory physics, created by the Massachusetts Institute of Technology
- Quest-based learning, created for New York City's experimental Quest to Learn school

> **Check It Out!**
>
> For examples and information about these types of partnering, see the following:
>
> http://new.pogil.org
>
> http://www.nmc.org/pdf/Challenge -Based-Learning.pdf
>
> http://icampus.mit.edu/projects/TEAL .shtml
>
> http://www.q2l.org

Note, for example, how close Apple's description of challenge-based learning is to what we have been discussing: "a collaborative learning experience in which teachers and students work together to learn about compelling issues, propose solutions to real problems and take action."[13] All these partnering variations are worth considering and using, especially if your school, district, or state has made an investment in one of them.

PARTNERING TIP

Check your state's web site for partnering resources, such as predesigned PBL examples tied to state standards. Contribute to these lists if you can.

The major points of distinction between all the various brands of partnering we have discussed are the degree of guidance or scaffolding provided to students and the breadth of the guiding questions. The latter determines, in turn, the length of each particular unit or exercise. Guiding questions can range from those answerable in a single period ("Why does it rain?") to those requiring an entire semester ("How can we best predict the world's weather?").

Although it is often helpful to start with a predesigned and pretested example, there is no "cookbook" for successful partnering. Ultimately, you will customize and perfect your own partnering method, combining from several sources what is best for you and your students.

TECHNOLOGY AND PARTNERING

Verbs and Nouns

Whatever level, type, or brand of partnering you choose, you will be working with students who are using some level of digital technology to find the answers to their guiding questions. Digital technology is the great facilitator that lies behind the renaissance of the partnering pedagogy in the 21st century, and although partnering can be done with whatever level of technology is available in your classroom (even none), the more technology that is available to students, the better partnering almost always goes. Having students make maximum use of whatever technology is available in your classroom is a required part of partnering. But two important questions still arise:

1. How do you partner using whatever types of technology are (and are not) available in your school and classroom?

2. How do you prevent technology from taking over the essentials that you are trying to teach?

The best way to answer both of these questions is to think in terms of *verbs* and *nouns* for learning.

Verbs are the skills that students need to learn, practice, and master. They include all the traditional things we want students to be able to do in the context of the content. Whatever subject we teach, we want students to be proficient at such verbs as thinking critically, presenting logically, communicating, making decisions, being rigorous, understanding content and context, and persuading. Verbs are, in a sense, the underlying learning, and pedagogy is typically about verbs, that is, how to provide students with the subject-specific and general skills they need.

What is extremely important to note is that the verbs important for learning do not change (or change very little) over time.

Nouns, on the other hand, are the tools students use to learn to do, or practice, the verbs. Nouns include such traditional tools as books and essays as well as more 21st century tools such as the Internet. Nouns are the way people generally think of technology: computers, PowerPoint, Wikipedia, and so on. Nouns include both hardware and software—the actual technologies available to your students. Most books on using technology in the classroom begin with the particular technologies (i.e., nouns) currently available, such as podcasts, wikis, or blogs, and explain how each one can be used for teaching different subjects. But nouns are only a means to an end.

And unlike learning verbs, learning nouns change increasingly frequently.

PowerPoint, for example, is a tool (noun) for presenting (verb). But it will likely be replaced in our students' lifetimes (and is already being replaced in many places) by Flash and other, better, presentation tools. E-mail is a tool for communicating. But it has already been replaced, among many students, by texting and even Twitter. ("E-mail is for old people," say many students.) Wikipedia is a tool for learning. But it is being supplanted by tools like YouTube and advanced search.

> ## PARTNERING TIP
>
> Discuss with your students the concept of verbs and nouns. Be sure they understand the difference and where to put their focus (i.e., on the verbs).
>
> Begin each year or semester by having students take an inventory of all the nouns that are available for their use (including hardware, software, Internet) in the classroom and in labs. You or they should then post that list (say, on a wall chart) for easy reference, adding more tools to the list as they become available. You and they can then list and discuss the various verbs for which each of the tools is helpful.
>
> As students partner to answer your guiding questions, they should choose tools from the list to use, depending on the verb they are doing. Ensure that over the course of the semester or year, all students get to try all the tools.

Begin With the Verbs!

Focusing the partnering and learning process on the verbs (skills), and not on the nouns (tools), is the way to avoid letting technology for its own sake take over students' learning. For a teacher who is looking to replace the pedagogy of telling with that of partnering, it is far better to begin by considering the various verbs through which students can learn material, and not get too attached to any particular nouns. There are a great many learning verbs that we would like students to be proficient in, representing skills that most educators (and people outside of education, such as employers) want students to know. In modern pedagogy, verbs get blended with the content we teach.

One great benefit of focusing on the verbs is that doing so makes it a lot easier for teachers to answer students' frequent "Why should I learn this?" questions. Typically the "this" students are referring to is a topic, or piece of content. But if you can show them that they are really learning and practicing skills that they realize they can use right away or will need in the future, they are often more willing to listen.

The Learning Verbs and the Associated Nouns

There are nearly 50 learning verbs that we use and want students to master, and over 100 nouns available to students to use in their efforts (see Table 2.1). Notice that all of the verbs have been around since long before digital technology came on the scene. Notice, too, that for each verb there are many tools and technologies available to help learn and practice it. To plan effective partnering instruction, rather than rush to figuring out which specific technologies or tools (i.e., nouns) to use, teachers should choose from the list the appropriate verbs that are key for the material and the group of students they are working with, and focus the lesson around blending those verbs with the content and technology.

As you browse though the list, think of which verbs might be most useful to you and your students for various things you teach. The verbs you choose will, in turn, suggest the roles for each of the partners (i.e., students and teacher) in learning the material.

Obviously, not all the nouns will be available to all students, and the answer to the question "How do you partner using whatever types of technology are (and are not) available in your school and classroom?" is that you start with the verbs and have students work with whatever nouns are available in your classroom or school at that time.

PARTNERING AND THE REQUIRED CURRICULUM

A frequently asked question is whether partnering can be used with the required curriculum that all teachers must follow. The answer is yes, absolutely. The partnering pedagogy can be used without any changes to the curriculum because—whatever pedagogy you use—the questions that students should be able to answer, and the skills they must master, remain the same. They are the questions we test on. Whether you tell your students about the Bill of Rights or they learn about it on their own, they still need to know what the document contains, why it is important, and what the issues are regarding each of the various amendments. And at higher levels, they still need to learn the skills of analyzing arguments regarding those issues.

The only thing that changes with the partnering pedagogy is the way that students learn those answers and skills. When partnering, students start with the questions and then learn the answers and skills for themselves, with the help of their peers and teachers. (This is, of course, the reverse of how things are done in the textbook.)

The two main connections between the partnering pedagogy and the curriculum are the guiding questions and the focus on verbs. Both of those together provide the explicit learning goals for students. When students know clearly what the goals are, it is much easier for the

Table 2.1   The Verbs and Associated Nouns

Verbs for Researching and Managing Information

Analyzing: spreadsheets, textual analyzers, parsers, spelling and grammar checkers, salience analyzers, factor analyzers, best fit, statistics, critiques

Exploring: search engines, hyperlinks

Reading: Internet, online readers, speech-to-text programs, rapid serial visual presentation (RSVP), cell phone novels, graphic novels

Searching and Finding: search engines, reading tools, RSVP, speed-ups, mapping tools, Really Simple Syndication (RSS), Listservs

Verifying: research tools, fact checkers

Watching and Listening: podcasts, YouTube, Big Think, TED Talks, video search engines, speed-up tools for audio and video clips, text-to-speech programs

Verbs for Thinking Effectively

Calculating: calculators, cell phones, spreadsheets, programming tools

Comparing: comparison tools, artificial intelligence tools

Deciding (Frequent Decision Making): decision-making tools, games, question generators, comparison generators

Ethical Questioning: scenarios, case studies, videos

Evaluating: logic tools, comparative shopping web sites, assessment tools, self-assessment tools, rubrics

Experimenting: data collection tools, cameras, probes, virtual labs, simulations

Modeling and Using Models: three-dimensional printers, simulations, spreadsheets

Observing: cameras, video, video cameras, games

Predicting: simulations, forecasting tools, scenarios

Problem Solving: decision trees, scientific method, data analysis

Reflecting: writing activities, after-action reviews, debriefing activities, wikis, blogs, Intuition

Socratic Questioning: logic trees, question generators, artificial intelligence

Thinking Critically: outliners, brainstorming tools, intuition

Thinking Logically: outliners

Verbs for Communicating and Presenting

Briefing: PowerPoint, Flash, multimedia, video, podcasts

Collaborating: collaboration tools, Google Docs, teleconferencing tools

Combining: mashups, video editing tools, multimedia creation tools

Connecting: social networking tools, genealogy tools, logic tools, cell phones

Cooperating: wikis, blogs, games, collaboration tools

Debating: research tools, online debating tools, blogs, YouTube, negotiating tools

Dialoging: e-mail, text messages, blogs, cell phones, wikis, YouTube

---

Verbs for Communicating and Presenting

Finding Your Voice: design tools, computer-aided design (CAD) tools, cameras, video, critiques, e-mail

Listening: podcasts, video, Skype

Negotiating: negotiation tools, research tools, historical videos

Networking: Internet, social networking tools, cell phones

Sharing: Listservs, YouTube, special interest blogs, cell phones

Writing: outlining tools, script writing tools, dictionaries and thesauri, blogs, games

---

Verbs for Constructing and Creating

Adapting: mods, hardware mods, "soft" mods

Combining: mashups, multimedia tools

Competing: games, contests, competitions

Designing: brainstorming tools, design tools

Imitating: memorizing tools, videos, podcasts, recorded books, plays, speeches, TED Talks, Big Think

Innovating: prototyping tools, iteration

Making: writing tools, video, programming tools, machinima, graphics, game-making tools, game-modding tools, CAD tools

Modeling and Trying: constructivist tools, drafting tools, brainstorming tools, digital manipulatives

Personalizing: interface tools, multiple intelligence tools

Planning: project planning tools, outliners

Programming: game creation tools, robotics, programming languages

Prudent Risk Taking: games, simulations

Simulating: simulations, games, role-playing tools

---

students to achieve those goals, each in his or her own way. Students have often said this to me, in their own language: "Just tell us where you want us to go and let us get there." I discuss these crucial connections between the curriculum and partnering in more detail in Chapter 5.

Ensuring the Connection Gets Made

In any pedagogy, the connection between the tasks students do and the learning they take away is not automatic and should never be taken for granted. Many students do make the connections on their own, of course, but it is still the teacher's job to point out the connections and ensure they get made. So the partnering teacher's final job in connecting the partnering pedagogy to the curriculum is to review—via discussions, presentations, blog entries, and other means, and on an ongoing, iterative basis—the answers to the guiding questions that students are finding (individually or in groups) and to provide feedback about the quality, rigor, and context of those answers. Partnering teachers should also continually (re)emphasize the underlying skills being learned. Figure 2.6 contrasts the old telling and new partnering approaches along several dimensions.

Figure 2.6   Telling Versus Partnering

Telling Pedagogy	Partnering Pedagogy
Objectives	Guiding questions
Lectures	Verbs (skills)
Worksheets	Nouns (tools)
Tests	Feedback/iteration

The Student's Roles in Connecting the Partnering Pedagogy and Content

It should not be forgotten that students also have roles in making the connection between the partnering work that they do and the curriculum, or content. The following are three specific roles that students need to play in making this connection:

1. Students need to see themselves as "partnering professionals," people whose job it is to be aware of what the important questions are in any subject they are studying and to answer those questions.

2. Students need to think of themselves as individuals who go about answering those questions in their own unique way, collaborating when appropriate and creating answers that others will understand and work that they can be proud of.

3. Students need to be aware of the verbs (i.e., skills) they are learning and practicing as part of the tasks they are currently doing and, as they work with the content, try to get better at doing each of them so that they improve at doing a wide range of required skills.

When the teacher and the students are each fully aware, through discussion and practice, of the roles they need to play in connecting the partnering pedagogy to the content and learning, and are playing those roles continually and effectively, much more learning—and much more effective learning—will take place in our classrooms.

PARTNERING TIP

Take some class time to review with your students their roles and yours in this process. It will pay off in terms of clarity of purpose and, therefore, results.

TAKING YOUR FIRST (OR NEXT) STEPS INTO PARTNERING

Partnering is, to a large extent, setting up a new relationship between you, the teacher, and your students. So when taking your initial steps into partnering, it is always a good idea to begin by talking with your students about what you are attempting to do and why. By making consultation with students your first step, you immediately change the relationship from the traditional top-down variety to one of equal partners.

For teachers who've never done it before, it can often be scary to leave the traditional position at the front of the class. Before you leap, it helps to do a number of things to ensure that your bungee cord is firmly attached and that you will not just fall into the abyss. These include talking with other partnering teachers who have transitioned successfully, watching videos of successful partnering in action, and visiting classes where partnering is happening.

And don't forget that the new relationship is something your students also have to get used to and accept. They too are likely to be skeptical at first and may have a hard time believing you are serious. Students are rarely, if ever, asked what they think about teaching methods, or how they prefer to learn, or even what they like, so when it is done (with a sincere desire to find out what they think) they are likely to react positively. The good news is that once both sides get over the initial awkwardness of doing something different, it almost always works out well.

Recently, students in one school were given three options for learning something: (1) participate in a traditional instructor-led session, (2) work in small groups with video tutorials and a PowerPoint handout, or (3) work individually with the video tutorials and a PowerPoint handout. Not surprisingly, not a single student opted for the instructor-led session.

Start Slowly

Although it is possible to jump right into partnering on the first day (and some teachers may find this better and even exciting), most teachers will find it preferable to ease into partnering a little at a time. You might begin with a partnering project, such as "How can we improve our school?" or "How can we improve our community?" Some districts do this as a school- or districtwide exercise. Or you can run one or two units, or one or two classes, using the basic partnering of guiding questions, verbs, students answering on their own, and reviewing the answers as a class, using what you learn from the first one to improve the second.

You can also begin at a more guided, structured, or scaffolded partnering level, basing your planning, for example, on the Teaching Matters examples discussed earlier. Or you can do a PBL project based on examples in any of the many PBL books or web sites available.

You might also try working with students to turn a lesson you have just taught into guiding questions, so that they get the idea of what you are up to, and then doing the same for the next lesson and guiding students to answer the questions themselves rather than you telling them.

What is important is that you start somewhere and that, whatever the initial results, good or bad, you do not give up.

Partnering Suggestions for Newbies

- Finish this book. Find and read other books on Web 2.0 and PBL.
- Find and talk with others who are partnering.
- Pick a lesson (or project) to start with.
- Create guiding questions and rubrics for evaluation.
- Discuss with your students what you are trying to do; get suggestions.
- Determine with your students what nouns are available for them to use.
- Try it for one to three days, handing out the guiding questions and letting students learn and present by themselves, with your coaching.
- Discuss and evaluate the results.
- Iterate, try again.
- Don't give up.

Overcome Other Barriers

If you are a beginner at partnering, your biggest step is probably going to be leaving the stage and getting yourself started along a different path. Ideally, as you do so you will get the support, encouragement, help, and guidance you want and need from your administration. That is how it should be and, in more and more cases, how it is. But not always. What do you do when partnering is not the preferred method on administrators' minds, or, as is true in some cases, they are actively opposed?

Once you decide to take the partnering route, it helps to resolve that, because this is in the students' best interests, you will not permit any outside barriers (or excuses) to stand in your way. Not enough technology? Just begin with what you have. Students having trouble taking responsibility? Start slowly, and let them discover the benefits. Not sure what to do next? Ask for help. Parents or others opposed? Do it stealthily. Unfortunately, if you wait for everyone to come around, you may never get started.

There are no prohibitions on trying to improve how you teach. Many partnering initiatives are actually begun by a single teacher because he or she knows it will work. If you are successful, it might actually spread!

Remember too that partnering always comes back to asking, and talking with, your students, individually and in groups. There is no way for me to overemphasize this or for teachers to overdo it. In the next chapter, we consider some of the things you should be talking with students about—particularly, and especially, their individual passions.

3

Think People and Passions Rather Than Classes and Content

Guiding Questions

1. Why is it important to know what each of my students is passionate about?

2. How can I use that information to differentiate learning?

3. How can my students and I live out the partnering roles and adopt new behaviors?

What ultimately counts in education (certainly from the point of view of the person being educated) is not standardized test scores, content, or curriculum. What truly matters is each student as an individual. Are these individuals (i.e., each of our students) learning what they need to know in order to go as far as their capabilities will allow?

Obviously we do some things on an individual, student-by-student basis, such as grading. But far too often, for a variety of what generally seem like good or necessary reasons, we think of teaching as being more about our classes and their content than about the different and differentiated individuals we teach. Most of the writing about teaching and learning is really about teaching and learning in classes (i.e., in groups). In many cases we have become so used to thinking of students in groups of 20–40 that we sometimes forget that our students are individual people, each with personal passions, personal interests, and personal needs that have to be met. Sadly, when this happens, the kids know and feel it. In the worst cases, they report being thought of as nameless, fungible "Saran Wrap kids" (i.e., their teachers see right through them) or being pigeonholed into a small number of types or categories such as "good student" or "slacker."

With all the increased focus on aggregating and comparing scores across classes, schools, and nations, how much do we really know about our students as individuals? According to what the students tell me, not nearly enough.

Students don't typically care at all what happens to their class—all that matters is what happens to them. This is not hard to understand. Picture yourself taking a class. How much interest do you have in your class's average scores and whether they are better than last year's? Your only focus is on how much you are learning and whether your needs are being met. In this respect, our students are precisely the same as us when we are learning—with one big exception. Today's students, who are catered to as individuals in so many areas of their lives (such as music, computer games, and other technology), have far less tolerance than many adults do for their individual needs not being met.

Outside of school, young people are increasingly treated as highly discriminating individuals, with the need (and the means) to differentiate themselves. Marketers of clothing, shoes, songs, movies, videos, cell phones, and other products offer young people enormous varieties of styles and models that allow each kid to totally individualize himself or herself (although often within a current fashion mode). To reach these people, we have to see them as discriminating individuals as well and differentiate our instruction for each one of them.

Differentiated instruction, of course, has now become a big educational buzzword. But what isn't as widely discussed is the best way—and often the only way—to approach each student as an individual and to motivate them at the same time. That way is through our students' passions—the things that truly interest them. Therefore, in partnering, students' passions are the main drivers of student engagement and achievement.

LEARN ABOUT YOUR STUDENTS' INTERESTS AND PASSIONS

Every one of your students has a main interest, or passion, if you will. These passions are extremely diverse and include everything (and anything) from nature, to sports, to reading, to music, to vehicles, to history, to medicine, to space exploration, to a wide variety of other, often unexpected areas. In some cases a student's passion may be still hidden from his or her own self-knowledge. And many students have more than one.

Knowing what those individual passions are, not just on the surface but in some depth and detail, is extremely important for partnering teachers. The reason is that students' passions are the routes and filters through which partnering teachers create individualized learning—learning that will stick in students' minds, be valuable in their lives, and make them want more.

Today, there is a new buzzword making the rounds: *passion-based learning.*[14]

Find Students' Passions

There is, of course, only one sure way to find out what your students' passions are: ask your students, one at a time, on an individual basis. I recommend you ask your students about their passions whenever you can, certainly at least once a term, and maybe more often. If a student replies, "What do you mean by *passion?*" a great definition you can offer is this: "Your passion is what you like to spend your time on when no one is making you do something else."

I recently polled a group of 200 teachers and administrators (using individual polling devices, or "clickers") on this question: "What percentage of teachers know the passion of each of their students?" A quarter said less than 10 percent. More than half said less than 20 percent, and more than three quarters said less than 40 percent. Only two people answered over 70 percent, and no one said over 90 percent.

Reflecting on this afterward, one teacher remarked, "I spend a great deal of energy putting my own passion into my teaching. It just didn't occur to me that each of my students has his or her own passion as well. Now I understand why, sometimes, when I say a particular thing, certain heads will suddenly perk up."

While most students have a passion, and can readily name it if asked, some students do not know or are not able to articulate what their passion is—or they may not have found it yet. They should be reassured that that's OK. But it is also important to point out to them how crucial it is for them to find this out and to keep thinking about it, because knowing their passion and following it is an important key to their success in life. Sometimes just listening to other kids talk about their passions helps students understand or find theirs, so it is good to encourage those students with similar interests and passions to find each other and talk.

PARTNERING TIP

On the first day of class, when you introduce yourself to your class(es) and ask each student his or her name, also ask, individually, what each student is interested in and/or passionate about. Write this down, and take it seriously. It will enable you to design ways to reach each of these students through his or her passion and to cluster your students, at certain times, by their common interests. You can encourage those students who are not able to identify a passion to try out the different clusters as they seek their own interests.

Remember, knowing and using your students' passions helps them *and* you. Your students want you to know what they are passionate about because it's part of knowing who they are. Knowing that you know and really care about their interests—and not just what you are teaching them—will often motivate them to do things they might otherwise not. At the same time, your knowing their passions helps you be the best coach and guide you can be.

Use the Passions to Individualize Instruction Daily

Another reason you want to know your students' passions is that you can use them to individualize (i.e., differentiate) your instruction for each student. It should surprise very few readers to learn that students typically report to me that they are bored in 50–100 percent of their classes, 50–100 percent of the time. In those times they are probably thinking about something that does interest them, and it would be great if we could make the connection. Knowing our students' passions is the best tool for doing this.

How exactly does knowing these passions help us differentiate instruction? First, it gives us more of an incentive to think about our students differently—as individuals who are our partners. We are in business, essentially, with each of our students, to get a job done—a professional learning job—every day. Just as in any professional law or consulting firm, each partner (i.e., student) needs to do the necessary work in his or her own way, yet always with an eye on the firm's (i.e., the teacher's) overall strategy. Because they are partners, students get a say in how the job gets done. Because they are people, students have individual ups and downs, good days and bad, and so long as the work does get done, as partners we need to respect that. And because they are individuals, all students' work and learning is filtered though their personal preferences, passions, likes, and dislikes.

In addition, knowing our students' passions gives us an idea of the breadth of interests we are working with—far broader, I would guess, than many teachers imagine. We can use those interests to bring far more diversity into our students' learning. Finally, knowing students' passions allows us to direct certain guiding questions (or subquestions) specifically to the different interests that our students have and to paths and resources that feed those interests.

Learn From Your Students

There are many topics that students are passionate about—of which technology is just one—where they may know much more than their teachers. Rather than let this threaten us, we should view this as a good thing, because in the partnering pedagogy we are all both teachers and learners. Today's students want (and need) not just to take in knowledge, but to mutually share what they know, including with teachers. In the words of one student, "If you want us to do what you like, you have to do some of what we like."

Figuring out what your students can do better than you, and then using that to improve instruction, is an important piece of partnering. Letting students do those things (e.g., use technology, teach their peers, go in directions that interest them) frees you up to do other things that otherwise you might not have time for and, in general, to be a better teacher. In fact, just asking students "What are your passions?" and finding out their interests puts you miles ahead on the first day.

PARTNERING TIP

Keep a log (online or off) of student passions that you have come across and ideas for reaching students through those passions. Share these logs with your colleagues (e.g., through a wiki). Search the Internet for suggestions from others on how they have used student passions. Even a small group of teachers ought to be able to build up a pretty extensive list over time, but using the experience of the world is much better. Twitter is one good tool for this (see Chapter 7), and you should be on the lookout for others.

Iteration Is Key

All professionals—be they product designers, marketers, or game makers—who connect successfully with their customers know that they cannot just design a product, or piece of advertising, or a game once and then use it over and over forever—even if it succeeds fabulously the first time. As teachers, we need to do much more of what other successful professionals do: iterate. Iteration means putting something out there, seeing how it works, and immediately changing those elements that don't work. In our case, immediately means as soon as the next class. Being aware of our students' passions and fluctuating interest levels ought to give us an incentive to try different things and to change our teaching frequently, which is exactly what our students are asking for.

Moving to a passion-based, iterative approach can help you reach your students in many new ways. For instance, instead of telling a misbehaving student to pay attention, you might say, "Taylor, you may not think you are interested in what I am teaching, but I do know you are interested in [whatever Taylor's passion is]. Can you think of a way in which what we are talking about relates to that? No? Well, perhaps I can give you some ideas. Did you happen to see [something that connects to the topic]? How many of you saw that? OK, what's the connection?"

PARTNERING TIP

Do you teach more than one section of a particular course? If so, make it a personal policy to never do the same thing in both and to ask students at the end of each class how you can improve it for the next group.

Make at least part of every class an experiment in teaching. Announce to your students that this is an experiment and you want their reactions to it. Afterward ask for honest feedback from your students about how the experiment went. Hearing "I hated it" should be just as valuable to you as hearing "I really liked it." In the video game business, when play testers give feedback that something "sucked" (that's a technical term in the game business), it is removed from the game immediately and for all time.

Get and Give Constant Feedback

To iterate, you have to continually figure out what is and isn't working for your students and change what isn't working—quickly and for all time. That means soliciting constant feedback from your students.

Imagine what you would do and how you would teach if Taylor were the only student you had, instead of having 20–40 students in a class. That is, imagine you were Taylor's personal tutor. What would you be doing differently than you do in class? For one thing, you would almost certainly be giving him (or her) constant feedback as well as getting constant feedback on what he (or she) was thinking and feeling. That would help you guide your teaching, changing course when something wasn't working and being sure that your one student wasn't bored and was happily working and learning all the time.

How do you do the same thing in a classroom with 20–40 students? Some teachers recommend "taking the temperature" of their students on a constant basis, and there are many ways to do this. One is to hand out cards that are red on one side, green on the other. You can ask at any time for a "temperature check," having students raise a green card if they are interested and a red card if they are bored, and see by the colors what's going on and who needs attention. Such cards are also a useful technique for getting the entire class to respond to binary questions when appropriate. Another, more technology-based way do the same thing is to use personal response devices, or clickers, when available (or the cell-phone-based equivalent of clickers—see www.polleverywhere.com—or even just cell phones using texting).

Many teachers encourage individual feedback from students via e-mail, texting, or posting to a class blog. Many respond to students individually. Some teachers even set up a live Twitter feed, which is visible to the class on a whiteboard or screen, on which students can post second-by-second reactions.

PARTNERING TIP

Be sure to set up a way to receive direct feedback from students in the classroom. It can come via "temperature checks," e-mail, texting, in-class polling, or even surveys if they are relatively frequent. Or you can leave a prepaid cell phone on your desk with this instruction: "Any thoughts you have on how we teach and learn in this topic/project/ semester, just text them to this number."

Do not wait until the end of the semester or year to solicit feedback. That will be useless for the students who are giving it. As a partnering teacher you need to continuously iterate and improve what you do, and real-time feedback is required for that.

Of course, getting feedback from your students on a day-to-day or even minute-to-minute basis can require a thick skin, at least at first. We are all concerned about our own feelings as teachers. And we should also remember to be equally concerned about the thickness of students' skin when giving them criticism or feedback on their behavior or learning.

But it is important to understand that getting feedback from students is not the same as being evaluated by them. In partnering, it is rather a route to improving our teaching for all.

Once teachers and students get the flow of honest two-directional feedback and communication going, students' interest, and the learning and teaching, almost always improve according to the vast majority of the teachers, principals, and superintendents with whom I have spoken. In fact, many teachers find that knowing what their students think helps make their teaching not only better, but easier.

PARTNERING TIP

If you are particularly sensitive about student criticism, one good way to get constructive feedback is to say to your students, "I am going to teach this same thing to another group of students again (tomorrow, next semester, or next year). What would you recommend I do differently to make the lesson (or class, or unit) better for them?"

Creating a working mutual feedback giving-and-getting process provides you with yet another important teaching opportunity: to help your students learn proper and effective methods of giving feedback and expressing opinions, especially when they are negative. In this age of incredibly offensive "feedback" posts to public web sites and discussions—often by adults—this is an enormously valuable skill for students to learn.

LIVING OUT THE PARTNERING ROLES

Partnering is just like many things in life—to learn to do it one cannot just talk about it; one must spend time living and "trying on" the various roles. A good analogy to think about is learning to become a doctor. It takes most medical students a good deal of practice to see themselves comfortably in the varying roles of caregiver, person in charge of patients, explainer to patients and families, caller of life and death, and so on. Similarly, it takes teachers and students a lot of practice and time to adjust to their new roles in the partnering pedagogy.

Living Out the Teacher Roles

Coach

Coach is a very powerful role, and great sports coaches are recognized and venerated by their teams and by society as much as, and sometimes even more than, great teachers. (Actually it's not "more than," because great coaches *are* great teachers.) Why are great coaches so venerated? It's not just because their teams or players win (which they do). It's also because the recognized role of a coach is to make the "coachees" better, both as players of their sport and as people.

In partnering, the kind of coach we are talking about is less the football coach, whose goal is for the team to win, and more the tennis, golf, or track coach, who focuses on individuals. What difference would it make to say to your class, "I am here to coach you through algebra" (or any other subject or grade level) rather than "I am here to teach you algebra"? It would sound to students like you are there to help them individually, and it would mean that the responsibility for success falls more equally on both parties, coach and coachee.

One thing to consider is that a teacher can teach and the students not listen, but a coach can't operate unless the students do something. Coaching is generally very heavy on feedback and motivation, with little if any telling. Living out the coaching role, therefore, implies approaching your students in a much more individual and personal way and certainly helping each student find and pursue his or her individual passion.

One option for living out this role that I have seen work is for all teachers and administrators in a school to be addressed, by each other and by students, not by their name, but rather just as "coach." Calling someone by their role instead of by their name (as we do when we say "Mr. President" or "Madame Speaker") emphasizes the role and its power. A coach's job is to help the individuals they coach succeed. Teaching them is a means to that end.

PARTNERING TIP

If the coaching role—or any of the roles of the partnering teacher—is new to you, or is one in which you are not totally comfortable, you can first try on the role.

Begin by discussing specifically with your students what you are planning to do. Ask them if they will see you differently in the new role and how you and they should partner. Ask what other coaching or guiding experiences they have they had and what made those positive or negative. Ask how they can give you feedback and make the role work for them and for you. Then set up some specific times, days, or units to try it out. Be sure to debrief how it went, and do not get discouraged if it is not everything you hoped for, because you will iterate and make it better next time.

Guide

Guide is also a powerful role. Literally and figuratively, the teacher leads each student through the learning wilderness to understanding. But as most know, it is extremely difficult to guide a group or an individual that doesn't want to be guided—this is often referred to as herding cats. On the other hand, if there is a place one does want to go, a good guide is an extraordinarily useful asset to have. So the guide role is less the motivator and more the helper of the motivated.

Being a guide, to a much greater degree than being a coach, requires that the students accept they need one and acknowledge that they are willing to take the journey. For this reason, living out the role of guide works best when you know and understand your students' passions. If what you are guiding students toward is perceived by them as somewhere they want to go (in the context of the curriculum), they will be much more likely to follow. For example, if you teach algebra and you know a student's passion is music, you might encourage him or her to think of songs as equations made up of different parts that need to be balanced properly. If you teach English you can encourage all students to read and write in the area of their passion and to find and post to web sites related to their interests. If students don't have or acknowledge a passion, you can send them on a quest to find one by suggesting they find 10 surprising things about a number of areas they choose.

Instructional Expert

The instructional expert is the most familiar of the teacher's partnering roles; it is in this role that teachers bring all of their traditional skills (with the exception, of course, of drill and telling) into the partnership. Living out this role means bringing out all your knowledge, imagination, and creativity about making learning effective and engaging, while still seeing yourself as a partner in the process.

Students do not want cookie-cutter lessons from books. Much better are creative approaches within the partnering framework. Some of these can be tied to current events (e.g., "The space shuttle is leaving today. Break up into crews of eight, assign one of these various specialties to each team member, and collectively answer the following questions, each doing research from your own role's point of view"). Others can be tied to student passions (e.g., "Which are the best sports stadium designs in the United States [or the world] and why?"). Still others can be tied to students' immediate reality (e.g., "How could we reconfigure the school parking lot to hold 10 percent more cars and still maintain a desired margin of safety?").

While instructional expert is the role in which most experienced teachers will likely feel the most at home, it is important for partnering teachers to not let it dominate, but to balance it with the other roles, such as coach and guide. It is also helpful to realize that the instructional expert role has several subroles, including the following:

Instructional expert: designer. Today's students want something new and fresh as often as possible—in many cases, almost every day. It is the teacher's job as designer to provide this variety within the framework of the partnering pedagogy. After formulating a topic's guiding questions, the teacher can provide or suggest a variety of activities such as reading a book, searching online, doing research for a video, or designing a game, which will lead to the answers to the questions. Being the designer is one of the most creative parts of the partnering teacher's job. It helps to approach it from the various passions and perspectives of your students, as well as your own. For example, "What are the elements of a good song from a [math, science, English, social studies] perspective, and can you write one?" might interest music-loving students in any class.

Should you feel you want or need help in being creative, there already exists in almost all our schools a group of teachers that has been doing this type of "learning design for partnering" for many years. These are our teachers of art and industrial arts. Not long ago, I had a conversation with an experienced industrial arts teacher who explained to me that an important (and challenging) part of his job was to create ideas for projects that would incorporate all the skills that he wanted students to learn and yet leave room for a great deal of individualization in how the task was accomplished and how the skills got learned. In partnering, this is a part of every teacher's job, and we can look for help to these colleagues more experienced in this role.

We can also look to art teachers for advice on teaching without telling. Art teachers rarely if ever give lectures and are, in many if not most cases, among our most experienced "partnerers." An art teacher who wants students to understand what colors go well (or not well) together will typically not spend much time getting kids to hear about and memorize the good and bad combinations—the teacher will go right to having students create their own examples (with guidance), which peers and the teacher can then critique.

Instructional expert: questioner. "Judge a person by his questions, and not his answers," said Voltaire. One of the best ways for a teacher to avoid telling is to ask questions in the most sophisticated way possible. There is much in the art of questioning that can be learned and practiced by teachers. This ranges from avoiding closed-ended questions entirely to asking Socratic (i.e., thought-provoking) questions such as "What things might cause students to spend more time on homework? Why?"

Partnering teachers should also work to be sure that each question they ask gets answered by every student, using either the technology of clickers or the nontechnology of colored answer cards. Abandon the voluntary "raise your hand" system, which allows many students to never answer a question at all. To help improve your questioning even more, in partnership with your students, you can create a rubric and evaluate both your questions and theirs, trying collectively as a class to continually ask better and better ones. It might contain questions such as these: "Is the question open-ended? Does it make the person questioned reflect and synthesize? Does it require complex understanding to answer correctly? Does it cause the person questioned to reevaluate his or her position? Does it make a listener say, 'That's a good question'?"

PARTNERING TIP

Try to ask as many questions as possible where the response is not an immediate answer, but rather "That's a good question!" (We often say that to students—think about what makes it true.)

Instructional expert: context setter. When getting students to answer questions on their own, as we do in partnering, there is a danger that some may miss the bigger picture or context in which certain information, facts, or conclusions need to be set. The horrible destruction of Hiroshima and Nagasaki, for example, needs to be seen in the context of the Second World War. Genetic research needs to be seen in the context of health and medicine. Certain decisions need to be set in the context of Western (or other) culture and morality. Ensuring that this context gets provided, in a variety of ways (other than telling) and to the right degree, is an important role of the partnering teacher. This includes the teacher discussing with students, and being sensitive to, the context of today and of tomorrow, including evolving ideas on topics such as copyright and intellectual property. In this regard, an interesting question might be "Do plagiarism and/or cheating need to be redefined in the new context of the Internet, mashups, and other new developments? Why or why not? If yes, how?"

Instructional expert: rigor provider. Rigor means putting down a floor under which work is not acceptable. Living out this role means not declaring any student "below standard," but trying to bring each student closer and closer to standard with each iteration and revision of his or her work. One of the big opportunities partnering provides here is to set up more peer-to-peer interactions between students who are above and below the rigor floor. It is important that students learn to judge for themselves whether work is above or below that floor. One way to help students do this is to give them lots of examples to evaluate in terms of whether or not they make the cut. The follow-up is to have students go out and find by themselves examples that are and are not rigorous, and then explain why.

Instructional expert: quality assurer. Living out the role of quality assurer means evaluating and critiquing student work. This is often a time-consuming role, but in the partnering context the time required can often be reduced by sharing the role with students. On the Internet, students are already commenting on and rating (typically with stars) all kinds of work, from artwork to blog posts to comments to books. Students can do this cooperatively with their peers, and you can oversee the results—online, if you have access and can get someone to set up the tools. This works well, for example, when all student work is required to be posted to a blog that allows ratings and comments. For examples of peer rating systems, see Amazon's book reviews or the techie site Slashdot.

PARTNERING TIP

Reflect on the different roles for the teacher in partnering and how they interact. Do they ever conflict? Which role is most important to students' success? Is there a different answer in the short term and the long term? How much of each role can be shared with students?

Living Out the Student Roles

Researcher

Researcher (i.e., finder, evaluator, synthesizer, and presenter of information) is a role that students should get to live out as often as possible. Whether or not your students have frequent or continuous access to the Internet, it is crucial that both they and you take this role seriously. (Note that the role of researcher does not require that students have Internet access; having access just makes the role easier.)

If our students are to be real researchers, it is important that the research we ask them to do has a real purpose in the world. A student who believes not only that it is his or her role to be a budding professional researcher but also that the research actually matters (i.e., will be used for something public such as a blog or online publication, or for a team or class consulting project) will likely behave much differently from one who thinks his or her work is only for the eyes of the teacher. When students get to post—on YouTube, SchoolTube, or TeacherTube—their videos on topics such as genetic modifications to food, disease in the developing world, and immigration, everyone in the world can see (and rate and comment on) the results of their research—including, not trivially, their parents.

PARTNERING TIP

Many students may not know, for example, that *researcher* is a real, professional job in the world. Bringing in a professional researcher, in person or online, to discuss his or her work would be really helpful to all partnering students. There are many professional researchers, from librarians, to journalists, to fact checkers, who can be brought in to talk to students. As you go through your teaching, collect questions that students might want to ask such a person.

Part of research is, of course, understanding what is true and not true—what is sometimes called truth finding or fact checking, and what Howard Rheingold, a longtime Internet guru, calls "crap detection." (That last term comes from a quote by Ernest Hemmingway: "Every man should have a built-in automatic crap detector operating inside him.") Separating fact from falsehood, whatever you call it, is an important skill for students to master. Rheingold has put all the materials and readings for his class online, and you are free to use them.

Check It Out!

Rheingold's "crap detection" readings can be found at http://www.sfgate.com/cgi -bin/blogs/rheingold/detail?blogid= 108&entry_id=42805

Having students fact-check information on Wikipedia is much more effective than banning students from using it. And as usual in partnering, rather than tell the students what the information and fact-checking problems are, it is much more effective to ask the class to list them, for you to complete the list if necessary, and for students to then find examples.

Technology Expert

Even though there will likely be students in your class who are not technology experts (at least at first), it is the role of all partnering students to become technology experts and to be the users of technology in the class. The best way for them to live out this role is for the teacher to let them use all technology and learn from each other and to never use the technology for them.

By virtue of being born in the digital age, our students are digital natives by definition, but that doesn't mean they were ever taught everything (or anything, in some cases) about computers or other technologies, or that all of them learned on their own. For partnering students to live out and get better at the role of technology expert, a partnering teacher needs to encourage as much peer-to-peer sharing and learning as possible so that those who are behind learn from their peers and catch up.

It is a huge mistake for a teacher to think that, before giving students access to or assignments in a technology, the teacher should wait until he or she has learned or mastered the technology. It is far better to let students master whatever it is by working together, teaching each other, and teaching the teacher. For example, after waiting weeks to give an assignment until she had personally mastered a particular piece of software, one teacher found that none of her students would even consider using that particular software to do the task she proposed.

PARTNERING TIP

If there are particular types or pieces of technology that your students don't know or don't understand at the level you think they should, consider having short class sessions during which those students who do know show those who don't. Give these student teachers the responsibility to follow up until they can certify that every student is proficient.

Thinker

Partnering students need to know, and be constantly reminded, that their job is not just to listen or even to find or take in information passively, but rather to think critically, logically, creatively, and in other positive ways. One way a teacher can help students live out the role of thinker is by providing them with good thought-provoking guiding and discussion questions. Modeling by providing students with many examples of both good (and bad) thinking should be done as often as possible. Some schools and teachers have introduced "thinking toolboxes" of various problem-solving and thinking tools and techniques such as brainstorming, mind-mapping, and de Bono's *six thinking hats*[15] for students to practice and master. Partnering teachers can create a daily or weekly puzzler (such as the hosts of NPR's *Car Talk* do) whose answers are not just trivia, but require some serious thinking.

PARTNERING TIP

Consider having a class discussion, structured for whatever level you teach, on what constitutes good thinking. It can include questions like these: "What makes some questions better than others? What is critical thinking? What is logic? What are inductive and deductive reasoning?" Be sure to show students multiple examples of the type of thinking you expect from them, and then let them go out and find additional examples on their own.

Together you and your students can review a large number of examples, including both good and bad ones, and then students can decide which are the good ones and why. This can be followed up by students looking for and posting examples of both good and bad thinking on a regular basis.

World Changer

To live out this role, students must try to relate every single thing they learn to making the world a better place in some way. As a partnering teacher, you should encourage them to do this. You can help by asking about this frequently, having students keep personal notebook or blogs, and collecting student suggestions. (It would be great to collect and share all of these on a school or public blog.)

Thinking in terms of everything being used to change the world is not just pie-in-the-sky fantasy. The City College of New York, for example, now has a required freshman course called Changing the World Using the Internet. But college is, in fact, quite late for students to begin living the role of world changer. This ought to begin in elementary school. Even elementary school students can change the world through online writing, supporting and publicizing online causes, making informational and public service videos and machinima, and creating original campaigns of their own design. Anything students create that "goes viral" on the Web reaches millions of people, and students should be continually striving to make this happen, with output that both does good and supports their learning.

Self-Teacher

"The object of education," said Robert Maynard Hutchins (president of the University of Chicago from 1929 to 1951), "is to prepare our students to educate themselves throughout their lives." Ideally, in every class they take, partnering students will learn new ways to teach themselves what they need and want to know. ("What they need to know" is defined by the teacher's guiding questions as well as the students' passion and their desire to improve the world.)

The more we expect students to live out the role of self-teacher, and the less we spoon-feed them, the better they will learn to do it. When students are motivated to learn by their own passions, finding out about new techniques and ways to do things better and more efficiently is something they will almost certainly be quite interested in. And this ability will serve them well for the rest of their lives.

More and more young people already use the Internet to decide what to buy, not only for themselves but for their parents, including electronics, appliances, and even automobiles. Today, purchasing a home, choosing health care options, getting insurance, selecting colleges to apply to, and finding a career or job are among the many things that require the ability to self-educate, often quickly.

Temporary Student Roles in Particular Situations

The creative instructional designer-teacher will set up many situations for students in which they will take on and practice the roles of real-world professionals. Students will benefit from assuming these roles as often as possible and practicing their associated skills seriously. To a greater and greater extent, role-playing simulations, as well as what are known as "epistemic" games (i.e., games in which you try to understand and do things from the point of view of a professional), are available to facilitate students doing this. Examples of role-playing games include SimCity (you play a mayor), RollerCoaster Tycoon (you play a theme park designer and operator), and the many other "tycoon" games in which you own and run almost any kind of business, from airlines to cruise ships to casinos to trailer parks. There are also many simulations of medical and health care professional roles, such as Emergency and Pet Pals: Animal Doctor. Prototypes for epistemic games described in David Williamson Shaffer's book *How Computer Games Help Children Learn* include *The Debating Game*, *Escher's World*, and *Digital Zoo*.

Even better than just using such role-playing situations as classroom exercises is to use them as real-world partnerships and apprenticeships and as producers of real outputs for a real-world audience. This is the famous lesson of Orson Scott Card's book *Ender's Game* (now required reading in many schools). In that book, the simulation that students use as a learning exercise becomes a true, real-world tool. Today's students, for example, can practice using computer-aided design (CAD) software as they actually redesign their school or classroom, a community center, or a park as real projects. Students can build web sites in class that they sell or donate to actual organizations and businesses. Students who have access to machine tools can practice making parts to specific manufacturer specifications and then sell the parts to the manufacturers who need them.

In every situation and in every class, students will be doing (i.e., learning, practicing, or perfecting) one or more of the verbs listed in Table 2.1. Students should never do this mindlessly, but should practice these skills consciously and mindfully, having been reminded by the teacher of the verbs they are working on and having been taught and asked by the teacher to reflect on their own learning. Students who are reading and writing ought to be aware that they are reflecting, questioning, and thinking logically and critically. Students doing computer projects ought to be aware that they are analyzing, verifying, modeling, deciding, and problem solving. Students making a PowerPoint presentation should be aware that they are presenting, briefing, connecting, and designing. Students doing a science experiment should be aware that they are analyzing, exploring, verifying, observing, and predicting.

PARTNERING TIP

At the start of the year, discuss all these teacher and student roles with your students. See what they think of them. Ask them to reflect, as you did on your roles, on how their roles interact. Do they ever conflict? Which role or roles are most important to the students' success? Does it depend on the student? On anything else? Is there a different answer in the short term and the long term? What suggestions do they have for doing this successfully?

MORE IDEAS

Encourage Open Teamwork and Peer-to-Peer Learning

Not only do most of the students I talk to in my panels say that they prefer to work with others (particularly their peers) than to work alone, but this is clearly what they will be required to do in their future life, no matter what job or profession they choose. In the 21st century almost all work will be done in groups, most often facilitated by technology. So working well with others, a skill that has always been valued, is almost certain to be even more valuable in the future.

But today, work teams do not have to consist only of peers and classmates. One thing networked technology allows for (when we have access to it) is the inclusion of people of any age from any place. So in a class with at least a certain number of networked computers, there is no reason a teacher couldn't ask a class to form teams, each of which includes, for example, x number of students plus an expert on the topic (say a professor) and at least one person over the age of 70. Without technology, this kind of teamwork in schools would be almost impossible; with technology, it becomes simple and, with experience, almost trivial. Think of the benefits to students of getting to work, in all grades, with experts and people with real-world experience.

Now that far fewer children than before live with their grandparents in the house, the vast experience of older people is often a resource that goes untapped in students' learning. But older people are one of the fastest growing groups on the Internet. While visits to retirement homes are nice but often impractical (and little, if any, serious classwork is likely to get done during them), any classroom with a computer and Internet access can reach out to older people and include their perspectives and experience in projects in social studies, science, writing, or anything else a creative teacher can think of. This includes, of course, historical archiving and ethnographic data collection, which can be combined, fact-checked, and cross-checked with other information for accuracy, just as happens in real life.

An additional way for partnering teachers to enhance teamwork is through peer-to-peer teaching and learning, as well as having older students mentor and create materials for younger students. Many students prefer to learn directly from their friends and other people close to their age (in part because their communication and references are much more direct and they feel freer to ask questions without fear of embarrassment), and partnering teachers should encourage this as much as possible. In partnering, all the teaching does not have to come directly from the teacher (although part of the teacher's job is to verify that it is happening correctly). Wherever and however partnering students choose to learn, what counts is that they do.

PARTNERING TIP

When you assign your students to do group or team work, have the groups or teams include members from outside your classroom, such as professionals, older people, even parents and grandparents. Making the outside person a team member sends a different signal to students than saying "Go interview someone" (although interviewing real people can be useful as well). Encourage classroom team members to be creative about how the outside members are found and about their participation. Use whatever technology is available (e.g., Skype can be used on individual computers to talk to the outside team member, an electronic whiteboard or projector with Skype can be used to bring someone from the outside in as a presenter to the whole class). Do not limit what you do in this area because of what you perceive as a lack of technology. There are many ways to create these extended teams—be creative.

Create Slacker–Free Group Work

The biggest (and often only) student complaint about group work is that there are students who coast while the other team members do the work. However, there are many solutions to this "slacker" problem. I have found that the best place to turn for these solutions is the students themselves. I have heard students suggest things from grading systems based on individual autonomous roles within the group (so if the history portion of the group's final presentation is weak or absent, one knows which individual to fault) to having students choose their own teams so they work with people they trust to do their part.

Some teachers have had success by putting all the so-called slackers into a single group and egging them on to beat the others. Paring potential slackers with certain inside (or outside) members of the team whom they might not want to let down can make a difference as well.

In general, creating slacker-free group work is a great way that you and your students can partner to find creative ideas and suggestions. And when you do, don't forget to share them via short videos that you or your students post online on YouTube, SchoolTube, or TeacherTube so that others can benefit from what you learn.

> **PARTNERING TIP**
>
> It is best to address the issue of slacking in group work upfront, when a project is first assigned. Hold a class discussion in which you lay out the problem, solicit suggestions from your students (and provide your own), and agree as a class on certain structures and rules to make group work more successful.

Circle the Chairs: Hold Class Discussions and Meetings About Learning

Many, if not most, teachers hold class discussions about what they are teaching; relatively few hold them about how the students are learning. I have been facilitating such student-teacher dialogues for years and can assure you that students find them worthwhile and—if done with mutual respect and the results are actually acted upon—they facilitate and improve learning.

> **PARTNERING TIP**
>
> Be sure your classroom is set up in a way that you can easily (and literally) circle the chairs. It is an arrangement that gives everyone's opinion equal value and that students consistently speak positively about. Set aside time periodically to ask students questions like "Is what we do in class the best way for you to learn? What would you like to see more of? Less of? Does the class meet your expectations?"

Use Students as Assistants

You may remember school safety patrol and blackboard monitors from your own school days. These are examples of partnering with students from an earlier time. What would the equivalents be today? "Tech Patrol" and "Technology Monitors!" Do you know which students in your class are the best with the technologies you have available? One Texas elementary school teacher proudly brought her two top student assistants to one of my presentations to show them off. "I couldn't teach without them," she said.

Often, students and teachers complain about classroom technology (such as computers or interactive whiteboards) breaking down and the teacher not knowing how to fix them, causing long interruptions in their use while help is arranged. Having a student assistant (or patrol) on call in such cases can save tons of time. (This is true even in the elementary grades.)

Student tech monitors (or a tech patrol) can be vetted for their knowledge and skill by the schools technology coordinator(s). They can be, and in many schools are, charged with maintaining all the school's technology in top working form. They can be given training in groups when new technology arrives and charged with training their teachers. They can also be made responsible for fixing anything that breaks and even for policing other students who are abusing technology. One tech coordinator described to me how the students in charge of maintaining the computer lab took their job extremely seriously and brooked no nonsense or messing around from other students (remember, technology is their passion). Such a group could also keep track of what technology is available in the school, help teachers use more of it, and help create and publish online videos of teachers' successes.

Having assistants works even with a small amount of technology. Even if you have only one computer in the room, for example, there can be a different student sitting at it each day during class whose job is to look up things that come up in the class discussion. In one history class I observed, on ancient Greek coinage, such an assistant could have been used effectively to answer questions that came up on coin values, the meaning of Greek words, where and for how much such coins could be obtained today, and a number of other questions that arose for which the teacher had no good answer.

PARTNERING TIP

Be sure to get as much technical assistance as you can from your students. Find out (by asking) who is the best at technology, and give them tasks to do. Trust them to do it right (lack of this trust is a huge complaint from students). Have those students meet with the tech assistants from other classes and with the tech coordinator if you have one. Then have them all meet with all the teachers to discuss what could be done to improve the use of technology in your school.

In the end, the more you think of your students as individuals, each with his or her own individual passions, and the more you use those passions to motivate students, the more you will be able to reach all students, including those who were previously unreachable. Partnering allows you to do this by freeing you from spending most of your time being the sage on the stage and by offering you a set of different teaching roles (coach, guide, etc.) in which you can work with your students and their passions individually.

In the next chapter, I will look at yet another way to motivate students as individuals and to help them find and use their passions—by making learning *real* (and not just relevant).

4

Always Be Real (Not Just Relevant)

Guiding Questions

1. What is the difference between real and relevant?

2. How can I always be real?

3. How can I teach for the future?

Do you think your students would be more interested in learning about the battles of the U.S. Civil War or about the lessons of that war for stopping civil wars in Africa? In learning about genetically inherited disease or about what the risks might be in their own family? In learning about exploring the universe or talking with someone who had actually been on a space mission? In memorizing dialogues in a foreign language or talking to native speakers their own age? Today's students—pretty much unanimously—prefer the second choice in each case. What makes the second choices preferable is that they are *real* to students.

While there's a lot of talk about relevance and authenticity among educators these days, I don't think that is really what all of today's students need or want. What they do need and want is for their education to be *real*.

What's the difference between relevant (or even authentic) and real? Relevant means that kids can relate something you are teaching, or something you say, to something they know (such as by your referencing a recent film or TV show rather than an old classic, or talking about the X Games rather than, say, polo). Relevant means taking readings, for example, out of the current newspaper rather than old textbooks.

Relevant is not wrong, of course. People do come to an understanding more easily when context is familiar. The problem with relevant is that it often doesn't go far enough.

Real, on the other hand, means much more and goes much further. Real means that there is a perceived connection by the students, at every moment (or at least as often as possible), between what they are learning and their ability to use that learning to do something useful in the world.

Unlike in the past, when kids really did have to be patient and wait to grow up in order to use whatever they learned, today's kids can experience immediate connections every day. Kids who learn to download, text, and tweet can immediately participate in profound social revolutions like crowdsourcing (and less profound ones, like voting for American Idol). Kids who learn to play almost any complex game quickly collaborate and compete with others around the globe. When they post to a blog about something they are interested in, kids are reaching a worldwide audience. By joining a Twitter campaign (such as *The New York Times* tech writer David Pogue's successful campaign to get phone providers to eliminate useless minute-eating messages), they help change policy in the biggest corporations.

It is one of the most important jobs of partnering teachers to help students make these real-world connections for everything they teach. For example:

Relevant is:	Real is:
"This applies to the environment."	"Let's measure Company X's carbon footprint and help them save money by going green."
"Let's read Harry Potter, because it's 'the thing' right now."	"Read any book that interests you, and use something about it to change your life."
"Let's talk about how technology changed the Iranian election."	"Let's look at the tweet stream from Iran and send our own tweets over there."
"This relates to baseball."	"Did you see in last night's game when this happened? Boy, what a great illustration of . . . ."

A NEW PERSPECTIVE

Once we adopt the perspective of making things real, and not just relevant, we can find so many ways to make what we teach immediately useful in students' lives. Sure, students can analyze all the forces at work in an extreme gamer's half-pipe jumps (relevant to some), but they can also ask, "How would I use that information to go higher when I am skating?" (Real.) Yes, students can learn about the techniques of persuasion (relevant), but can they actually persuade someone they know to do something? (Real.) Of course students can learn about online economics (relevant), but can they run a successful online business? (Real.) Yes, kids can learn about our country's deteriorating infrastructure (relevant), but can they actually estimate when and why a particular structure they use will fail? (Real.) Or use something from of science to change their family's eating or drinking habits or improve the local drinking water? (Real.) In some classes today, students do all of these real things, and that is, to a great extent, what engages them about their learning.

MAKING OUR SUBJECTS REAL

It is possible, with some imagination, to make *everything* we teach real for each of our students. The desire and ability to go beyond "I'm teaching this because it's in the curriculum" to "Here's how this relates to each of your worlds in a real (and not just a theoretical, relevant) way" is something students highly appreciate and value in their teachers.

The best thing a partnering teacher can do to keep learning real (and not just relevant) is to make everything he or she is teaching come directly from the world of the students—either their world of today or their world of tomorrow. (And, of course, not just the world, but the part of that world they are passionate about.) Going further, the partnering teacher should make learning not just about students' world, but about changing and improving their world. Can you think of a better answer to "Why should I learn this?" than "To make your world a better place"?

Partnering itself is already more real than traditional classroom learning, which is typically removed from the world. In partnering, students use real-world tools to access and analyze publically available information (as opposed to textbooks created only for school). When students use web sites that are open to anyone, and understand that if they feel there's a problem with those sites they can take action by changing wikis or posting messages, that is real. When they post their work for others to see, that is real as well.

We can and should do this with everything. To spark your imagination, I offer the following suggestions on how to begin.

Making History and Social Studies Real

How do you make history and social studies real? Say you are teaching about the French or American Revolution. How do you connect what happened a long time ago to what kids are interested in today? You might begin by thinking what revolutions today's kids are living through. The Internet/information tech/nanotech/human enhancement revolutions, certainly. How are those revolutions affecting them and each of the things they are passionate about?

Can we start there and work backward? What might be the contemporary equivalents of storming the Bastille? The Reign of Terror? The Thermidorian Reaction? The winter at Valley

Forge? The Declaration of Independence? The U.S. Constitution? Who are today's Jacobins, today's Robespierre, today's George Washington, today's Thomas Jefferson and Lafayette? Why?

With technology, partnering social studies students can increasingly virtually visit historical cultures and sites where things happened; these tours have become more and more widely available and interactive online. If they become interested, students can sign up to receive further information about the place and times. When students visit the historical sites in person, they can often use their cell phones to get a guided tour, such as at Lexington and Concord in Massachusetts.

Even more real is for students to add to existing sites or to create local tours for others to use. In conjunction with studying historical battle sites, such as Gettysburg or Antietam, students can use simulations to replay the real battles, taking the roles of the various commanders.

And student work can get even more real. Virtually or in person, students can help restore historical sites, join recovery expeditions and architectural digs, and help clean up pollution. With their teacher or others as partners, students can form historical preservation societies to preserve something in their own town or neighborhood, perhaps even raising money or other resources online. Students can research real local or national historical records—more and more of which are online—and find and graph changing demographic and naming patterns. Using increasingly sophisticated genealogical and search web sites and software, students can find their ancestors and trace their historical lineage and family tree. Using their cell phones and other voice or video recorders, students can collect oral histories from their relatives and other older people. They can see how much lives have changed, look for useful things from older civilizations, and suggest improvements for the future.

Via webcams already in place, students can observe real life all over the globe and look for differences and ways to improve both those people's lives and their own. In many cases they can communicate with families or students through secure worldwide e-mail services such as ePals. There may also be opportunities to bring this closer to home by having students communicate with senior citizens or people who are homebound who have Skype or webcams. There are also lots of government meetings that students can attend virtually via C-SPAN and sometimes even participate in via the Internet.

Students can create imaginary Facebook pages for world leaders and historical figures and take on these people's roles by sending e-mails or tweets between them. They can find out the Internet addresses of, and write to, actual world leaders, some of whom may answer. They can participate, many times, in real unfolding events by e-mailing, texting, or tweeting to people in places where those events are happening.

What if history and social studies became for students less about "What happened?" and more about "What can we learn or use from other civilizations, times, places, cultures, and people to improve our own lives?" A great historical example of this happening was the establishment of the modern Olympic games. At the end of the 19th century, Pierre de Coubertin, inspired by the ancient Greek Olympics, proposed an international competition, which became the first Modern Olympiad. (The rest, as they say, is history.) What good things could *your* students bring us from the past?

Making Math Real

The day the bridge in Minneapolis collapsed in 2007, I said to myself, "I hope every math class in America is using this as an example today." What a perfectly *real* illustration that mathematical calculations (in this case, of the stress on truss plates and rivets) can make a life-or-death difference in students' lives. All kids in America live near and travel on structures that could be similarly threatened. What should they be thinking about when they use those structures? What a great lead-in into geometry, statistics, force and stress analysis, and more!

The way to make math real is to make every problem about something that is actually happening—a bridge collapsing or being built (computing forces or stress), an election that's taking place (probability, percentages), a space launch (trajectories, fuel consumption, rates of speed and acceleration), a golf tournament (parabolas), baseball or football (statistics), a song being recorded (timing, notes, compression, sampling rates).

Kids need to relate math not to real-world or relevant experiences, but to *real* experiences actually taking place. Are roads or buildings being built near you? Find out from the engineers what math they use (perhaps even get the actual plans) and let your kids do the same calculations and see if they get the same answers. Is there a space launch coming up? Get some actual NASA data (go to www.nasa.gov and search for "data") and compute some answers, which can be done at any level, from adding to calculus. Want your students to do *real* arithmetic or statistics? Use the federal budget data that is in the news every day. Let them do the calculations to see who is correct and who is exaggerating, and discuss how different groups can start with the same facts and reach such different conclusions. Teaching estimation and large numbers? Try the income and budgets of actual sports or rock stars (or lottery winners) in the news. Let students see just how easily fortunes can disappear if not managed carefully.

There is another important area for making math real: programming. Programming is using applied math to make a machine (computer, robot, etc.) do what you want it to. In the world of increasingly powerful machines, programming is something that students can and should do much more of, and it is a use of math in which students can immediately see real results and get real feedback. Both multimedia programming and robotics competitions such as FIRST Robotics or humanoid robot competitions feel real to today's students and can motivate them to learn math, even on their own. "How did you do that?" I once heard a teacher ask. "I used the arctangent function" was the student's reply. Interestingly, the more the programming involves humanoid robots that can be programmed to move and dance, the more girls start becoming interested in programming, and the math behind it as well.

Making Science Real

Here's a great example of making science real. For a class in failure analysis, a teacher was able to get, from NASA, actual pieces of the destroyed space shuttle Columbia to analyze. The class later presented their findings to real NASA scientists.

Today's partnering science students can participate in actual, worldwide experiments done by real scientists, such as the Search for Extraterrestrial Intelligence (http://setiathome.berkeley.edu) or molecule folding (http://folding.stanford.edu/). Students can collect real data on the environment that gets added to actual databases used by real scientists. They can record and analyze microweather and climates, or compute local rates of forest or fish depletion as evidence for climate change.

Science is one of the easiest subjects to make real, because students are living with it every day. Do students have earbuds in their ears? Ask them, "What are they made of? Why? How do they work? Why do some cost so much more than others? What happens if the music gets too loud? What are the scientific steps in getting the ideas in a musician's head through the playing and recording process, through the distribution process, onto your iPod, and into your head?"

Who in the class is wearing microfibers? Have them find out what they are and how they are made. What's inside your students' cell phones? What happens when they text message their neighbor across the classroom? Why are our school computers often so slow? How could students make them faster?

All of today's science students should be talking frequently, in person or via technologies such as Skype, to actual scientists. These people can suggest projects or give students real work related to their own projects to do and real problems to solve. Science students can join international multistudent teams and competitions, not only in robotics, but also in creating science games, space exploration, and other technologies. New competitions and prizes are being announced daily and should be continually searched for.

To fill a shortage of biotech workers in their state, Arizona has set up a high school program to teach real, cutting-edge biotechnology research tools. High tech job training in high school—that's pretty real.

Making English Real

How do you make English real? Do your students text? (Duh! as they would say.) You can have them become English-to-English editors, translating documents from formal English to textspeak and back again. They can focus on all the kinds of English available and what is appropriate to use where. Ask them, for example, what they think of textspeak (or a spelling mistake) on a formal wedding invitation. Then apply that to a résumé.

English is a really simple subject for making things real because it is so easy to tailor readings and tasks to student passions—all you have to do is allow and encourage it. English students can read, write, and give speeches about whatever they are passionate about, not only to their class, but by posting online, to the world. They can write public service announcements, record them in audio and video, and make them available online for others to use and emulate.

> **Check It Out!**
>
> For an inspiring public service announcement made by and for kids, see www.youtube.com/watch?v=uWxNBuNPS1I.

Today's English students can participate in the very real change of having more and more books available online by finding and reading books about their interests that were previously unavailable until recently scanned by Amazon or Google. After discussing why books used to go out of print and how this is changing, students can further participate in this change by helping to scan more books, and by setting up sites and channels to review them.

English students can write and post blog entries about their real lives that get shared, commented on, and critiqued by their peers in terms of grammar, structure, and content. They can write and edit their own (or others', such as a relative's) life history—as a Facebook page, a web site, an animation, or a formal résumé—and think about which might be the relevant form to submit for different types of applications. (They might even look for job openings and submit what they've written.)

English students can write and post comments to real professional journalists' online blogs (some even answer!) and submit real online letters to the editor on topics they are passionate about. They can submit real op-ed articles to print and online publications. They should be encouraged to write articles for real publications that deal with their passions.

In doing this, students can and should learn to express themselves, particularly online, in a civil and constructive way. One way to accomplish this is by having students critique online posts that aren't civil. Some sites, such as Slashdot, have users rate others' comments as to their appropriateness and usefulness. You can encourage your students to do this as well.

Making Foreign Language Real

Language should, in many ways, be the most real subject for kids, because it is about actual communication with their peers. Students say consistently that they do not want to learn languages for the literature or grammar, but rather to speak with their peers and make new friends in other places. And they are already doing a lot of this on their own by texting, tweeting, Skyping, and exchanging YouTube videos in every language.

One partnering teacher used the virtual world Second Life to bring together two classes—one from the United States and one from Japan—in a collaboration to build a virtual island together. The kids communicated through text and voice in both languages and, by the time they met in person, had gotten to know each other really well.

Today's language learning has to be about real (i.e., actual) communication, not "dialogues" and pretend. Our students live in the age of instant Internet translations, so improving the automated translations of real documents the kids want to read (such as game or fashion sites) is a great place to start. Today's students can (and frequently do) communicate with peers in other places who speak a language they are studying—via e-mail, YouTube, Skype, Twitter, and a host of other applications. Language teachers should be encouraging them to play their favorite games in foreign language versions and join online game teams that speak the language being studied. Students can read online graphic novels in those languages and even create and post in this genre.

Today, there is no more learning a language for "someday when you go there." As often as possible in the language class, students can and should travel "there" virtually and connect in the foreign language around their real lives and passions.

Making the Future Real

School typically doesn't spend much time (certainly not enough) on the future, but there are lots of real future issues for students to get involved in. Partnering students ought to be thinking about the long-term future, reflecting on and dealing with questions such as these:

- How long until we run out of coal or oil, and what will replace them?
- How many songs (and other types of media) will eventually fit on an iPod, and what will it look like?
- How will people communicate in 2050? In 2100? In 3000?
- What are the math, science, and psychology of deep space exploration?
- What parts of the U.S. Constitution might become obsolete or need new interpretations?
- Will video ever replace writing?
- When and how will artificial intelligence equal the brain?

And students should also focus on the short-term future, asking questions such as these:

- What infrastructure should we be building in our communities?
- How should we be using our resources?
- How should schools and other institutions deal with budget cuts or windfall monies?

Reading and discussing appropriate science fiction stories—both the near-term variety, such as the works of Cory Doctorow (*Little Brother*) and William Gibson (*Pattern Recognition*), and the longer-term variety, such as the works of Isaac Asimov, Greg Bear, David Brin, Orson Scott Card, Ray Kurzweil, and others—can get students thinking about problems they are likely to confront in their own lifetimes, which, in many ways, will certainly be science-fictional to us older folks.

MORE WAYS TO MAKE THINGS REAL

There is just no need, in the early 21st century, for any problems or units of study to be totally made up, totally from (or about) the past, or totally unconnected to the present or future real lives of our students, because there are so many ways to make connections to their lives and passions.

Have Students Make the Connections

If you are at a loss for how to make these connections, and make things *real* for your students (either in general or in a particular case), the first thing to recognize is that you don't have to do it alone. Try looking for connections online, or, even better, try asking your students. The more your student partners are equipped with technological research tools (such as Internet access), the more they can be asked to find, as an essential part of their work, more and deeper connections between the real world and anything they are studying. Students should not only be encouraged to do this, they should be required to do so.

If after working together and doing lots of research, you and your students can't make a single connection between a topic in the curriculum and the real world, you might want to flag that topic to your administrators as a candidate for deletion from the curriculum.

Find Groups of Passions

Differentiation and individualization in students' learning is a goal that everyone supports in principle, but a big issue is that it is not always possible, in the time available, to design for 20–40 students individually. One strategy for making your teaching *real* for all your students, without always doing something totally different for each individual, is to group them for certain work according to their passions and interests. The ability to group students in this way flows from the initial class or classes when you asked (and recorded) what each student's passions are. You might see that there are several students whose passion is sports or music or video or people or saving the world.

Say you are studying a civilization in history. One group might enjoy finding out what we can learn from its music, another about what we can learn from its business practices, transportation, medical practices, sports, military organization, or architecture.

Or you might be studying a principle in science. Can one group apply that principle to sports, another to film and video, another to medicine, and yet another to music?

Grouping students into such affinity groups is rarely done, yet many students find it more interesting to be grouped that way. Grouping students by their passions can also be an incentive for students who haven't found their passion to keep looking for one; they might try out the various groups or be combined into a group of seekers. (Be sure to discuss this way of grouping with your classes, though, before doing it.)

In many ways, this type of grouping reflects what is done in schools that follow a program based on multiple intelligences, except in that case the grouping is based on supposed abilities or talents. What makes affinity grouping and planning easier is that it is based purely on interests and requires no assumptions about intelligences or talent.

Far too often we underestimate students' potential, because success doesn't emerge until later in the person's life. Because so many of our students grow up to surprise us, it is generally a mistake to make any assumptions about any student's talent or potential. As Sir Ken Robinson so nicely points out in his book *The Element*, a person's full potential begins to emerge when that person finally finds his or her passion. So partnering teachers should assume that every student has great potential, and that their job is to help each student find his or her passion and bring it out.

Connect Students With Peers

Having students connect with their peers and learn from each other is something that, ironically, we used to do a lot more of, particularly before students were strictly isolated by grade. I believe there will certainly be a lot more of this type of learning in the future, but today we do relatively little of it.

Part of this is due to our testing system, which puts such a premium on what students know independently. That, of course, is not how the adult world works at all—we work together, we ask each other, look things up, and learn from our colleagues on the job. Our students' future, in just about any job or profession they go into, will be about working and learning together with their peers (mediated to a great extent by technology). So it is in our students' interests for us to encourage peer-to-peer connections and learning—in person and via technology—whenever possible.

Students in all subjects and contexts—not just language classes—are eager to connect with their peers around the world. Partnering teachers should take the time to find out how, in the context of what they are teaching, students want to connect; whom they want to connect with; what they want to say; and what they want to learn. Teachers should then help their students accomplish those things. Learning about content is important; learning about it by hearing what kids in other places think, and whether they share the same interests and perspectives, will provide the kind of real context that gets students motivated.

Connect Students With Practitioners and Models in the Real World

It is terribly important that partnering teachers help connect today's students with as many real-world workers, practitioners, and people as possible, to serve as models. In any subject, a class segment in which, every few days, a person in a different job came in and answered questions for just 10 or 15 minutes could be more valuable to most students than much of the curricular content they might learn in that class. If this can't be done in person, it is becoming easier and easier to do it virtually, using technology. Experts can connect with a class or with individual students via texting, Skype, prerecorded presentations, blog posts, Facebook messages, and many other ways, with new ones continuing to evolve.

Even well-known experts are often willing to donate their time to students. For example, one class started a blog about *The World is Flat,* and Tom Friedman, the book's author (and *New York Times* columnist), added a comment. The e-mails of all politicians and many journalists are publicly available, and there are certainly real issues about which students can contact them (and expect to get responses and results).

> **PARTNERING TIP**
>
> Take the time to find out what your students' parents do, to talk with community organizations and organizers, and, in general, to learn who knows who in your community. Find out who might be willing to visit your class or serve as an advisor to students with a particular passion. If you can, find a "passion-based" advisor for every student in your class. You and your students can find many e-mail addresses online, and you can "cold e-mail" various experts in what you teach, with a "Hi, I'm a teacher and could use your help . . . ." Many will respond.

Real as College Prep

Making learning real is not confined to K–12. More and more colleges and universities are building *real* into their curricula, and making "real learning" a big recruiting tool. This, for example, is from the web site of the College of the Pacific, in Stockton, California:[16]

"Real life learning" opportunities spark students' imaginations, embolden their thinking and often set them on a path of intellectual inquiry that helps to shape not only their years at the College of the Pacific, but their lives beyond as well.

In all of its majors and minors, the College provides opportunities for students to acquire practical skills and knowledge through a variety of internships, fieldwork and research projects.

Whether working with Disney on a public relations project, dealing with foreign policy in Washington, D.C. or helping to catalogue and preserve historical documents at Stockton's Haggin Museum, internships through the College offer real life experience that allows our students to apply and expand their classroom learning.

Fieldwork assignments have included sending photography students into downtown Stockton to document historic buildings, to the Delta to calculate water chemistry, and into local immigrant communities to study the criminal justice system and its inequities.

Student research projects have been as varied as our students' interests: from protein production to economic modeling of U.S. immigration policy and the gendered iconography of Aunt Jemima advertisements.

This is from Northeastern University, in Boston:[17]

Real-life learning is central to your education at Northeastern. Our experiential learning opportunities, anchored by our signature cooperative education program, enable you to discover your path before you leave college. These broadening experiences provide you with a competitive edge. Co-op and more. Curricular partnerships. Service learning, lab research, and great preparation for graduate school. An education truly like no other.

You can mentor students in local schools, volunteer at area social-service organizations, and help plan charitable events and fundraisers.

The senior capstone, an advanced-level course within or related to a student's major, requires students to integrate what they've learned in classroom with their co-op, research, service-learning, and global experiences.

And this from Coe College, in Cedar Rapids, Iowa:[18]

In addition to service-learning experiences . . . the department offers a number of opportunities to learn outside the classroom.

Communicating Common Ground—National Service Learning Initiative in Multicultural Education with Elementary schools

African American Museum

Lakota Culture & Communication on the Reservation

Elements of TV & Radio Broadcasting

Speaking Center—The Speaking Center provides individual consultation for students interested in improving their speaking skills. Faculty and staff also use the center and participate in Teaching and Learning Workshops that address how to integrate oral communication into any classroom.

Writing Center—The Coe Writing Center is a place for conversation and composition. Students can bring papers in any stage of writing, from assignment to final draft, to the Writing Center.

Bicycle Writing

Nature Writing—Taught during the summer at the college's Wilderness Field Station in Minnesota's Superior National Forest this course investigates strategies for writing about the natural world in an informal workshop format.

Writers Colony—An intensive workshop taught off campus during May term. Recent Writers' Colonies have been held at Tybee Island, Georgia; Inner Mongolia; and the Lake District in England.

There is no reason why, even within the constraints of public schooling, many such experiences can't be integrated into K–12 classes as well.

ALWAYS THINK FUTURE

One of the important and useful things about a true partnering pedagogy is that the teacher, in the role of coach and mentor, is always thinking about the world that students will be going out into, and preparing them for that world.

One of the great differences between teaching in the 21st century and teaching in the past is that in the past things didn't change very fast. So teachers prepared their students for a world that was pretty much the same as the one they were living in then. But that situation has now changed dramatically. The world our students will live and work in will certainly be radically different than the world in which they, and we, are now living. The past is to be respected, of course, but our students will not live in it.

How does partnering help deal with this? For one thing, it makes the assumption explicit that the future will be different and tries to deal with it now. So while partnering teachers prepare students for their exams, they also prepare them for their future, when little if any of the stuff on the exams will likely matter. While partnering teachers still help kids graduate and go to college, they also help them find their passion so that they will know what they want to do in, and after, college. And while partnering teachers prepare their students for today's world, in which most information is written, they also prepare them for tomorrow's world, in which most information will likely be in forms other than written. These are big, new jobs for teachers. And I am convinced that it is only through partnering that these jobs can be accomplished.

Meanwhile, of course, we have to get through the curriculum. Partnering teachers do this, in great part, by turning that curriculum, which has traditionally been a list of topics and skills to teach, into guiding questions for students to answer and, in so doing, learn what they need to. Constructing good guiding questions, however, is not trivial. In the next chapter, I take up this important partnering task.

5

Planning

Content to Questions, Questions to Skills

Guiding Questions

1. What is planning in partnering?

2. How do I translate the curriculum into guiding questions?

3. How can I focus on the appropriate verbs?

One big benefit of partnering is that it frees the teacher from the tedious task of planning by preparing lectures (or the repetitious task of reusing lectures prepared in the past). But the fact that the old style of planning is no longer appropriate for the partnering pedagogy is not to say that planning itself is outmoded—far from it. So what does "planning" mean in the partnering pedagogy?

Of all the pieces of partnering planning, the most important is almost certainly translating the content of lessons into the questions you will ask to guide students to the information and learning they need, without you having to tell it to them. The next most important part of partnering planning is figuring out how to make an explicit connection to the underlying skills, or verbs, that the students are learning and practicing as they answer the guiding questions and learn the content of the lesson. In this chapter I discuss both of these aspects of planning.

CREATING GUIDING QUESTIONS

The Primary Link Between Partnering and Content

In general, questions are the device that frames, guides, and ultimately evaluates all learning. The partnering pedagogy is all about asking students the questions before, rather than after, they are answered by the content of lessons. Therefore the teacher's primary task in connecting the partnering pedagogy to the curriculum is to turn the content into a series of questions, and to make sure that all students understand up front, and in a crystal-clear way, what the important questions to be answered actually are for the content in question.

In the partnering pedagogy, planning always begins with formulating a series of guiding questions for students to answer. Guiding questions (also known as driving questions, inquiry questions, or challenge questions) are the primary way teachers translate the curriculum they are required to teach into the partnering pedagogy.

No matter what subject or topic you are teaching, what you are really after is to have all of your students be able to answer the key question(s) that you are focusing on that day, or in that topic. For students, knowing what the guiding questions are, and checking which ones they can (or can't yet) answer, is a great way to self-assess their progress and to study for any test. And once the students can answer those questions, they should be able to do well on any test you give or, for that matter, on any standardized test.

Guiding questions come in two varieties:

1. Big or overarching questions, which some may refer to as the goals or objective of the lesson (but in question form). Here are some examples:

    -   Why and how do we multiply fractions (or, in a different class, binomials)?
    -   Why did the United States have a civil war?
    -   What is irony, and how do we use it?
    -   Why does the Earth move, and in what ways?

2. More detailed incremental or supporting questions. Here are some examples:

    -   How do you find the common denominator?
    -   What was the role of slavery in causing the Civil War?
    -   Where is the irony in *Romeo and Juliet*?
    -   What is precession?

PARTNERING TIP

When planning, always think about what you can ask students, rather than what you can tell them. In fact, always consider how little telling you actually need to do in the class. Then cut that in half. And cut it some more. Try to be sure that any talking you do in the classroom is not telling, but rather asking and discussion. Your students and you will almost certainly be better off.

Making Your Guiding Questions Better

Creating good guiding questions is an art, and you should always strive to make yours better and better. Go through several iterations if possible. Consider this checklist for guiding questions:

1. Can my students understand the guiding questions?

2. Are the guiding questions open-ended, and do they require a complex answer?

3. Will my students need to learn important content knowledge and a variety of skills and tools to answer the guiding questions?

4. Do the guiding questions allow me to create a local context for the topic(s) under study and have students solve a real problem?

SOURCE: Adapted from Buck Institute for Education unpublished documents.

The best guiding questions are generally about a *why* followed up with a *how*. Even when we are teaching specific skills, the *why* should come first. "Why did we have a civil war, and how can we help prevent other such wars?" "Why do we have seasons, and how can we predict when they start and end?" "Why are some numbers irrational, and how can we calculate with them?" "Why is our city or community hurting, and how can we help?" "Why would we want to measure the area under a curve, and how do we do it?"

Reverse the Tests and Textbooks

A good way to think of guiding questions is to think of what you (or others) might ask your students in order to check their understanding of the material you are teaching (say, on a test). Boil those questions down to the 5 to 10 most important. Then, rather than waiting until you have taught the material (i.e., told them the answers), give the questions to the students, on paper or online, and tell them their job is to be able to answer them.

Sometimes you can lift, or derive, the guiding questions right from the textbook or planning guide you are using, by working in reverse. Try turning the chapter names or subheads (which are almost always presented as topics) into questions. Also look at the questions offered as homework at the back of the book. How many of these are useful guiding questions for your class? (How many are not?) Do take the time, however, to rethink the questions, asking yourself the following:

- How interesting/motivating will these questions be for my students?
- How could I make them more so?
- How can I relate them to my students' passions?
- What interesting activities can my students do to answer these questions and to show me they know the answers?

PARTNERING TIP

Always spend a large part of your planning time on figuring out the big, overarching question and the detailed/incremental questions for each lesson. Write them down and hand them to students (and/or post them online). Ask students how they would like to answer them. If students say, "You tell us the answers," ask them, "How would you get the answers if I weren't here?" Then let them do that.

One of the key reasons you are teaching in this partnering way is that you want to encourage your students to be questioners. So whenever you give them a list of questions, always ask what questions they might want to add. Encourage your students to think about questions in the manner you are illustrating to them, that is, in a hierarchy of big and overarching questions to smaller and narrower ones.

Examples of Guiding Questions

The following are all guiding questions that can be used in various subjects at various levels. Some are more specific than others—this is good when students actually get to do the tasks mentioned. You can adopt these, and make up others like them, for whatever subject/level you teach.

- What are the positive and negative results of genetically modifying organisms?
- What effect do plants in your environment have on the air quality?
- How are sounds made?
- How could we make our community better for its citizens?
- When is war justified?
- What makes someone a hero?
- How can we design the best networking plan for a school or business?
- How can we use mathematics to design a roller coaster or holes for a miniature golf course?
- How could global warming affect our community?
- Can we capture the spirit of our city in art, music, and poetry?
- How can we plan an effective campaign to prevent water pollution in the lake?
- How can we design a web site for teenagers about books they like?
- Is our soil healthy enough to support a vegetable garden?
- How do architects use geometry?
- How can we design a theater that meets specifications with the greatest number of seats?
- How does technology make war more or less humane?
- How can childhood memories show who we are today?

SOURCE: Adapted from Buck Institute for Education unpublished documents.

Take the first question, for example: "What are the positive and negative results of genetically modifying organisms?" Without any lecture from the teacher, students can begin investigating what genetic modification is, where and how it is done, and what the benefits and risks are. As students work on the topic, the teacher provides more detailed questions and guides students into forming more of these on their own. Students can come to their own conclusions about whether or not we should genetically modify organisms, backing up those conclusions with evidence. This would then be a subject for a lively class discussion.

One seventh-grade group that studied this particular question concluded that the United States is "the world's greatest feeding experiment" and that the risks of genetically modified food were important enough to avoid eating it. They made a short movie about their perspective, titled *Frankengenes*.[19]

Bad, Good, and Better Guiding Questions

Here are some criteria you can use to evaluate your guiding questions:
Guiding questions are bad if they

- can be answered simply, with a right answer;
- do not have multiple solutions and subquestions for students to explore;
- do not fit in the time frame available (too broad or too narrow);
- are phrased in too academic or jargon-based a style;
- have no actions associated with them, that is, the answers don't cause students to do anything.

Guiding questions are good if they

- have multiple solutions and no simple answer,
- have local and global implications,
- have practical results.

Guiding questions are even better if

- students react by saying, "That's a good question";
- they can be adapted to different student interests and passions;
- they lead students to real actions that change the world.

So, for example, the question "Is war good?" is a bad guiding question because it can be answered with yes or no. "Why do we have wars?" would be a good guiding question. An even better guiding question would be "How can understanding why we have wars help us prevent them?"

Creating Individualization and Differentiation Through Guiding Questions

A great advantage of giving students the questions, rather than the answers, is that each student (or team of students) can approach finding the answers in his or her own way. It makes no difference at all, in partnering, whether the students get the answers to the guiding questions (assuming they are correct) from the teacher's mouth, from a text, from the computer, or from their best friend. All that matters is that the answers be right and that the students learn them.

So when partnering, there is generally no need for a teacher to spend class time introducing or teaching lessons or topics from the front of the room. In the partnering pedagogy, the teacher need only hand out or post the day's questions—both the overarching question and the more detailed, incremental ones—and then act as a coach and guide as students use the resources at their disposal to answer those questions. (In some instances, of course, the questions themselves might merit a discussion before the students begin to answer them.)

Students choose whether to work individually or in groups, and use any combination of the different nouns, or tools, available to do this. (I discuss these in Chapter 7.) After a certain amount of time (often one-third to one-half of the total class time for the topic), students make short presentations and/or the teacher (or a student) leads a discussion to verify whether the questions have been answered correctly and the material learned.

Obviously, it gets boring to do this exactly the same way every day. So the teacher and students need to think of variations on this basic approach. Examples might include the following:

- Students working all as individuals, or all in teams
- Teams of different sizes
- Competitions between teams or individuals to find answers more quickly or more completely
- Everyone searching for new sources
- Everyone debunking an existing source or myth
- Project-based learning or lessons
- Focusing on certain tools (e.g., only ones students don't know or haven't tried)
- Constraints, such as no computers, no Wikipedia, or no collaborating
- Internet-based information hunts, such as webquests
- Having different types of presentations (e.g., PowerPoint, audio, video) and different lengths (e.g., 30 seconds, 1 minute, 5 minutes)

For example, if the overall guiding question for unit is "What is poetry?" one day might consist of groups of students trying to answer that question, another day might consist of individuals finding and posting poems they like (answering the more detailed question "What makes a good poem?") and other students looking for criteria, and another day might consist of students writing and posting their own poems (answering "Can anyone write a poem?") and of peer-to-peer and teacher critique.

Relating Guiding Questions to Student Passions

In order to make the guiding questions interesting to all students, and to motivate all students to want to answer them, a key job for teachers is to help each student relate the guiding questions to his or her own, individual passions. This can be done in a variety of ways—individually or in groups, in advance or on the fly—but thinking in advance about how to do it is an important part of the planning process. A lesson with the guiding question "What are fractions, and why do we need them?" can, like many lessons, be pitched to different students or groups in terms of music, sports, computers, science, art, and many other student passions as well.

To get to each student individually, partnering teachers take a different approach to planning than many teachers are used to. The partnering alternative to preparing a lesson plan each day to deliver to all the students in a class is this:

- This is my plan for Student 1, given what I know about his or her passions and progress.
- This is my plan for Student 2, given what I know about his or her passions and progress.
- This is my plan for Student 3, given what I know about his or her passions and progress.

Doing this every day in great detail may not be realistic or even possible. Even if you have only 20–30 students, it is difficult to always plan individually for each one of them. Fortunately, there is help. You can get your students to coplan with you by making sure they know it is their responsibility to link what you are discussing to their own passion. In fact, you should encourage (and even require) them to make this connection every day. A personal notebook or a personal or class blog would be a good place for students to record these connections. Teachers should record them as well for future use and sharing with colleagues.

PARTNERING TIP

Have each student keep a notebook area, blog, or other method of the student's choosing titled "Relating What I Am Learning to What I Like." Be sure that students take a minute every day or two to fill this in. If they can't think of anything, they should ask you or the class for help.

Here are some examples of what I mean.

Say you are teaching fractions. The big question of the day might be "What is a lowest common denominator, and why do we need it?" A student whose passion is music might understand this best in terms of notes. The sports person, in terms of stats. The politics buff, in terms of polls. The coin collector, in terms of coin values.

Or say you're teaching the First Amendment. The student whose passion is music might understand this best in terms of lyrics. The sports person, in terms of political comments by athletes. The politics buff, in terms of TV campaign spots. The coin collector, in terms of advertisements and fakes.

And, of course, you will strive to make all these connections not just theoretical, but *real*. Knowing each of your students' interests and passions gives you tremendous and immediate advantages in your planning. In addition to the ones already discussed, you can also take these steps:

1. Enlist the students who are actually passionate about the subject you are teaching as peer-to-peer instructors.

2. Research how the subject you are teaching relates to your students' interests and passions, and use this to make your suggestions more appealing.

Examples

1.   You know that one of your students is passionate about coin collecting. How could you approach this student differently . . .

- . . . *as a math teacher?* You could cast this student's questions in terms of different currencies. Currency conversions use both multiplication and division skills. Old English currency uses base 12 and base 20. The Internet, if there is access in your classroom, provides enormous opportunities for research.
- . . . *as an English or English language arts teacher?* Realizing that every coin has a story that can be read about or written about, you could ask about those. You could have the student connect with literature in which money figures prominently, such as *Ali Baba and the 40 Thieves* or *The Merchant of Venice.*
- . . . *as a social studies teacher?* You could ask the student to research the coinage of the period or culture you are studying, seeing what it reveals about people, places, cultural behaviors, and relative costs.
- . . . *as a science teacher?* You could ask the student about what coins are (and were) made of, and why, as a lead-in to materials science and chemistry.
- . . . *as a language teacher?* You could ask how coins help tell the history of the culture whose language this student is learning.

2.   You know some of your students are passionate about music (this will almost certainly be the case). How do you gear your teaching to their interests . . .

- . . . *as a math teacher?* You could ask your questions in terms of rhythms, structure, and the other mathematics of music.
- . . . *as an English teacher?* You could ask about song lyrics, opera libretti, or other musical forms.
- . . . *as a social studies teacher?* You could ask students how they would enter whatever period or culture you are studying through the music of its time or the music written about it.
- . . . *as a science teacher?* You could ask students about the effects music has and the ways we perceive it as an entry to the realm of human biology and psychology.
- . . . *as a language teacher?* You could ask students how the music and lyrics of a culture provide entry into the language.

Passions are much more differentiated and are probably far easier to identify than other differentiators, such as learning styles or Howard Gardner's multiple intelligences (and in both of those cases, there is controversy over whether they even exist). Passions certainly exist, and your students will tell you what they are. Again, the thing that makes passion-based differentiation possible (and even relatively easy) to do is that, as a partner, you don't have to figure out everything by yourself—you can ask the students!

It is highly likely that once the students get the idea of relating their schoolwork to their passions, they will want to do more. If you work with students by asking questions about their passions in the right way (and it will almost certainly take some time and iteration to figure out exactly what that right way is for you and your students), you will likely be quite pleasantly surprised by the results.

Letting Students Choose Their Own Path to the Answers

In partnering, as we have seen, each student (or group) gets to choose his or her own path to answering the guiding questions—and you need to plan for this. You will want to think about your room arrangement, as I discussed earlier, and expect it to change over the course of a class as teams form and break up. If possible, you might want to arrange for passes for a certain number of students to be able to use the library. You might need to get some web sites unblocked, temporarily or, even better, permanently (this can often be arranged by consulting your tech coordinator). If YouTube or other useful sites are permanently blocked, you may want to record or download some videos or other materials at home for students to have at their disposal. You might want to let some students or teams do their work on your interactive whiteboard if you have one.

All of this does mean, in general, a looser and almost certainly more noisy classroom than a traditional one where the only voices heard are those of the teacher or of the student who has been called on. It means you, the teacher, will likely not be found in the front of the room, but rather walking around, giving students and groups advice, guidance, and suggestions on where to look and how to begin. It may even require you getting permission for some students to be in the halls or even out of the building doing their research. (Of course, this needs to be cleared with administrators. More and more superintendents and principals are becoming more understanding about, sympathetic to, and supportive of this new style of learning.)

What partnering definitely does *not* mean is that your classroom should, or ever will, devolve into total chaos. Part of introducing partnering is to make sure that this is understood and accepted by students. An important part of partnering is creating a shared understanding with your students that they are being given responsibility for their own learning (which they may not have ever had) and that they have to act responsibly. Taking responsibility is a huge part of the students' learning experience in partnering. For some teachers, it means having students follow, at all times, what I call the Three Rules of the Classroom:

1. Always try to behave ethically.

2. Do your best to learn.

3. Don't disturb anyone else in the process.

A student not doing his or her own work is unethical and is therefore unacceptable. Slacking, that is, not doing one's best to learn, is also unacceptable. So is causing any disturbance that prevents others from learning, such as noisily joking around or taking videos unrelated to the task at hand. On the other hand, a lively debate or discussion focused on the guiding questions, with all participating—even if it gets loud or raucous—should be fine.

FOCUS ON THE VERBS

The Link to the Required Skills

The second important connection between the partnering pedagogy and the curriculum, used in planning, comes through the verbs, or skills, that are connected to and appropriate for answering the guiding questions. The verbs are the skills that are mandated in the curriculum (and most curricula are becoming more and more skill based) and that students learn through their partnering work.

In planning, it is the job of the partnering teacher to figure out ways to make these skills explicit, because it is important that students understand that it is skills they are learning, not just facts and content. Students may be finding and learning important dates, but underneath they are (or should be) practicing such skills as developing research techniques, verifying, conducting historical analysis, and thinking critically.

Just as students need to always know what questions they are answering, they also need to know, at every moment, precisely what skills they are being asked to learn, practice, and master as they answer those questions. Many complex computer and video games are good at helping players understand this. They give the player a score, or level, in each of a number of skills based on what the player has accomplished in that area, and they require proficiency in all skills for a "level-up" promotion. Partnering teachers should do something similar—articulate the skills being learned and help students understand how good they are at each skill. Partnering teachers should never assume that students have automatically made the mental connection between the work they are doing and the skills they are learning; these connections need to always be made as explicit as possible.

In this verbs-focused planning step, teachers think about what they want students to do with the content, that is, reflect and decide on the underlying (and overriding) skills they want students to learn, practice, and master through the answers they will find to the guiding questions. In planning and designing, it is very important for teachers to focus their thinking strongly on the verbs and not move too quickly to the tools or technology that will be used.

What learning skills should the students be practicing as they answer the guiding questions and learn the content? Reading? (Possibly.) Memorizing? (Probably not.) Analyzing? Researching? Thinking critically or logically? Making decisions? Combining? Debating? Collaborating? Or should students be figuring out for themselves what to do with the content? As you plan, take the time to think carefully about the skills involved in what you are teaching and focusing on (through the partnering pedagogy), and choose which verbs you are interested in having your students "do" with the content. That will lead you to the appropriate technologies.

As we saw earlier, Table 2.1 includes all the learning verbs considered in this book. Each verb has associated with it particular nouns, or tools, that are useful and appropriate. I suggest you now go back and peruse that list carefully.

Here are some ways you can use the list.

- Look through the all verbs, and decide which are applicable to each of the various lessons you will teach.
- Focus on specific verbs that you would like to encourage your students to use, practice, and improve in.
- Take some of your existing lessons and/or content, and try to rethink it in terms of the verbs being learned as students master that content.

Two Special Verbs

Most of the verbs on the list are self-evident and need no special explanation. However, let me single out two of them, frequent decision making and Socratic questioning, for some discussion.

Frequent Decision Making

Perhaps surprisingly, one of the things most students do relatively infrequently in class is make decisions. When teachers ask questions, they are often content to let volunteers raise their hands, without obliging everyone to decide. And students don't rush to decide if they don't have to. This is not particularly good for students' learning, since making decisions (and getting feedback about whether those decisions were good) is one of the primary ways we learn. Kolb's so-called learning loop of action, observation (or feedback), reflection, and abstraction is widely known and acknowledged as the way most learning takes place.[20]

Even more curiously, the situation in which we have students make the most decisions is on tests—and then the decisions are separated from the feedback (which only comes much later, if at all), so that the decisions don't help the learning. Our students would be well served if we introduced a great deal more frequent decision making into their learning. (This is one of the reasons kids learn so well from games—they typically involve a decision, with feedback, every half second or so.)

Here are some strategies a partnering teacher can use to introduce more frequent decision making:

1. Ask more questions.

2. Require an answer to all your questions from every student—if a question is worth asking, every student should answer it. Ensure particularly that all students answer the guiding questions.

3. Get each student to commit to a position. During discussions, cards (e.g., one side red and one side green) can be held up by all students to indicate their answer, or students can write an answer on an index card.

4. If your school has "clickers" (personal response systems), use them. They force each student to give an answer. (Cell phones can also be used for this, either via texting, Twitter, or combined with the web site www.polleverywhere.com.)

5. Have students create templates (say, using PowerPoint) that let them make and get feedback on multiple decisions in a short amount of time (see Figure 5.1). This is similar to flash cards, but with more sophisticated problems and decisions. In an art class, the decisions can be about which is the real work of art and which is a forgery (and why students think so). In an English class, decisions can focus on which of two alternatives is the best opening, or closing, sentence and why.

Figure 5.1   Sample Decision-Making Feedback Templates

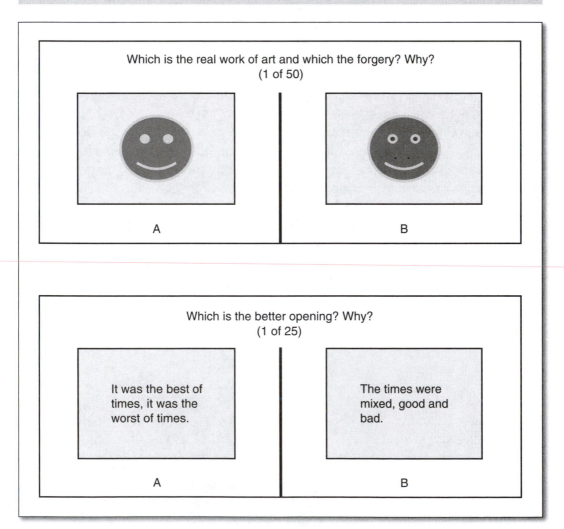

PARTNERING TIP

Discuss with your students ways to increase their decision making as part of the partnering work they do. Groups or teams might use templates to test each other on their decision-making ability in whatever area they are studying.

Socratic Questioning

Another important skill today, little used by teachers outside of law schools and rarely taught to K–12 students, is Socratic (i.e., thought-provoking) questioning. Although the word *Socratic* is often heard (and generally misused), true Socratic questioning means asking open-ended questions that make the person being questioned recognize logical contradictions in his or her own position and that force the person to reconsider his or her position on the topic under consideration.

A good description of Socratic questioning comes from the web site of the Science Education Resource Center at Carleton College, in Northfield, Minnesota:[21]

> Named for Socrates (ca. 470–399 B.C.), the early Greek philosopher/teacher, a Socratic approach to teaching is based on the practice of disciplined, rigorously thoughtful dialogue. The instructor professes ignorance of the topic under discussion in order to elicit engaged dialogue with students. Socrates was convinced that disciplined practice of thoughtful questioning enables the scholar/student to examine ideas logically and to be able to determine the validity of those ideas. Also known as the dialectical approach, this type of questioning can correct misconceptions and lead to reliable knowledge construction.
>
> Although "Socratic questioning" appears simple, it is in fact intensely rigorous. As described in the writings of Plato, a student of Socrates, the teacher feigns ignorance about a given subject in order to acquire another person's fullest possible knowledge of the topic. Individuals have the capacity to recognize contradictions, so Socrates assumed that incomplete or inaccurate ideas would be corrected during the process of disciplined questioning, and hence would lead to progressively greater truth and accuracy.
>
> During Socratic questioning, the teacher is a model of critical thinking who respects students' viewpoints, probes their understanding, and shows genuine interest in their thinking. The teacher poses questions that are more meaningful than those a novice of a given topic might develop on his or her own. The teacher creates and sustains an intellectually stimulating classroom environment and acknowledges the value of the student in that environment. In an intellectually open, safe, and demanding learning environment, students will be challenged, yet comfortable in answering questions honestly and fully in front of their peers.

When discussing education, for example, a Socratic question might be "Why do we have school?" When discussing World War II, it might be "What was good about Hitler's Germany?"

Partnering students should be taught, and have a chance to use, the skill of Socratic questioning. While a teacher can and should demonstrate Socratic questioning, it is also something that students can research and then practice with each other.

PARTNERING TIP

Try to hold discussions in a completely Socratic mode, with you and the students asking questions that get people to reflect on their own positions.

As you plan and consider your partnering classes, constructing your guiding questions and focusing on appropriate verbs, also remember, and think about, your various roles as a teacher in the partnering pedagogy. Instructional expert, certainly, but also particularly the roles of coach and guide. It is typically much easier to think of yourself in those last two roles if you have planned principally in terms of guiding questions and verbs, rather than content.

Keep in mind that, just as the answers to the guiding questions are to be found by students and not the teacher, the verbs (skills) are also for students to do and practice with the content, using a variety of differentiated activities that teacher and students agree on mutually.

The tools that your students will use to do these activities are many. Some will be the traditional nondigital tools that you are familiar with and may have used with your students for years (books, for example). But many more will be new digital tools. And the digital tools available to your students will continue to increase in number and variety.

How do you, as a partnering teacher, ensure that as many of these tools that are available in your school get used to your students' maximum learning advantage? That is the subject of the next chapter.

6

Using Technology in Partnering

Guiding Questions

1. What is the role of technology in partnering?

2. How can I ensure that students use all the technology available?

3. How do I choose the appropriate nouns, or tools, for students to use?

In the previous chapter I discussed the verbs (i.e., skills) of learning. In this chapter I will look at the nouns, the actual technology tools used by students to answer the guiding questions, practice the over- and underlying skills, make presentations, and, in so doing, learn the material.

The reason I emphasize so strongly the important verb/noun metaphorical distinction is that it helps partnering teachers (and all teachers, for that matter) keep the focus on what is most important in education, which is not the technology itself, but rather the underlying skills our students must learn and master—with or without technology. So while I am a big proponent of our students using digital technology—these are the tools of their time and will certainly be what they use in almost any job as adults—technology for its own sake will get us nowhere.

As I have discussed, the verbs of learning (e.g., understanding, communicating, presenting, persuading; see Table 2.1 for all of them) are unlikely to change for 21st century students. They are the stuff of education, the skills we want all our students to have, and the part of education that we want to carefully preserve. In the old metaphor of the baby and the bathwater, verbs are the baby.

NOUNS: THE TOOLS STUDENTS USE

So what, then, are nouns? Nouns are tools for "doing" the verbs. And unlike the verbs, nouns change. They change with the times and with improvements in technology. Of course, technology is hugely important in today's education. Using as much of it as possible is kids' birthright as students in the early 21st century, and it is crucial that we all strive, as educators, to provide students with as many technology tools as possible. But technology is, and will always be, just that—a tool.

There is a useful saying (from researcher Alan Kay) that "something is only 'technology' if it was invented after you were born." We already use many forms of technology in our teaching (books, encyclopedias, writing boards, even paper and pencils) that we no longer think of as technology. Educational technology tools (nouns) did change in the past—from the scroll to the book, from the pen and inkwell to the ballpoint pen, from the blackboard to the whiteboard, from chalk to the marker, from the private tutor to the class teacher. But they generally changed very, very slowly, over decades and centuries. Because this pace of change was so slow—and often over the course of one's entire career no change in tools happened—some teachers may have gotten the idea that the nouns of education are fixed.

But that is not the case. The verbs stay the same, but the nouns do change. And suddenly that change is accelerating wildly. We have entered a period—the digital age of the 21st century—when new learning tools are emerging, changing, and even disappearing at a speed never before experienced, a pace by which tool change happens in months and years, rather than decades and centuries.

TECHNOLOGY IS THE ENABLER

Once the partnering teacher has given the guiding questions to students and made certain that students understand the appropriate verbs (i.e., once the partnering students know their goals), the teacher's job is to let them work, on their own and with their peers (and with the teacher's guidance and coaching), until they have convinced themselves and the teacher that they know the answers to the questions and have mastered the required skills.

To learn (both the content and the skills) on their own, students need tools. Part of the partnering teacher's job is to be sure students are aware of all the available and appropriate learning tools at their disposal and are using the best ones for the job. As I have said before, while teachers should never use the tools for students—and are not required to use the tools themselves—it is important that partnering teachers know what tools exist, understand what each of the tools can do, and, to the extent that the tools are available in the school, make them available to students and encourage their use.

As partnering teachers, we want to use as much (modern) technology in our teaching as possible, precisely because it will help students learn the skills better. Digital technology is the enabler, allowing students to teach themselves in ways they couldn't in the past. Students know that digital technology represents the tools of their time as people growing up in the early 21st century, and they want to use these tools, as deeply as possible.

Technology's role, therefore, is to support the partnering pedagogy. For that to happen, partnering teachers need to know what modern technologies are (potentially) available to students, what they do, and how they support learning, both in answering guiding questions and in practicing skills. In Chapter 7, I present this information, tool by tool, and encourage you to supplement what I tell you with further inquiries, classes, and especially consultations with your students around any tools you think might be of help.

TECHNOLOGY AND EQUITY

To Each His or Her Own

Of course, not all technologies will ever be available to all (even the richest). But that is OK as long as all students have access to a minimum. More and more, this minimum is becoming each student having his or her own networked personal computer (and, of course, cell phone).

If you don't have one-to-one computing (or, as one teacher put it, 2:1 with the phones) in your school today, you should expect it tomorrow. And as a partnering teacher, you should prepare for it today by thinking about what you would do if your students did have access to that level of technology in your classroom. There are a number of things partnering teachers can and should do in the interim to approximate 1:1, such as teaming.

Partnering teachers need to be proactive about finding out what technology is available in their schools today, what's coming tomorrow, and what to ask for that's not. It is also very important that partnering teachers continue to encourage the use of technology and not hold back because some students do not have the same access as others. Students who don't have the technology need to be accommodated by putting them on teams or partnering them with those who do and by making sure labs, libraries, and other places with the technology are open long enough so that all can have access. Many schools now keep their computer labs open on weekends and until midnight during the week to accommodate students who need this access.

LET THE STUDENTS USE ALL TECHNOLOGY

Viewing all the technologies available to students today (more than 130 are listed in Chapter 7, and more come daily) can seem overwhelming to teachers who are not technophiles or who have never paid much attention to this area before. But there is really no cause for alarm. The partnering teacher's job is simply to know about these technologies and how they can aid student learning. It is not to use them; using them is the students' job.

Many of the teachers who are the most successful at using technology in partnering say, "I never touch the stuff. My students do it all." And their students use a great deal of technology.

And by the way, this is not an unfamiliar position for a teacher. To teach about books and essays, novels and poetry, teachers do not have to actually write them. To teach about science, they don't need to actually research and publish. To teach about films, they don't have to make them. The teacher's (i.e., coach's) role is not to do these things for the students, but rather to help students do them for themselves, to give them feedback, and to help them improve.

Which is not to say that students can't benefit from expert advice in using various technology tools. On the contrary. But their teachers do not have to be the experts at using these tools. There are outside experts who know, in great detail, how to use Web 2.0 tools effectively or how to make good videos or podcasts. Such expertise can be brought in, in person, virtually, or through reading and YouTube. And when these experts do interact with the class, they should talk directly to the students (with the teacher present, of course), not first teach the teachers so that they can later (and much less expertly) teach the students.

The Prensky Apostasy

So in partnering, it is the students' job—not the teacher's—to use whatever technology is available, just as it is the students' job to answer the guiding questions, use the verbs, and master the skills. When it comes to technology, the teacher is the guide, the coach, and the quality controller, not the user.

PowerPoint? Not for the teacher. Only students should be allowed to use it. Interactive whiteboards? Again, not for the teacher; students (only) can and should present on them. Computers, smartphones, blogs, wikis, Facebook, Twitter, or other technologies? Students, not the teacher, should be setting them up and using them. Interestingly, this is true (perhaps more true) even in the elementary grades. The only exception is that teachers can, from time to time (if they are able), model the kind of use(s) they expect. But even that is not absolutely necessary. Many, if not most, kids can learn on their own if good feedback is provided.

It should be noted that this is not a universal point of view, which is why I call it an apostasy. Many think that teachers should use the tools, and many teachers ask for and receive training in their use. But I think this is the wrong way to go.

My view is based partly on comments from students, who say things like "Teachers make a PowerPoint and they think they're so awesome, but it's just like writing on the blackboard" or "Don't try to use technology yourself—you'll only look stupid." It is also based on my observations of teachers using technology at only a fraction of what it is capable of doing for learning, and not letting students (who are dying to) use it instead.

This, of course, is not to say that teachers shouldn't use technology to communicate with their students. They should. But not via PowerPoint. Rather via texting, e-mail, and posting online, which are often the best and easiest ways to communicate (at least from the students' point of view). And, of course, there is certainly nothing wrong with a teacher who really knows something about a technology communicating that to students, just as a peer might.

But, overall, I think this should be the rule: partnering teachers should never, ever use the technology *for* their students.

I recently came across this blog post from a longtime teacher:

> Throughout my career I have believed that in order to bring a learning tool into my classroom I had to be fairly adept at using the tool myself—after all, how could I require my students to use a tool without having the personal expertise to show them how to use it effectively? . . . I must admit that it is rather unnerving to give an assignment that requires students to use a technology in which I have little expertise. But, to my surprise, students appreciate the fact . . . that they know more than I do and that I am more than willing to learn from them. Rather than undermining my credibility and impact as a teacher, my students view my "openness to new technological experiences" as cool, and a way for us to build a deeper connection than my content knowledge and expertise ever could.[22]

Teachers who are especially fluent in technology (and proud of it!) might be very tempted to use the technology for students (e.g., to set up blogs for them, to create their own PowerPoint presentations). They should, I think, resist this temptation. In the long run, students can use technology much more effectively than (most) teachers can, and when they can't, they need to learn to do so and not have it done for them.

So let's be clear. Should a lot of technology be used in the partnering classroom? Absolutely! Should it be the teachers who are using it? Rarely—only using it for something students can't or shouldn't use it for (e.g., giving a test) or when modeling or preparing technology-based materials out of class for students to use in class. It's great for a teacher to create (out of class) an alternate reality game or some other type of game for students to play, or to make a podcast of something for students to listen to. In class, though, teachers who know how should be showing and getting the students to do these things for themselves.

For skeptics, in a sense this is no different from dealing with older technologies. Should teachers who have great essay writing skills be writing for their students? Do students benefit (except in special cases) by being read to by teachers? (We may bring in an actor or great speaker sometimes to demonstrate how to read dramatically, but most would agree that reading should be the students' job.) In the case of those older tools, I think we can all agree that it is the students' job to use and master them on their own. The same is true with digital tools. The difference, though, is that the kids already have a head start with these modern tools.

The Teacher's Roles With Regard to Technology

So what exactly are the partnering teacher's roles in this area? The teacher should

- point out to students all technologies that are available. Teachers should know about all those listed in the following chapter and be constantly checking for new ones.
- watch carefully as students use the technologies and present with them, to be sure that students are producing high-quality, rigorous work. (If not, teachers should request revisions.)
- encourage, or even require, students to make use of as many different technologies as possible over the course of a semester or school year.
- point out (through well-constructed questions rather than telling) potential pitfalls and mistakes that are often made by students when using technology, and help students become better at critically assessing the tools they use. Teachers can point out, for example, web sites that are not what they purport to be (e.g., the now-famous instance of the Martin Luther King Jr. site that is actually run by a hate group). But teachers should always follow up by asking students to find additional examples on their own.

> **Check It Out!**
>
> See my article "Search vs. Research" at http://tinyurl.com/mu7hhz.

Partnering teachers should also point out important distinctions that students might not recognize on their own. Example might include the difference between search (where anything goes) and research (which has traditions and rules) or the difference between fair use (OK) and plagiarism (not OK.)

Four Special Cases

Before we get to the full technology list in Chapter 7, let me say something additional about four technologies that I think partnering teachers should particularly focus on.

Web 2.0—What's Happening Now

As I write this, it is hard to attend or read anything related to technology and schools that does not mention the great benefits of Web 2.0 for learning. In case you don't know, what people mean by Web 2.0 is that, in addition to being a medium for reading and watching (which it was, mostly, a few years ago), the Web is also a medium for publishing (of words, videos, etc.) by anyone. This is not especially new, since the inventor of the Web, Tim Berners-Lee, said many years ago that "what people put into the web is much more important than what they take out."

Web 2.0 is a shock only for those who internalized the model of the Web as a library, a place for reading and watching, and have not watched it evolve. What has happened is that tools for extremely easy publishing of words, images, videos, and other media have been developed that allow any student to be a publisher of his or her work. Because publishing one's work (and getting feedback from the world) is important for learning, improving, and sharing (not to mention pride in oneself), this is an important development for students. They should be encouraged to use Web 2.0 tools, such as blogs, wikis, YouTube, and others as much as possible.

And stay on the lookout for Web 3.0, the "semantic web," where you can search any work ever created for anything and link any pieces together. It's just around the corner.

1:1—The Coming Wave

Beginning with small programs in the State of Maine and other places, the idea of giving each student his or her own computer (laptop, netbook, or even cell phone) to use, maintain, take home, and, essentially, learn on is finally taking hold. It is being adopted in more and more countries, districts, and schools around the world. For example, the prime minister of Australia recently announced such a program for the whole country. Any teachers, no matter where they teach, would be foolish to think this will not be coming to their classroom within the next several years, and ought to be preparing for that day.

The issue, of course, is what do you (or more precisely, in the partnering pedagogy, the students) do with computers, particularly in class. Most students will have no trouble (especially if coached by their peers) in using the computers outside of class for homework, research, connecting with teachers and assignments, turning things in, and so forth. But in some colleges and universities, where students have had their laptops in front of them for some time, teachers have citied disappointment that students in class use their computers for non-class-related activities such as Facebook. "Computers have become the new spitball," wrote one teacher.

It is extremely important for partnering teachers to understand that when this happens, it is not the fault of students (or the teachers) but rather of the pedagogy the teacher is using. Technology, particularly laptops in class, does not support lecturing or telling pedagogies at all. Given nothing interesting to do on the powerful machines in front of them, students will use them as they wish.

A partnering teacher whose students have their own laptops (or netbooks or even cell phones) in class has an obligation, therefore, to be sure they are used regularly as part of students' required work. This can mean researching answers to guiding questions, meeting in groups and with people outside involved in student projects, creating and posting online in writing or other media, and preparing presentations. Ideally, there should be no time in a partnering class for a student to throw a new spitball (although reality tells us there will always be some).

PARTNERING TIP

If you do get 1:1 computers in your classroom, begin your work with them by holding a conversation with your class about using the computers. What are the responsibilities of each partner (i.e., you and the students) with regard to these tools? How can they best be used? How can abuse be minimized or prevented? Although it often goes against teacher or administrator instincts, students almost universally ask for fewer restrictions and more responsibility in this area.

Cell Phones—The Computers in Students' Pockets

Cell phones are a technology that merits a discussion of its own, if only because so many educators are so confused about what to do with them. Should we ban them? Can we use them? What about students who don't have them? These are all important questions, all with a variety of answers.

As I write this, the policy in many schools and districts around the country and the world, including my hometown of New York City, is to ban cell phones on the grounds that they can be a disturbance in class and an opportunity to cheat on quizzes or exams. Obviously, no one wants a cell phone going off in the middle of a lecture, and no one would encourage cheating. But what about cell phones in a partnering classroom? What is the role of cell phones there? It is different. Should we have different policies? It is important for us to think about a good role for cell phones in students' education for a number of reasons:

1. Cell phones have become so ubiquitous, and they are such an important tool in students' lives out of school.

2. They are an area where there may be a digital divide, which as teachers we need to help overcome.

3. Their power and the useful things they can do for education are growing rapidly and enormously as they morph into smartphones and full-fledged computers, which is already happening with the iPhone and other phones like it.

For more and more of today's young people (and for many of us from the older generation), our increasingly powerful cell phones are a tool we can't do without. Phones are now practically ubiquitous in many high schools, and their penetration is quickly growing in middle and even elementary schools. So it makes sense to find ways of incorporating the cell phone's benefits into our teaching while eliminating its distractions. Banning cell phones—as easy a solution as it seems—will in the long run only make our education weaker.

Luckily, attitudes toward cell phones in schools are changing rapidly, with more and more teachers finding ways to incorporate them into students' education. They are doing so, at times, despite official bans, asking forgiveness rather than permission. (Note: I'm not advocating, here or anywhere else, breaking rules. I am just reporting what is happening, and happening frequently.) Consider these examples:

- Many science teachers have students use their cell phones for unit conversions and data collection, often using the phones' cameras.
- Many math teachers have students use their cell phones as calculators (there are downloadable applications for turning many phones into graphing calculators).
- Many language teachers have students use their cell phones to connect to students in other countries, particularly via texting.
- Many social studies teachers have students use their cell phones to follow breaking news and to e-mail politicians.
- Many English and English language arts teachers have students use their cell phones to interview experts, practice business speaking and writing, and post to blogs and other web sites.

Open-phone tests? For a number of years I have been advocating these, whereby students can use their phones (individually or in groups) to find elements of the answers to complex questions. It took a while for a student to finally tell me, "Most of our tests *are* open-phone tests, you guys just don't know it." Open-phone tests are now being used by teachers around the world (along with, of course, appropriate redefinitions of cheating in these instances). Recently, such a use by a teacher in a private school in Sydney, Australia, made the front page of the country's biggest newspaper. As a result, the school received inquiries from as far away as Central Asia!

Using cell phones in class represents big changes in how we think about education and technology, but these changes are both societal (i.e., happening far beyond just school) and appropriate to the new capabilities we have as users of these technologies.

For an interesting discussion of the many ways phones have been used in class, along with a set of available tools, I recommend Liz Kolb's excellent book *Toys to Tools* and her blog "From

Check It Out!

Here's the article from the *Sydney Morning Herald* about the use of cell phones in class: www.smh.com.au/articles/2008/08/19/1218911717490.html.

Check It Out!

Liz Kolb's blog on using phones is class can be found at www.cellphonesinlearning.com.

Toy to Tool" (see sidebar on previous page). It is important to consult the blog since, with the rapid advances in phone technology, many of the tools she mentions in the book have already been supplanted by better ones.

The bottom line for partnering teachers is that we need to find ways to make good and appropriate use of students' cell phones. These already powerful tools will soon be far more powerful and useful than anything a school can provide.

PARTNERING TIP

Hold a discussion with your students about whether and how they want to use their cell phones for learning. That discussion should include questions like these: How and when can we best use them? How will we prevent their use from becoming a distraction? What will we do about students who use their phones inappropriately? How will we deal with students who don't have them?

If necessary, work with students to contrast legitimate student needs with outdated and fear-inspired school policies, and advocate for policy changes in your school. Doing this certainly qualifies as making learning *real* for students.

As for the issue of equity—dealing with the fact that every student may not have a cell phone or a phone as good as his or her classmate's—I recommend that partnering teachers work hard to become digital multipliers (rather than digital dividers). One way to do that is by placing students into groups around the number of phones available. Another is to get donations of used cell phones. Note that more and more cell phones can use a Wi-Fi signal (often available for free in schools) in place of the carrier's network, which can often mitigate the cost related with data usage. I recommend talking to your school's tech coordinator about this.

PARTNERING TIP

If not all of your students have cell phones, I suggest looking at this positively, as a glass half full. The "glass half empty" way is to think, "Half my students don't have a cell phone. I can't use them." The "glass half full" approach is to think, "Great! 100 percent of pairs of my students have a cell phone. Let's go!"

I am often asked what I would recommend as 1:1 technology for a school or district that is starting from scratch and wants to buy new tools for all its students. At this point in time, with the way things are going, I would definitely recommend purchasing a smartphone (such as the iPhone) for each student, rather than laptops or even netbooks. Today's iPhone, for example, has means for easy reading and writing, a still camera and a video camera, and over 100,000 useful downloadable programs, many of which are usable in the classroom. These capabilities will only get better in future versions. In my view, the smartphone is the 1:1 device of the future and one that is likely, with software upgrades, to be useful for some time and for students at all levels.

Games—The Great Potential Motivator

Many teachers use games already (especially minigames such as versions of Jeopardy!), and all partnering teachers are encouraged to do so and to explore the category further. I have written much about the potential value of computer and video games as learning tools, particularly for generating engagement (see my two previous books, *Digital Game-Based Learning* and "*Don't Bother Me Mom—I'm Learning*"). Games can be used in the partnering context in a variety of ways:

- Some existing off-the-shelf commercial games can be used directly to help answer guiding questions or to acquire and practice skills. Games about periods of history are some of the best at this, as are logic games for younger learners.
- There exist some "learning games" within curricular subject areas that can be used for answering guiding questions and for skills practice. Examples include *Dimension M* and *Lure of the Labyrinth* for math, *SlinkyBall* and *Waste of Space* for physics, *Darfur Is Dying* and *Food Force* for social studies, and *The Grammar of Doom* for English. These games, widely scattered around the Internet and of varying size, quality, and complexity, have been created by individuals, companies, and foundations looking to engage kids in different types of learning. Most of the existing games are collected and rated on the Spree Learning Games web site.
- There are many tools that students can use to design and create their own games, such as Game Creator, GameStar Mechanic, Flash, and various "modding" tools. Students can create games as answers to guiding questions, as tools for learning and practicing potential skills, and even as presentation tools. One way for students to demonstrate their learning is to make a game that teaches what they have just learned to students who have not yet learned those things. Contests for older students to create games for younger ones have begun popping up around the world and are becoming more and more popular.

> **Check It Out!**
>
> For a list of learning games, see www.spreelearninggames.com.etc.

- Game tools can be used to make machinima (noninteractive animations made using game tools) as presentations that answer guiding questions.
- Even if your students lack access to any or all of these games or tools, it can be useful to work with students to design a theoretical or hypothetical game about the questions or skills you are working on. This has the advantage of requiring no technology at all, other than brain power.

PARTNERING TIP

Ask your students if any of them play a game that relates to what you are learning. If the answer is yes, ask them to present it to the class, and integrate it into their learning.

Work with your students to invent a theoretical game that, if one were to beat it, would prove that a person had answered the guiding questions and/or learned the skills in question. To do this, ask questions such as these: "What decisions would the player have to make? What would the conditions for winning be?"

NO TECHNOLOGY AVAILABLE?

What if, in your school, students have access to no technology at all that is remotely up to date? Or perhaps your school lacks the specific technologies you would like your students to use for certain purposes (or the technologies exist, but are blocked from student use). What can you do in such cases?

Fortunately, there is a good solution for a partnering teacher, which is to say to students, "Let's assume (or pretend) we have the technology. How would we use it? What would we do? What might we search for? What terms and strategies might we use? What should we be wary of?" Done well, this type of discussion can often be more powerful than the students actually using the technologies, because it gets directly to the question of *why* we are using technology: What verbs are we supporting? What do we hope to learn?

This approach can be even more powerful when thinking about simulation, in any subject. Rather than students using an existing simulation and observing the results, if no simulation is available you (or they) can ask, "How would we design a simulation for this? What are the relevant variables? What are the relationships between those variables? What are the key decisions to be made by the user?"

The point is that a partnering teacher need never feel totally stymied by a lack of technology available to students (even while always pushing for more). From the learning perspective, pretending is often equally good (or at least a close second).

USING THE APPROPRIATE NOUNS FOR THE GUIDING QUESTIONS AND VERBS

Finding the appropriate tools for students to use to answer the guiding questions, practice the verbs, and in so doing learn the content and skills they need to learn is not always an easy or obvious task. Because there are so many tools, and they change so frequently, some people have adopted the strategy of learning only a few of them and then sticking with what they know. That, however, is a losing strategy for both teachers and students in the 21st century and in partnering. Partnering teachers should instead read widely, striving to familiarize themselves with as many tools as possible (by "familiarize" I mean understanding the tools and what they do, not necessarily using them or using them well), and encourage all students to use as many appropriate tools as possible.

The annotated list in Chapter 7 consists of a great many (more than 130) technology tools (nouns) that students can use, if available. As you read or browse the list, please bear in mind the following things about the items:

1.   These are not technologies that you as the teacher (or even students) have to, or even should, totally master. They are means to an end, the end being answering the guiding questions and practicing the verbs.

2.   The tools on the list represent varying levels of digital technology, from zero to cutting edge. Some tools do almost the same things but in different ways; deciding which to use is merely a matter of what is available, up to date, and of personal preference.

3.   The preferred or so-called best tools for any particular use will change over time, often quite rapidly and frequently. Therefore it is very important that teachers not get too attached to any of them, or let their students do so. Despite what you may hear, in cases of rapidly changing technology there are no best practices to follow, only good practices.

The idea that the best tools for particular tasks or skills will change frequently is a major disruption for many teachers, who are used to using the same tools over and over, year to year. While in some ways this makes the teaching job more complex, it also makes it far more interesting, and that is how I recommend partnering teachers look at it.

PARTNERING TIP

Review the list of nouns in Chapter 7. Make a list of those that are unfamiliar to you, and then ask your students how many they are familiar with. Find out which of your students know a lot about technology, and then (1) use them as your own tutors and (2) pair them up (or put them in groups) with students who know less.

Think about the next things you will be teaching and the underlying skills related to each. Then find the tools that relate to those verbs (see Table 2.1). Suggest those tools to your students, and discuss them.

Working the List

The list in Chapter 7 describes the major tools available to students today (not all tools are available to all students, of course). I recommend browsing the list and then using it as a reference. You can of course read about all the tools if you wish, or you can just quickly search for any that you may not know about. Once you identify all the tools you are interested in, check with your school to find out which are available to your students. You can then suggest that students use certain of these tools, alone or in combination, to help answer guiding questions and practice required skills (verbs).

The tools are listed alphabetically, not in order of importance. Clearly, the list is selective and hardly includes every tool, or even every type of tool, out there. I have attached to most a selection of verbs that the tool might be useful for in terms of learning, practicing, or doing.

Although today we hear a lot about blogs, wikis, podcasts, and other Web 2.0 tools—and these are extremely important as tools for our students—one thing that I hope you will quickly notice is that there are far more tools available than just those. As important as those are, they should not get all our attention just because they are new.

Also note that additional new tools will appear on the scene frequently, so updates to this list should always be sought from the Web; from this book's web site; and from books, other teachers, and students.

Finally, although I have occasionally provided specific product names and URLs, when of special interest, the best way to find a specific tool to use with or to recommend to students is to search for the term in a search engine or look it up on Wikipedia. (Until only a few weeks ago I would have written that the best way is to Google it, but now that Microsoft's Bing has appeared on the scene, who knows what will be the preferred search engine by the time you read this.)

And so it is with all of these tools—expect them to evolve and change. And now to the list.

7

Understanding the Nouns, or Tools

Guiding Questions

1. Am I familiar with all the types of tools available?

2. Can I guide students to the right tools for the skills they are learning?

3. How do I get more information when I need it?

The purpose of this chapter is to serve as a reference for the great many nouns (tools) available for your partnering students to use. If you wish, you can read only what interests you or what you think you need, returning later, as required, after you have finished the book. As you read or use this list, please keep in mind the following:

- The tools are listed alphabetically, not in order of importance.
- Nouns change rapidly. This list may need updating by the time you read it.
- The list is selective and doesn't include every tool, or even every type of tool, out there.
- **(cf)** refers to another entry in this list.
- To find more information and examples for any listing, search for the term in Wikipedia.

1. **3D (Three-Dimensional)Printers**—These machines take the output of a design that a person has created using a computer-aided design (CAD) or other program and, by both adding and sculpting material (e.g., plastic, wax), create a complex 3D object such as an engine part or a fantasy creature. That object can be held, painted, modified, and used to get a feel for the final, manufactured object. These printers are used by design firms all over the world as well as by engineers, toy makers, and other manufacturers. Previously quite expensive, these machines have been quickly coming down in price to the point where most schools can afford one. They are a fantastic way to excite and motivate students by letting them see and hold 3D examples of their ideas and designs (see www.zcorp .com/en/Solutions/Education/spage .aspx). **VERBS supported by these tools**: exploring, experimenting, modeling, designing, innovating, tinkering, making, presenting.

2. **After Action Reviews (AARs)/Debriefing**—Also known as reflection, this is a highly effective tool for building understanding and drawing lessons from what has just happened in any situation. It is used extensively in the military. In education, holding an AAR with a class after completing a unit or project helps students get more out of everything they do by going over how everybody experienced it. An AAR requires no technology, only talking and listening (although audio and/or video recording tools can be used to enhance its value). **VERBS supported by these tools**: listening, observing, reflecting, thinking critically, planning.

3. **Aggregation Tools, or News Aggregators**—These are tools for automatically downloading and collating information from a variety of sources. Using an aggregator, a political science class could subscribe to, and receive daily, all the political columns and blogs in the United States or the world. A science class could aggregate columns and topics from major journals, magazines, and newspapers. The most widely used example is the **Really Simple Syndication (RSS) (cf)** aggregator, now built into many Internet browsers. However, other aggregation tools exist, such as the Alltop news aggregator for combining stories from a variety of sources, and new ones are constantly appearing. **VERBS supported by these tools**: finding, comparing, combining, planning.

4. **Alternate Reality Games (ARGs)**—These games involve combinations of computer and real-life elements that require players to solve complex puzzles and problems by combining information from a wide variety of sources. These include both real sources and public information as well as artificial resources (such as web sites) set up specifically for the

game. Players work individually and in teams, combining their information and findings to reach solutions. Many ARGs are extremely complex, but they can also can be relatively simple, set up by students and/or teachers, such as was done recently by a seventh-grade world history teacher in California (www.classroom20.com/forum/topics/so-i-terrified-my-students). **VERBS supported by these tools**: analyzing, exploring, finding, listening, reading, searching, verifying, watching. ARGs are also useful for thinking logically, collaborating, cooperating, and taking leadership. Setting up and then playing an ARG can be a great way for students to stimulate, or test, their creation and problem-solving abilities.

5. **Animation Tools**—These tools allow students to easily create their own animations on any topic. Examples include Adobe **Flash (cf)**, Toonz Harlequin, CelAction, Anime Studio, Toon Boom Animation, and AniMaker. **VERBS supported by these tools**: writing, creating, designing, making. See also **Comics Creation Tools**, **Graphic Novel Creation Tools**.

6. **Artificial Intelligence (AI) tools**— These programs try to make a computer approximate what a human might do. AI tools range from the very simple (e.g., Liza, a program that mimics a psychoanalyst asking questions) to extremely complex (e.g., robots that can respond to their environment and to humans). AI is used extensively in most computer games. Students can use AI tools to try to understand and mimic human behaviors, such as reproducing a particular author's or composer's style or a particular style of questioning. **VERBS supported by these tools**: analyzing, deciding, predicting, planning, programming.

7. **Assessment/Grading Tools**— Assessment and grading are often a burden to teachers, but in many cases much of this work is now being automated, which can potentially take a large load off of teachers' plates. Tools such as Scantron allow for automated marking of papers, using a scanner. There are now automated tools for the grading of short paragraphs and essays. Teachers who want to save time should look into these technologies and see if they can be made available in their school. **VERBS supported by these tools**: evaluating, providing timely feedback to students.

8. **Audiobooks**—"Reading with your ears" is the way one writer describes these recorded books. These were once known as "books on tape," but these days very few are on actual recording tape. Almost all recorded books are available on CD or as MP3 files that can be shared and played on any iPod or other music player. (Those on CD can easily be "ripped" to a computer.) Some may object to students' using recorded books because it obviates the need to practice decoding and understanding written words. But if the verb in

question is not decoding but rather understanding what is in another person's (i.e., the writer's) mind, recorded books are a perfectly acceptable way to do that. They have additional advantages as well. Playback hardware can speed up voice recordings, which can in many cases be taken in at speeds of up to four times faster with no loss of understanding. The "reader" (i.e., the person doing the recording) is, of course, important when it comes to recorded books. Although today there is often only one choice, in the future there may be multiple interpretations of books for various people to prefer and enjoy, much like with music, where one can generally choose one's preferred interpreter between the composer and listener. A potential activity or project for partnering students is to make recordings of books for other students or for the blind. **VERBS supported by these tools**: reading, listening, finding, reflecting, thinking critically, personalizing.

9. **Augmented Reality Tools**—Augmented reality is the superimposition of information on real, or photoreal, images. Examples include seeing the names of the peaks superimposed as you view a mountain range through your camera, or seeing labels appear on the fly on all the objects and buildings as you view an image of a city. Augmented reality is made possible by the combination of GPS (see **Geolocation Tools**) and accurate 3D geographic coordinates for objects.

Any data, including descriptions or historical information, can be added to and superimposed on any location. It is quite possible for students to use and add augmented reality information. **VERBS supported by these tools**: researching and managing information verbs, such as analyzing, exploring, finding, searching, verifying.

10. **Avatar Creation Tools/Character Generators**—An avatar is a graphic representation of a person that is often dynamic (i.e., changing according to context) and used to represent that person in online games, virtual worlds, or other computer programs. Tools, both built-in to programs and stand-alone, allow students to create increasingly detailed and sophisticated avatars of many kinds, human and otherwise. Students can also use these tools to create such things as historical costumes, characters from stories and novels, and animals with certain properties. The "creature creator" tool from the game Spore is an excellent example in which the character's behaviors are based on its physiology. **VERBS supported by these tools**: creating, modeling, designing, innovating, personalizing.

11. **Best Fit/Regression Tools**—These are statistical tools for students to use when they have collected data and want to see whether there is any correlation between two or more data sets. For example, by doing a regression analysis on the number of students absent from class versus

the average daily temperature, students would learn if there is a strong correlation between the two. **VERBS supported by these tools**: analyzing, verifying.

12. **Big Think**—This web site (www .bigthink.com) solicits, creates, and posts short videos from well-known experts in a variety of fields. These videos are essential for students to use in researching any subject. They can be accessed directly at the Big Think site or via **video search engines (cf)**. **VERBS supported by this tool**: listening, evaluating, thinking critically, communicating, finding your voice.

13. **Blogs and Blogging Tools**—A blog is a web site that records postings (typically one or more paragraphs of text, sometimes with pictures and video) in order of date. These can be the postings of one person or of everyone who has permission to post (e.g., a class). Comments and feedback from readers of the blog can be allowed (or not) and are generally tied to specific posts. Blogs are good for a variety of partnering tasks, including collecting student opinions or explanations and collecting student reactions to something that is posted by a student or teacher. In addition to the students, the teacher can also be a blogger, as can anyone else (e.g., an outside expert) given permission to blog or comment on the site. Many tools exist for creating and setting up blogs (easily done by

students) and for posting to them from a variety of devices, such as cell phones. A number of good books exist on using blogs creatively in classrooms, and I suggest you search for and consult them. **VERBS supported by these tools**: reflecting, thinking logically, collaborating, writing, thinking creatively.

14. **Brainstorming Tools**—These tools allow individuals or groups to come up with a variety of ideas on any topic and then sort and organize those ideas into useful groups. One brainstorming tool used in many schools is **Intuition (cf)**. Others for groups to use include collaboration software and the nontechnological "six hats" of Edward de Bono. Brainstorming tools are useful for students to use in organizing individual work, and for groups to use in generating new ideas and finding interesting solutions to problems. **VERBS supported by these tools**: exploring, finding, comparing, questioning, collaborating, writing, innovating, thinking creatively.

15. **Calculators**—The use of calculators by students is often highly controversial, but there is really little reason for this controversy in the 21st century. After a long fight, graphing calculators are now accepted in most high school math classes and can be used in many exams. Using a calculator for arithmetical calculations is the best 21st century method (just as the slide rule was the best method in the

early to mid 20th century). Cell phones all have calculators built into them, and many can download graphing calculator programs. Of course, students need to be taught carefully when to do various arithmetic operations, but the best solution for how to do them in the 21st century is clearly the calculator. **VERBS supported by this tool**: analyzing, finding, verifying, calculating, comparing, deciding, evaluating, predicting.

16. **Cameras (Digital)**—Having digital cameras available to groups of students, or to each student individually, should be a boon to any teacher of any subject. Social studies teachers can have students illustrate their personal lives and environments. English teachers can have students use their cameras to illustrate words or phrases, and to take interesting pictures for caption contests. Math teachers can have students take pictures of mathematically based phenomena in nature, such as fractals. Science teachers can have students use their cameras to collect data. All of these pictures can easily be integrated with any presentations students make. It is very important that partnering students learn the value of a camera as a learning and educational tool, and not be prohibited from using them in their schoolwork. **VERBS supported by this tool**: exploring, finding, observing, communicating, modeling and trying, finding your voice.

17. **Case Studies**—These are a useful tool for analysis that can be done with or without technology. They are basically a description of a real situation, typically with a problem or question at the end, regarding the best thing to do. Case studies can be created on paper, or dedicated technology tools can be used to create them in a systematic way that allows users to arrive at the proper conclusions in an iterative fashion. Several examples of case study creation software exist. **VERBS supported by this tool**: analyzing, verifying, deciding, evaluating, thinking logically, prudent risk taking, stimulating, having good judgment, making good decisions, problem solving.

18. **Cell Phones/Mobile Phones**—These are carried by more and more students in today's schools. It is important to realize that many of these phones are also enormously powerful computers. Although many schools currently ban students using them in class, this is a short-sighted policy because of the many potential learning opportunities these tools offer from a partnering perspective. For examples of how cell phones can be used for learning (in or out of class), see my article "What Can You Learn From a Cell Phone? Almost Anything!" (http://tinyurl.com/r678x) and the book *Toys to Tools,* by Liz Kolb, as well as her blog (www.cellphonesinlearning.com/). **VERBS supported by this tool**: used creatively, cell phones are a useful tool

for learning and practicing almost any verb.

19. **Cell Phone On-Screen Readers**—Cell phones are becoming better and better at displaying text from books, periodicals, and other sources for on-screen reading. One excellent example is the Kindle iPhone application, on which a book or periodical can be easily read, and to which most books can be downloaded for a price and many classic novels can be downloaded for free. (I use this tool frequently and find the format and the backlighting better than the dedicated Kindle reader.) Other cell phone readers that exist use the International Digital Publishing Forum (IDPF) standard rather than that of the Kindle. **VERBS supported by these tools**: reading, writing, copying/imitating, creating, finding your voice. See also **Electronic Books and Readers.**

20. **Cell Phone Novels**—More and more novels and other writings are designed to be read on a cell phone. This type of reading is available no matter where a person may be and is easily sharable with others. Students can benefit from studying, reading, and writing such works, which typically require different overall, paragraph, and sentence structures than writing for paper does. **VERBS supported by this tool**: reading, writing, copying/imitating, creating, finding your voice.

21. **Clickers**—"Clickers" is the popular name for audience response tools, handheld units that allow all class or audience members to input answers to a question or series of questions, with the answers compiled and viewed on a presentation screen. Several brands exist, and versions range in capability from simple numerical entry only to the ability to enter free text. It is worth asking about whether clickers have been purchased by your school and are available for you to use. If not, a very similar effect can be achieved with cell phones and the web site www.polleverywhere.com. In the not-too-distant future, it is likely that cell phones will take over entirely the functionality that now requires separate clicker devices. **VERBS supported by this tool**: exploring, researching, comparing, deciding, predicting, questioning, planning.

22. **Collaboration Tools**—These software tools enable individuals and teams at various computers to work together from anywhere in the world—whether in the same room or spread out around the globe. The telephone, or cell phone—particularly using conference calling—is an often-used collaboration tool. While normal calls can be prohibitively expensive for educational contexts, Internet-based calls, using such tools as Skype, can be much cheaper, or even free. Virtual meeting tools are another type of collaboration tool. So are online

work tools, such as shared documents (e.g., Google Docs). **Wikis** and **blogs (cf)** are also collaboration tools. ePals is collaboration software that allows safe e-mail and blogs. In partnering, students should be encouraged to use all the collaboration tools that are available to them. To find out which are available in your school, I recommend having a conversation with your tech coordinator (if you have one). **VERBS supported by these tools**: almost all verbs.

23. **Comics Creation Tools**—This software makes it easy for students to create and tell stories in the multiple-panel style of comic books. Today these stories are often known as graphic novels or, in Japan, manga. Several of these tools exist, including Mashon.com, Comic Book Creator 2, and Comiq Life. Students can use them to write their own stories, which is sometimes more engaging for students than the traditional essay form. These tools can be used for foreign language learning as well. **VERBS supported by these tools**: writing, creating, designing, making. See also **Graphic Novel Creation Tools**.

24. **Communication Tools**—This is a broad category, ranging from traditional handwritten letters to **e-mail**, **cell phones, texting,** and **Twitter (cf)**. Partnering students should certainly be exposed to as many of these tools as possible, and learn to use them all effectively and appropriately.

VERBS supported by these tools: all communication verbs.

25. **Comparison Generators and Comparative Shopping Tools**—These tools automatically present side-by-side comparisons of products or features. Suppose you had a set of items (e.g., pictures, sentences, formulae) that you wanted to display side by side, two at a time, so that students could make decisions about which one was better, real, more effective, and so forth. For example, English teachers might have students decide which title, opening line, paragraph, or closing is the strongest from tens or hundreds of compared examples. For one or two examples, you could make a PowerPoint presentation, but for many you would want an automated program. (These are easily written in no time at all by students who are good at programming.) Comparative shopping sites, such as Shopping.com, PriceGrabber.com, and Yahoo! Shopping are a **mashup (cf)** of the comparison generator category that finds and displays real data and prices from other sites. **VERBS supported by these tools**: analyzing, searching, evaluating, negotiating, having good judgment, making good decisions, personalizing.

26. **Computer-Aided Design (CAD) Tools/Drafting Tools**—These are the basic tools of design in industry and architecture. In those worlds, pencil-and-paper drafting tools have been almost totally replaced by

2D and 3D CAD tools. Students can use these latest tools to design a wide variety of objects, many of which can be printed out as solid objects on a 3D printer. Students can also use CAD tools to design their own spaces, such as classrooms or lobbies. Exposure to, and basic use of, CAD tools should be included in partnering students' mathematics and other curricula. Some CAD software requires high-end computers, but it is now becoming cheaper and more accessible. **VERBS supported by these tools**: calculating, designing, experimenting, innovating, modeling and trying, planning, tinkering, finding your voice. It is worth inquiring whether any departments in your school are using CAD currently.

27. **Contests and Competitions**—These are a useful way to spark student interest and enthusiasm, and technology can make it easy for students to set up and administer them. Many competition formats already exist on the Web, including caption contests, Photoshop contests, question contests, and others. For whatever contest you and your students decided to hold, online contest tracking and ladder ranking software is also available. **VERBS supported by these tools**: searching, comparing, deciding, evaluating, prudent risk taking, making good decisions, self-assessing.

28. **Critiques**—These are used often in the art and architecture world to provide feedback to creators on their work. Critiques can be used equally well in the realm of writing or in any other creative endeavor that students do. Critiques are valuable not only for the person whose work is being critiqued, but also for those doing the critiquing. Although critiques can be done with or without technology, the technological tools that can be used to facilitate critiquing include collaboration tools such as wikis and blogs. **VERBS supported by these tools**: analyzing, listening, comparing, evaluating, observing, questioning, reflecting, thinking critically, thinking creatively, designing, behaving ethically, having good judgment, finding your voice.

29. **Crowdsourcing**—Crowdsourcing involves using software to gather the opinions of large numbers of people (often from around the world) in order to arrive at new or unexpected solutions to a problem (although it may not provide a "right" answer). Technology tools that can be used by students for crowdsourcing include e-mail, Facebook, and Twitter. **VERBS supported by this tool**: exploring, finding, evaluating, modeling, predicting, problem solving.

30. **Data Acquisition/Collection Tools**—These tools include search engines as well as scientific probes, sensors, cameras, video cameras, and voice recording software (e.g., for interviews). Technology presents great opportunities for students to collect a variety of data in ways that were previously impossible. Data collected

can then be put through various **data analysis tools (cf). VERBS supported by these tools**: analyzing, exploring, finding, comparing, deciding, evaluating, experimenting, observing, questioning, thinking critically, connecting, designing, problem solving, planning.

31. **Data Analysis Tools**—A great many tools are available to students—frequently online—for analyzing data of all types. These include textual analysis tools ranging from the simple word count, spelling, and grammar checkers and vocabulary grade-level analyzers built into Microsoft Word, to frequency analyzers, salience analyzers, style analyzers, and other more sophisticated tools, such as version comparison tools, which are useful in historical analyses. Countless numerical analysis tools, such as spreadsheets, statistical tools, Mathematica, and Wolfram Alpha, are also available to students. **VERBS supported by these tools**: analyzing, exploring, verifying, calculating, deciding, evaluating, predicting, connecting, thinking long term.

32. **Data Mining Tools**—Data mining is the finding and extraction of useful information from large sets or databases. Because databases have gotten so big, it is often useful to "cut" and cross-index them in various ways to look for previously unseen patterns. Although companies such as Google use very sophisticated proprietary tools to do this, students can often data mine large online databases using widely available programs such as spreadsheet software. **VERBS supported by these tools**: analyzing, exploring, finding, observing, questioning, thinking critically, connecting, problem solving.

33. **Data Visualization Tools**—Data visualization tools take large quantities of data (e.g., stock market tables over time, seismic or weather data) and display it in graphic ways that are easier for people to intuitively understand. The weather satellite maps we see on television are a sophisticated example. Increasingly sophisticated data visualization tools are available to students both online and through universities with the large amounts of computing power that data visualization often takes. Examples of data visualization tools include mind maps such as TheBrain (www.thebrain.com/), all the various types of graphs in Excel, the program Mathematica, and 3D worlds such as Second Life. The free tool Graphviz from AT&T Labs is also worth a look. **VERBS supported by these tools**: analyzing, exploring, finding, verifying, experimenting, evaluating, modeling, observing, predicting.

34. **Database Tools**—Databases are a basic building block of technology, and all partnering students should be familiar with how they work and be able to create and use them. Databases come in two kinds. Flat databases are essentially just lists. They can be sorted, but they are hard or impossible to search on specific

criteria. Relational databases have each criterion stored in a separate field, so searching is much easier. Database tools allow you to select from the data and communicate with the database. There are a great variety of database tools, from simple (e.g., structured query language [SQL] tools, Microsoft Access) to extremely sophisticated (e.g., Oracle). **VERBS supported by these tools**: Since data on anything at all can be stored in a database, they are useful for most verbs.

35. **Decision Support Tools**—These tools, or systems, are software that helps people make better decisions by supporting those decisions with data and information as well as helping decision makers communicate more effectively. They include search (for relevant information) and tools such as **decision trees (cf)**, which mathematically weigh various alternatives, and Groove, a business tool that supports a wide variety of decisions. Examples in education would be tools that allow a teacher to call up all of a student's work before making a grading decision. **VERBS supported by these tools**: analyzing, verifying, debating, planning, taking leadership.

36. **Decision Trees**—These are a type of decision support tool that graphically portrays the various alternative outcomes of a complex, multi-stage decision and assigns them probabilities. By combining probabilities along each path, one can assess the combined probability of each course of action. Decision trees can be constructed on paper, and are also found in statistical packages such as SAS. **VERBS supported by these tools**: analyzing, comparing, deciding, evaluating, planning, making good decisions.

37. **Design Tools**—Design is an area in which using good tools can be of enormous benefit, and there are numerous design tools that partnering students can use. Design tools such as **CAD (cf)** are used by professional designers to create most of our physical products, from cell phones to cars, airplanes, and architecture. A wide variety of drawing, painting, photo manipulation, and layout design tools exist for on-screen and printed materials. In addition to tools like Photoshop and Flash (CF), specialized tools, such as 3d Studio Max, exist for creating games. All 21st century students should be exposed to as many design tools as possible. **VERBS supported by these tools**: exploring, experimenting, modeling, copying, creating, innovating, tinkering, adapting, thinking creatively, finding your voice.

38. **Dictionaries and Thesauri**—These tools, which formerly required separate volumes on a bookshelf, are now built into most word-processing software. But they don't always get used, or used well, by students. This is an obvious place for coaching by partnering teachers. **VERBS**

supported by these tools: verifying, comparing, thinking logically, debating, writing, communicating.

39. **Digital Manipulatives**—Manipulatives have been used forever by students to learn concepts via the interaction with physical objects, such as Cuisenaire rods. Most of these manipulatives can now be re-created, and manipulated, on the computer screen. Examples include virtual Lego blocks and interactive computer beads from MIT. **VERBS supported by these tools**: analyzing, exploring, calculating, experimenting, observing, predicting, problem solving, thinking logically, designing, innovating, programming, playing, thinking creatively.

40. **Electronic Books and Readers**— Paper (e.g., books, magazines) is only one medium for reading in the 21st century; today much of what young people read is on a screen. More and more books and periodicals are being published in electronic form, either simultaneously with printed editions or on their own. There is a wide variety of electronic reading software, such as Microsoft's ClearType, various web sites, Amazon's Kindle and other "dedicated" electronic book readers, and even e-readers for cell phones such as the iPhone (which I now use for almost all my personal and professional reading and which works wonderfully). Although there are some inconveniences to reading electronically, such as the inability to write notes on the page (now being added in various ways) or the inability to thumb through pages, there are also many advantages, such as the ability to change text size, look up and go to particular words and phrases, and embed hyperlinks in other documents or materials (not to mention not having to carry heavy, bulky books around). It is important that you, the partnering teacher, provide, as much as possible, the electronic reading experience to your students and that you discuss with them the benefits and drawbacks of each medium, with both you and students keeping an open mind. **VERBS supported by these tools**: any that involve reading.

41. **E-mail**—E-mail has become so ubiquitous that we often don't think of it as a tool. But it can be an enormously powerful tool for learning, especially when used to communicate across cultures, for example, using safe e-mail programs such as ePals. In some circumstances, e-mail can also be used effectively for teacher-student communication. However, among today's student population, e-mail has largely been supplanted by texting as the preferred means of electronic communication. **VERBS supported by this tool**: connecting, cooperating, dialoguing, writing, planning, taking leadership, communicating, reflecting, finding your voice.

42. **Facebook**—This social networking tool has grown extremely rapidly, and as I write this, it is a favorite of many students. Although Facebook and other social networking tools (e.g., MySpace, Twitter) certainly have potential applicability to learning, we are still in the process of discovering where and how this is true. Examples of interesting uses of Facebook in classroom learning exist and can be found via an online search of "Facebook classroom." Imagine, for example, a Facebook account for every fictional and historical character, writer, inventor, scientist, and so on maintained and replied to in the voice of the character. There is currently some debate as to whether Facebook and other social networking tools that students use in their personal lives should also be used, without change, for educational purposes—this may be like mixing one's work life too closely with one's personal life. But the ability Facebook provides to connect with people of particular groups and to see their frequent comments, as well as to reply to those comments, is potentially a very important one for education and should be explored, and thought about, by every teacher. A Facebook-like tool such as **Ning (cf)** can be considered as an alternative. As an example of how fast nouns change, MySpace, recently a popular networking tool, has now become mainly informational, such as for following favorite bands. **VERBS supported by this tool**: listening, watching, deciding, evaluating, reflecting, thinking critically, collaborating, connecting, dialoguing, personalizing, planning, communicating, finding your voice, being proactive, behaving ethically.

43. **Factor Analysis**—This tool is used by statisticians and analysts to evaluate and isolate the importance of each of the many factors that go into a particular result or outcome. For example, factor analysis might be employed by students to answer the question "To what extent is increased life expectancy a result of better nutrition, better healthcare, less smoking, and other factors?" A number of software programs exist for factor analysis, and similar types of statistical analysis, such as the statistical package SAS, which can be used in any subject. **VERBS supported by this tool**: analyzing, evaluating, predicting, reflecting, thinking critically, thinking creatively, planning.

44. **Flash**—This software program sold by Adobe, is the tool now used for almost all the animation found on the Web, and the free Flash Player is built in to every new web browser. Flash has become, for the moment, the de facto standard tool for creating animated multimedia, animated presentations, and games on the Web. Ideally, all students should be exposed to (and taught, if possible) Flash creation. Although this program is not free, it is one tool well worth paying for. One of Flash's great advantages is the large number of preprogrammed objects that

exist for free on the Web and that can easily be combined by students into their own programs. Flash Lite is an associated tool that enables creation of many of the same results on smartphones. It is worth asking if your school has acquired any Flash licenses that may be available to your students. **VERBS supported by this tool**: communicating, presenting, designing, persuading.

45. **Forecasting Tools**—We all know about weather forecasting tools; these are currently huge simulations running on the biggest and most powerful computers. But there are many other forecasting tools, a number of which students can use. Spreadsheet models (built in, say, Excel) are probably the most widely used forecasting tool. These combine many different factors and dependence relationships in order to predict an outcome. Other forecasting tools, such as iThink, allow the inclusion of nonlinear relationships as well. Students should be encouraged to use these tools, which are widely used in business. **VERBS supported by these tools**: modeling, predicting, questioning, evaluating.

46. **Game Creation Tools**—One of the most exciting learning tasks for students is the creation of their own computer games. There are several tools available to facilitate this, at all grade levels. For elementary grades, there is Game Maker as well as the newly developed Gamestar Mechanic. By middle school, kids who started

early can be making games in Flash. And in high school, students can use C++ as well as modding tools that come with many games. In addition, many graphics tools can help contribute to the process. **VERBS supported by these tools**: analyzing, exploring, calculating, experimenting, modeling, reflecting, thinking logically, innovating, competing, programming.

47. **Game Modding**—Modding (i.e., modifying) is a way for a person or team to take an existing complex computer game that is purchased in the store and modify it almost completely (using the core functionality of the game's underlying software "engine" along with tools provided) to create an entirely new game of their own design. Creating game mods is a great way for more advanced partnering students to create their own complex games related to what they are studying. An interesting example is a project at MIT in which the commercial game Neverwinter Nights was modded into a re-creation of a 18th century New England town on the eve of the American Revolution. Soft modding, a term coined by Elizabeth Hayes and James Paul Gee, involves students (often girls) using game-based tools to tell stories. Partnering students (and teachers) doing any kind of storytelling should explore modding further. **VERBS supported by this tool**: analyzing, exploring, experimenting, modeling, combining and connecting, designing, innovating, making.

48. **Games**—Games, both computer and video games—with appropriate content—and even older board games, are extremely useful tools for student learning because they bring with them enormous levels of engagement. There are many ways to use games in the partnering pedagogy. I discussed games in some detail in Chapter 6 as well as in previous books (*Digital Game-Based Learning*, "*Don't Bother Me Mom—I'm Learning*") and articles I have published. **VERBS supported by these tools**: In one form or another, games are useful tools for almost all the verbs.

49. **Gaming Devices**—There are a number of gaming devices, both consoles (attached to TVs) and handhelds, that many students already have and use. These include, at the moment, the Nintendo Wii and DS, the Microsoft Xbox 360, and the Sony Playstation3. There are times when these devices, and the games that can be played on them, can be relevant and useful to partnering students' learning. It is worth asking your students whether they think this is true and encouraging them, when it is, to bring in and share these tools. **VERBS supported by these tools**: depending on the games, potentially all of them.

50. **Genealogy Tools**—Excellent tools exist for tracing and displaying family trees. It could be an interesting learning exercise, in many subjects, for students to trace their own, or historical or fictional, family trees.

VERBS supported by these tools: exploring, searching, connecting.

51. **Geolocation Tools and Global Positioning System (GPS)**—Geolocation tools enable students to find and use the coordinates (exact longitude, latitude, and altitude) of any specific place on Earth. Many free databases of geolocation data exist (e.g., Google Earth). Geolocation tools also allow students to view data in many forms (e.g., maps, images), post notes and search for hidden things (geocaching) and places (geotrekking), and combine this data with other software and data sets in **mashups (cf)**. GPS is used to collect the data from the geostationary satellites that give the geolocation data. **VERBS supported by these tools**: exploring, finding, comparing, connecting, modeling.

52. **Graphic Novel Creation Tools**—What were once derided as "comic books" now have been given the much fancier title of graphic novels (or, in Japan, where they are much more common, manga). These interesting and often highly stylized stories are very appealing to today's students. While graphic novels can be drawn by hand, there are also software tools that can be used in creating them, in terms of storyboards, layout, and art. Sometimes labeled comics creation software, these tools are fun for students to use in honing their storytelling and graphics skills. **VERBS supported by these tools**: writing, creating, designing, making.

See also **Comics Creation Tools, Animation Tools**.

53. **Graphics Creation/Modification Tools**—The term *graphics* has taken on greatly expanded meaning in the 21st century, with graphics now coming in a variety of electronic forms, both still and moving. There are many ever-evolving tools for creating both newer, electronic graphics and video and traditional, print graphics. Basic graphics creation programs generally come preinstalled for free on new computers. Advanced programs, such as Photoshop, are so well-known that their names have become verbs themselves. ("to Photoshop" a picture or photograph means to alter it using that, or a similar, graphics program.) Many 3D graphics tools exist, such as 3ds Max, Maya, and Softimage, and there are many free alternatives to the commercial packages. All students should use and become proficient with graphics creation tools during their K–12 years. **VERBS supported by these tools**: creating, designing, making, innovating, modeling, personalizing, finding one's voice.

54. **Hardware mods and upgrades**—The term *mod* (again, short for modification) got its start with hardware, that is, the physical computers themselves. In an attempt to improve and speed up their computers (often to be better for computer gaming), users began taking the computers apart and modifying them: speeding up the microprocessor's internal clock, adding a more powerful graphics card or a better fan, and so forth. Sometimes they add custom outside cases, with windows and special lighting. Hardware modding is a terrific potential learning tool for partnering students. Since many schools have old computers that have basically become obsolete, it makes sense to let students use them for modification and learning, rather than just donating them to charity or recycling them. In fact, any teacher who possibly can, ought to have his or her students open a computer and be able to identify, and know the function of (if not actually replace), the important components parts. **VERBS supported by these tools**: exploring, adapting, modeling, tinkering, designing.

55. **How-To Videos**—These videos show you, step by step, how to do something—from how to dissect a body to how to fix an engine, from how to write a story to how to draw an eye. It is truly amazing how many how-to videos now exist online. In addition to general video sites such as YouTube, there are entire sites, such as WonderHowTo, that are devoted to how-to videos. Such videos are, in fact, often the younger generation's favorite way to learn to do something. So no matter what subject you teach, you should encourage your students to use how-to videos to learn and to make their own videos about things they know. People can educate themselves for almost

any career—certainly those involving computers—using free, online how-to videos. These videos are often made by students' peers and are therefore potentially easier for students to understand. For many if not most topics, there is more than one video, so students have a choice of explanations. And as important as it is that students use how-to videos, it is even more important that they create them, particularly on underrepresented topics. **VERBS supported by these tools**: exploring, imitating, trying, watching, evaluating, questioning, reflecting, thinking critically.

Check It Out!

Students are already posting how-to videos for other students, both informally and in more formal programs such as "kids teaching kids" (www.mathtrain.tv/cate goryhome.phpcid=Student-Created%20 Videos) and NASA's Kids Science News Network (http://ksnn.larc.nasa.gov/for_ kids.html).

---

56. **Image Editing Tools**—See **Graphics Creation/Modification Tools**.

57. **Interactive Whiteboards**—On these large surfaces, sold under a variety of brands and typically installed in the front of a classroom, one can write, display images from the Internet, and use and display a number of interactive programs (or the screen of, say, an individual student's computer). Interactive whiteboards are being purchased by schools and districts for many teachers and classrooms, and numerous examples of their use can be found on the web sites of Promethean (www.prometheanworld .com) and SMART Technologies (www.smarttech.com). While interactive whiteboards can be powerful and useful tools, unless used thoughtfully they can easily devolve into just another, fancier version (i.e., with pictures and videos) of traditional "writing on the board." As I discussed previously, in partnering, interactive whiteboards—and all other technology— are far better used by the students than the teacher. **VERBS supported by this tool**: used thoughtfully, this tool can support almost any verb.

58. **Interface Tools**—These tools enable a student to partially or totally redesign a software program's interface to be closer to what he or she prefers. If you use computers at all, you have certainly experienced the pain of using a badly designed interface, such as menus that are unclear and poorly organized; buttons that are too small, missing, or in the wrong place; features that are not what or where you expect or want them to be; missing capabilities; and so on. Users can correct some of these deficiencies with interface tools. Some are included as parts of well-known programs and systems (e.g., Windows, MS Office, browsers) as design and personalization options. Some come in separate design programs, such as GUI Design Studio, and others are programming tools. In any subject, designing one's own interface for a

product is a great learning experience for any student. **VERBS supported by these tools**: experimenting, modeling, problem solving, designing, innovating, programming.

59. **Internet**—The Internet is the electronic system (wired and wireless) that connects all the world's individual computers, machines, and sites, and allows communication between them. It is not the only network in the world—phone companies and the military have networks of their own—but it is the largest and the one available to anyone with a computer and a connection. Rather than being owned and maintained by a single company or government, the Internet is a conglomeration of parts owned by individuals and companies and is managed publically, in a variety of ways. The advantage of this open setup is that, at least for the moment, the Internet is an "innovation commons" available to all for all kinds of information and new ideas. Every U.S. school is now connected to the Internet, although the capacity of that connection varies widely. (Having stronger connections—more bandwidth or, in the vernacular, "bigger pipes"—allows more people who are connected at the "ends" to get faster service.) The information on all the world's computers that is available for public (or security-enabled) access is considered to be "on the Internet." All information travelling on the Internet travels in small packets, each of which contains information about where it came from, where it's going, and what it belongs to so that it can be reassembled when it arrives. An e-mail message requires relatively few packets and so arrives relatively quickly; a multimedia program or feature movie requires many more packets and so takes more speed (and/or bandwidth) for quick delivery. Streaming is a way to deliver and use the packets a few at a time, again so that things can go more quickly. Partnering students need to understand how the Internet works, particularly in the context of the subjects they study. In math, students should learn to understand and calculate the Internet's quantitative statistics; in science, the Internet's structure and scientific issues; in social studies, its social consequences; and in English or foreign languages, its capacity for communications. **VERBS supported by this tool**: collaborating, communicating, creating, exploring searching, verifying, writing.

60. **Intuition**—Intuition is a product widely used in schools for organizing one's thoughts. As such, it is a type of **brainstorming tool (cf). VERBS supported by this tool**: exploring, comparing, questioning, writing, innovating, thinking creatively.

61. **Iteration**—This tool is actually the process of creating something as a prototype, using it with an audience, collecting as much (sometimes brutal) feedback as possible, redoing it, eliminating anything where there is a large group disliking it, collecting feedback on the next version, and continuing to build and test versions

until there is nothing in the product that any meaningful group of users finds objectionable (as opposed to individual opinions about different things). Iteration is the opposite of engineering, whereby someone designs something once in its entirety and that is the way the finished product will look for all time. Teaching and lesson planning have typically been done via engineering; in partnering I strongly recommend iteration as a better tool. Iteration can be used for many things, including games, products, reports, and papers. It is a recommended tool for improving the quality of student work (with as many iterations as there is time for). **VERBS supported by this tool**: every verb.

62. **Kindle**—the Kindle is the **electronic book reader (cf)** designed and sold by Amazon. **VERBS supported by this tool**: all that involve reading.

63. **Listservs**—These are e-mail lists to which people subscribe (i.e., sign up) based on their desire to hear from others about a certain topic and to share their own thoughts on the topic. Any e-mail that a member sends to the list goes to all members on the list. Any K–12 class with access to e-mail could certainly (and should) be subscribing to several Listservs around topics the class is studying. A class can also be running one or more Listservs (which requires special software, but this is often made available by the e-mail provider). The real power of a Listserv is that it can include people from anywhere in the world who have an interest in the topic. Millions of Listservs exist, and they cover every conceivable topic. Teachers should encourage their students to subscribe to Listservs about all subjects that interest them. **VERBS supported by this tool**: exploring, finding, listening, deciding, questioning, collaborating, connecting, debating, problem solving.

64. **Logic Tools**—There are many tools that can help partnering students improve their logical thinking. Among these are the puzzles built into many computer games. A simple logic tool is the checker for circular reasoning (i.e., one cell referring back to itself at some point) built into Excel and other spreadsheet programs. Other logic tools include logic trees and flow diagrams. **VERBS supported by these tools**: analyzing, verifying, thinking logically.

65. **Logic Trees**—One particular logic tool is logic trees, which describe the paths one can go down via successive choices, with some paths being independent and some interlinked. **VERBS supported by this tool**: analyzing, verifying, thinking logically.

66. **Machinima**—These are animations built with game creation tools. They have the look of video or computer games, but tell linear stories and are not interactive. Machinima are very popular around the world and are

based on a wide variety of games with great diversity of styles. It is certainly a presentation style your students can try. For examples, see www.machinima .com. **VERBS supported by this tool**: watching, creating, persuading, presenting, storytelling.

67. **Mapping Tools**—These tools include Google Earth, GPS (built into individual devices and cell phones), and other location devices such as radar and sonar. Increasingly, various mapping tools are being incorporated, that is, via **mashups (cf)**, into each other in new and useful ways. Mapping tools should be used by students to learn about the physical world (and the universe): what it looks like, distances between places, finding your way, reading maps and directions, and so on. It is often instructive to compare the new mapping tools of today with the old ones (e.g., atlases, dead reckoning) to see what each of the different tools offers and does better. Mapping tools are increasingly making use of **augmented reality tools (cf)** as enhancements. **VERBS supported by these tools**: analyzing, exploring, finding, observing, searching, combining.

68. **Mashups**—Mashup is a term for the combining of different sorts of media and data into a new, more useful, and often unexpected project. One example of a mashup that got wide distribution was the Obama campaign's "Yes We Can" commercial by will.i.am (www.youtube.com/watch?v=jjXyqcx-mYY). Another example of a mashup

is how Google Earth combines and overlays map, satellite, and ground view data. Mashups are fun for students to make, often highly expressive and useful, and hold great promise as learning tools. Students (and teachers) can combine any separate data that is usefully viewed at the same time, such as buildings with dates, events with people, or objects with the mathematics or engineering behind them. **VERBS supported by this tool**: experimenting, modeling, predicting, problem solving, combining, designing, adapting, innovating, personalizing, finding your voice.

69. **Memorizing Tools**—Memorization, often out of favor in our schools today, is still important to actors, those who give speeches, and others. In my view, it is important that partnering students learn by heart at least a few short, useful writings (e.g., the start of the Declaration of Independence, the Preamble to the Constitution, the Gettysburg Address, Emma Lazarus's poem on the Statue of Liberty) so that they can recall them from time to time and reflect on their meaning. Electronic tools, findable and usable by students, can help students memorize more easily. **VERBS supported by these tools**: listening, memorizing, reflecting.

70. **Modding Tools**—Modding, as described under **Game Modding (cf)**, is the changing, or modification, of existing commercial computer games in to new (and sometimes very different) games,

using tools that come with the games as well as other scripting, programming, and graphics tools. If you ask your students, it is likely you will find some who know how to do this. They might be able to construct some mods that are useful for learning, such as the MIT re-creation of the pre-Revolutionary New England town described earlier. **VERBS supported by these tools**: creating, presenting, storytelling, modeling, innovating, simulating.

71. **Multimedia**—This catchall term (actually in use since multiple slide projectors were combined with music) today describes the combination of animation, video, sound, music, text, and other electronic (and sometimes nonelectronic) elements into a single product. As tools advance, multimedia keeps getting more and more sophisticated, and at the same time, with the newest tools, it becomes easier for students to create. Among our most advanced multimedia is much of TV and Internet advertising, of which our students get to see huge quantities. Products that combine different media (e.g., machinima, games, graphic novels) are often more interesting to today's students (at least on the surface) than products such as text-only books, which don't. **VERBS supported by this tool**: creating, persuading, presenting, storytelling, modeling, innovating.

72. **Multiple Intelligences**—Howard Gardner's theory is included here as

a noun, or tool, because it is a way of looking at students that is often used to engage them in learning according to each student's particular intelligence spectrum or preferences. In this respect, it is similar to the idea of finding and using students' passions, which I discussed earlier. Although both approaches may have advantages, it is probably easier to find students' passions than their preferred intelligence, and the range will certainly be wider. **VERBS supported by this tool**: adapting, reflecting, differentiating.

73. **Music Creating and Editing Tools**—Music is so important to today's students that it is not surprising that there should exist a number of tools students can use to create and edit it. All partnering students should be encouraged to use these tools, adding appropriate music (and sound effects) to their PowerPoint presentations, podcasts, multimedia presentations, games, and almost any other project they do. Examples of products include Audacity, Audition, eJay, and Magix. **VERBS supported by these tools**: creating, experimenting, listening, adapting, designing, making, innovating, programming.

74. **Negotiation Tools**—Negotiation is a skill that is taught much less frequently in school than it ought to be, because it is used so often in life. Since it is not a skill, or verb, that students typically study and learn, students often come out on the losing

end of confrontations with banks, businesses, and others. However, many tools (both computer based and on paper) exist for becoming a better negotiator, and partnering teachers should encourage their students to use them. Examples include Parley and Negotiator Pro. **VERBS supported by these tools**: analyzing, listening, deciding, ethical questioning, evaluating, observing, predicting, questioning, reflecting, cooperating, negotiating.

75. **Ning**—This social networking tool can be used by educators to reproduce and benefit from many of the features of sites such as Facebook, without all the added baggage of the non-school-related uses. Although other tools exist (and more will emerge in the future), Ning is of particular interest because its creator is Marc Andreessen, the extremely intelligent programmer who also created the first web browser. Many classrooms, schools, and school districts, as well as content-centered groups, have set up their own Nings, and you should consider having your students do this. **VERBS supported by this tool**: searching, sharing, collaborating, combining, connecting, cooperating, writing, designing, personalizing, programming.

76. **Note-Taking Tools**—There are a number of tools designed to help students organize their ideas and notes from their work and readings (not, of course, from the lectures their partnering teachers don't give). Students should be encouraged to

find and use these tools, and to share the best ones they find with their peers. **VERBS supported by these tools**: analyzing, verifying, comparing, observing, reflecting, listening, writing, personalizing.

77. **Online Bookstores**—One of the great advantages of using an electronic reader such as the Kindle (or the Kindle app on the iPhone, the Sony Reader, or even a reader on a computer) is that any book that you want to read can usually be purchased online and downloaded in seconds (provided, of course, that you have the right device, are connected to the Internet, and have an account set up for payment). The cost for older books whose copyright has lapsed, which includes most "classic" literature and writing, is typically zero. It cannot be long before libraries offer this service as well. This is one more step on the way to allowing students to read anything they want to that relates to whatever it is that the class is studying. **VERBS supported by these tools**: reading, searching, writing, personalizing.

78. **Outlining Tools**—Outlining is a verb often taught to students as a way of organizing their thoughts. Many electronic tools exist to make this process easier. Perhaps the easiest to find and use is the one already built into Microsoft Word (and other word processors). Teachers of writing should become familiar with this tool and encourage their students to use it when appropriate.

VERBS **supported by these tools**: analyzing, exploring, comparing, deciding, reflecting, thinking logically, writing, planning.

79. **Parsing Tools**—There are times when parsing (i.e., dividing into meaningful parts) is the verb you want students to do. This can be in grammar, programming, or other subjects, and electronic tools exist that can help students understand the process and do the work. Wikipedia does a good job of listing and discussing these. **VERBS supported by these tools**: analyzing, writing, programming, thinking logically, innovating.

80. **Photo Sharing Tools**—These tools, such as Flickr, are a form of both collaboration and social networking. They allow people to upload photos (or videos) to a dedicated place online and grant access in any way the poster desires (e.g., to all, to a group, to a particular individual). **VERBS supported by these tools**: collaborating, connecting, sharing, creating.

81. **Plagiarism Detection Tools**—As the number of students who copy and paste others' work without attribution (or, worse, attribute it to themselves) increases, software tools have emerged to detect this. Turnitin is probably the most widely used. Google itself also can be used for this purpose. Students as well as teachers ought to understand that these tools exist and how they work. **VERBS supported by these tools**: verifying, deciding, evaluating, thinking critically.

82. **Podcasts and Podcasting Tools**— A podcast originally meant an audio recording that was posted online for people to listen to or download if interested. The term has now expanded considerably. There are video as well as audio podcasts, professional as well as amateur podcasts, podcasts that you have to search for, and podcasts that are automatically downloaded to your computer or cell phone. Today, a podcast is usually an explanatory or educational audio or video file that can be downloaded. Podcasts exist in all sorts of places and on every conceivable topic. They are, for example, a great way to keep up with what is happening in a particular field. (You could search, for example, for "best technology podcasts.") Creating their own podcasts is an easy way for students to collect and share information. I have been interviewed by many students, using their cell phones as audio or video recorders, for podcasts to be put on their web sites and used for class projects. Because they reside on the Web, podcasts can be easily shared with other students, teachers, parents, and the entire world. There exist hundreds of tools for creating and sharing them, many listed at www.mashable.com/2007/07/04/ podcasting-toolbox and www.only podcasting.com. **VERBS supported by these tools**: listening, collaborating, creating, making, sharing.

83. **PowerPoint**—Microsoft Power-Point, while only one brand of presentation software, deserves its own mention here because it is so widely used. Like any tool, it can be used well or badly ("death by PowerPoint" is a common complaint). Reducing too many things to bullet points and putting too many words on a screen are frequently cited mistakes. Because of its ubiquity in the business world, PowerPoint is no doubt a good tool for students to learn to use at some point in their schooling. One group of Texas students, asked by teachers "In what grade should students start using PowerPoint and in what grade should they stop?" responded with first and sixth grades, respectively. Their point was that the tool is easy enough for first graders to use, and by sixth grade kids should have mastered it enough to go on to a more sophisticated presentation tool, such as Flash, which allows a much higher level of animation and interactivity. In partnering, teachers are discouraged from using PowerPoint at the front of the room. It is much better to let students use the tool with the teacher and their peers as their critics. **VERBS supported by this tool**: briefing, writing, designing, persuading.

84. **Probes**—These devices attach to a computer or cell phone and are used to collect data on a wide variety of information, from temperature to weather to chemical composition. More and more of these (e.g., digital microscopes, telescopes) are available for student use each day. Partnering science teachers should encourage students to use such probes as much as possible. English and social studies teachers can think of voice and video recorders as probes to collect information from people. **VERBS supported by these tools**: exploring, finding, searching, observing, predicting, analyzing, thinking critically.

85. **Programming Languages**—These languages are the tools used to create the instructions that control all machines, and they exist at many levels. The menus we use to record TV shows or set up our cell phones are examples of higher-level programming languages. Tools such as Microsoft Word, Excel, and PowerPoint are in themselves programming languages and, for more sophisticated work, have other programming languages (known as macros and scripting tools) built into them. Web creation tools such as HTML, PHP, and Drupal are types of programming languages, as are modding tools. So-called lower-level programming languages, such as Basic, Perl, and C++ (among many others), let programmers start from scratch and create almost anything they or you can imagine. The lowest level of all, the instructions that the computer can read directly, is called assembler and is usually written automatically from a higher-level language by software known as a compiler. Learning and understanding programming languages, at the lowest level they can, is a very useful and

important task for partnering students. Programming is a verb, or skill, that will certainly have more and more importance in their future. Partnering students should realize the extent to which they already program today on their devices, such as when they download and configure software or set up playlists on their iPods, and should be encouraged to learn to control their machines (i.e., to program) as much as possible. Programming tasks can be created for (or suggested to) students at all levels and in all subjects. **VERBS supported by this tool**: analyzing, exploring, verifying, calculating, evaluating, experimenting, modeling, thinking logically, connecting, designing, innovating, programming, simulating.

86. **Programming Tools**—Programming languages are just one variety of programming tools; there are others that not everyone would describe as languages. These include visual programming tools that you would use to, say, wire up an online robot or create an online program by connecting pictures representing components with lines representing wires and logic. They also include scripting tools, which is programming using the English language rather than just symbols. Finally, they include tools like game-making software, such as Gamestar Mechanic in which almost all the choices are controlled by menus. **VERBS supported by these tools**: analyzing, comparing, deciding, evaluating, experimenting,

modeling, predicting, problem solving, thinking logically, combining, connecting, innovating, planning.

87. **Project Planning/Management Tools**—There are a number of electronic tools used by professional project planners and managers that can be of great benefit for students. They include PERT chart generators (PERT charts help prioritize tasks by showing which things have to be done before others), Gantt chart generators (Gantt charts are bar charts that illustrate start and end points of elements in a project schedule), and others. Students should be encouraged to use these tools for planning and managing their own projects. **VERBS supported by these tools**: analyzing, deciding, predicting, problem solving, thinking logically, designing, innovating, planning.

88. **Prototyping Tools**—More and more often, a project (e.g., software project, new car or airplane, TV show) is preceded by a prototype, a small version of the whole, or of some of its parts, that shows (for a relatively small investment of time and money) what the final product will be like. Rapid prototyping has become a new creation methodology. Prototypes make ideal student projects, as they do not have to be completely worked out or professionally polished. Examples of prototyping tools include Axure, EasyPrototype, and well-known tools such as Flash, PowerPoint, and Visio. **VERBS supported by these tools**:

exploring, comparing, deciding, observing, thinking critically, designing, innovating, modeling and trying, personalizing, simulating.

89. **Rapid Serial Visual Presentation (RSVP)**—This is a highly effective (although little used) way of presenting textual information for reading. It consists of a presentation by the computer of a single word at a time on the screen centered on a single point. The words appear at a speed preselected by the reader. Because the eye remains in the same place, this can be a much faster reading method than reading serial words on a page. In fact, "normal" reading rates of 200–400 words per minute can often be increased, with little practice, to rates of over 1,000 words per minute. RSVP lends itself particularly well to reading on a small screen such as that of a cell phone. There are a number of different RSVP readers that can be downloaded and tried by students, who should be encouraged to search online for the latest versions. **VERBS supported by these tools**: reading, reflecting, personalizing.

90. **Really Simple Syndication (RSS)**—RSS is an **aggregation tool (cf)** that should be continually in use in any classroom that has at least one computer connected to the Internet. It consists of software (often part of the web browser) that allows students to subscribe to any RSS feed available on the Internet. Such feeds can include opinion columns, blogs, news bulletins, and other sources of information. When a class subscribes (in partnership with the teacher) to a selection of RSS feeds, a constantly renewing daily stream of information on topics of interest starts coming into the classroom. A different student each day can be appointed as the RSS monitor, whose job it is to collect these stories and present them to the class. **VERBS supported by this tool**: exploring, finding, searching, evaluating, connecting, debating, personalizing, programming.

91. **Recorded Books**—see **Audiobooks.**

92. **Research Tools**—The number of useful online research tools for students to use increases every day. You are probably aware of Google and Wikipedia (and their limitations: they are typically good for search, bad for research). Are you and your students also familiar with, say, Google Scholar (for finding journal articles) or Scholarpedia (for finding peer-reviewed articles)? It is very important for partnering teachers to stay abreast of developments in this area and to share them with their students in order to ensure that partnering students are using the very best tools for their research. **VERBS supported by these tools**: researching, exploring, finding, searching, comparing, observing, questioning, reflecting.

93. **Response Systems**—See **Clickers.**

94. **Robotics Tools**—Robotics is a subject that is of interest to many students

(for some, it is their passion). Today, robots can be created or purchased, and programmed to perform a wide variety of tasks, a great many of which are within the reach of K–12 students. FIRST Robotics (For Inspiration and Recognition of Science and Technology) is an organization that provides competitions and tutorials in all sorts of robotics, using LEGO robotics for middle schoolers and custom-built robotics for high schoolers. There are also special competitions for humanoid robots, with divisions at many levels. (Since humanoid robots can be programmed to dance, this form of robotics is often appealing to girls.) iRobot, the company that makes the Roomba floor cleaner, also makes a kit of parts for students to use to build their own robots. Partnering teachers should look for places where students can use (or discuss the potential for using) robotics within the subject they are teaching. **VERBS supported by these tools**: analyzing, exploring, calculating, experimenting, modeling, observing, predicting, questioning, problem solving, thinking logically, collaborating, negotiating, competing, designing, innovating, making, programming.

95. **Role-Playing Tools**—Role-playing has been used forever as a teaching tool, and now there are electronic role-playing programs that can greatly aid in the process. Some are simply creative uses of online student discussion forums and chat. (see http://tinyurl.com/yg74jz9). Others, such as character creation and map tools from Sound Forge and RPTools, come from games and online worlds, which are often used for role-playing outside the classroom. Many role-playing tools and games can be adapted or modded for classroom use. This is an area in which talking with students and encouraging student initiative and creativity can produce especially interesting results. **VERBS supported by these tools**: exploring, finding, listening, decision making, questioning, reflecting, Socratic questioning, thinking critically, collaborating, cooperating, dialoging, listening.

96. **Rubrics**—A rubric, or evaluation scheme, is a tool for achieving consistency in evaluating student work. The term is little used outside of education, and may even be educational jargon, but the concept of a standardized evaluation or marking system is a useful one. A number of rubric-making tools exist online and can be used by teachers or students. **VERBS supported by this tool**: verifying, comparing, deciding, evaluating, observing, thinking critically.

97. **Salience Analysis**—Sometimes in a string of words, symbols, or numbers it is important or useful to know which ones have the most important meaning or carry the most meaning. One way of finding this out is salience analysis, and there are several tools available. Students could use such a tool, for example, to create an automated

program that says, "Parse this text, find the salient words, and then, for each, do something." Will Wright (the well-known game designer of SimCity, the Sims, and Spore) wrote such a program to take an Emily Dickenson poem, perform a salience analysis, go to Google Images, pick the first image for each salient word, and display the pictures in order while the poem was read aloud. The result, totally automated, was extremely powerful. Students can design and do similar projects. **VERBS supported by this tool**: analyzing, searching, comparing, deciding, evaluating, thinking logically, adapting, combining, making.

98. **Scenarios**—These are stories, typically short, that are used to set up a problem for analysis or to illustrate a particular point. They are also used in computer games, particularly role-playing and war games. There are specialized software tools for creating and analyzing scenarios, such as Visual Explorer and tools included in many game packages. The advantage for students and teachers in using these tools: is that the scenarios created in a class (and often the analysis as well) can be saved and then used later. In addition, other people's or classes' scenarios can be retrieved and reused in the future. **VERBS supported by these tools**: exploring, comparing, deciding, ethical questioning, evaluating, modeling, observing, questioning, reflecting, thinking critically, debating, writing, creating, simulating.

99. **Scientific Method**—The scientific method is a noun that consists of several verbs: observing, reflecting, hypothesizing, experimenting, and analyzing. It is, of course, a tool that partnering students should use constantly.

100. **Scriptwriting Tools**—Scriptwriting, particularly for television and film, requires a highly specialized presentation format; to make it easier there is software that does this formatting automatically. Any students involved in scriptwriting or creative writing classes should be introduced to, and consider using, scriptwriting software. **VERBS supported by these tools**: writing, experimenting, observing, thinking logically, collaborating, dialoging, adapting, innovating.

101. **Search Engines**—Almost all students are aware of the search engine Google. But there are other search engines that do particular things very well. For example, Microsoft's Bing allows you to preview search results without leaving the browser. Others, such as AltaVista, allow easier searches into the origin and history of pages. Google Scholar allows research of articles published in professional journals, and Google Images, as well as the image searchers in other engines, allows searching of still images online. As of this writing, there are specialized search engines for video, but that capability is becoming integrated into the general search engines as well. **VERBS supported by these tools**: exploring, finding,

searching, verifying, comparing, deciding, reflecting, thinking critically, personalizing.

102. **Search Tools**—There are other search tools in addition to search engines (as they are usually thought of). An example is **plagiarism detection tools (cf)**.

103. **Self-Assessment Tools**—Self-assessment is an extremely important form of assessment in partnering (and in life), as I discuss in Chapter 10. Many electronic tools exist for self-assessment, along a number of dimensions. Students can self-assess, for example, their reading speed and comprehension, their level and proficiency in a variety of subjects, their preferences and interests, and many of their psychological traits. Students should be encouraged to find these tools and use them frequently to gain self-understanding and to see whether they are improving. **VERBS supported by these tools**: analyzing, finding, evaluating, observing, questioning, thinking critically, planning.

104. **Shared Lists**—Technology allows individuals to share with others their preferences for just about anything. Tools are available for sharing bookmarks, reading lists, and favorites in just about any category. Such lists can be very helpful to partnering students, who should be encouraged to share their own preferences as well. This is an area of great fluidity in which new tools are emerging often. If you need such tools, search for them and consult your students about what they have found and like to use. **VERBS supported by these tools**: finding, searching, collaborating, connecting, cooperating, writing, combining, personalizing.

105. **Simulations**—These tools attempt to model certain states of things or processes, and how those states change over time based on different inputs. Simulations allow users to ask "What if?" over and over, under a variety of conditions. Simulations can exist purely in the mind (e.g., thought experiments), with physical equipment (e.g., tabletop battles, chess, flight simulators), or entirely in software (e.g., weather prediction). Simulations are enormously important tools for partnering students to use, because they allow students to try different strategies and alternatives and immediately see the consequences of their actions. Simulations exist in all fields, including English (simulations of writing styles), social studies (simulations of the environment or cultural evolution), science (simulations of almost all processes from micro to macro), and math (simulations of topology). A great many existing simulations, such as the Oregon Trail, are usable by partnering students even in elementary school. Although simulations and games are not the same thing, they are closely linked. Typically while the simulation presents the more or less accurate model of what happens, the game elements provide the motivation to use it.

When using simulations, partnering teachers need to help student users recognize the choices (and often biases) that go into the creation of every simulation model. Simulations also provide excellent material for the discussion of causes and connections in any subject. No partnering student should go without using some form of stimulation—with or without technology—in all of his or her classes at various times. **VERBS supported by these tools**: exploring, watching, deciding, experimenting, modeling, observing, predicting, problem solving, innovating, planning.

106. **Skype**—Skype is one brand name of a tool generically known as Voice over Internet Protocol (VoIP). Skype has now expanded to include texting and live video as well. Because VoIP uses the Internet, and not telephone carriers' private networks, it can be free, or almost free. Skype (and more generally VoIP) is a wonderful tool to use in the classroom to connect with the other classes and students in different parts of the world and to connect with professionals who may be able to interact with students in some way. **VERBS supported by this tool**: listening, watching, observing, communicating, collaborating, debating, dialoging, listening, personalizing.

107. **Social Bookmarking Tools**— These tools are a subset of **shared lists (cf)**. People share their favorite bookmarks (i.e., web sites) for others to see. Delicious is an example.

108. **Social Networking Tools**—This is a generic term for tools that allow users to interact in a variety of ways with groups of people of their own choosing. Important social networking tools include **Facebook (cf)**, MySpace, **Twitter (cf)**, and LinkedIn, as well as virtual worlds such as Second Life and the young peoples' worlds of Whyville and Club Penguin. **Ning (cf)** is an example of a social networking tool that can be created and customized by students and teachers. Each social networking tool has somewhat different features and works in somewhat different ways. One of the major differences between tools lies in the limitations and changes that users can impose on whom they connect with and how they connect with them. While it appears that social networking provides many features that are useful for education, it is far from clear that the existing commercial tools such as Facebook and Twitter are the right ones to be using with students. Social networking is an area in which rapid innovation and change is sure to happen, and it should be both explored by partnering teachers and watched carefully for new developments. **VERBS supported by these tools**: exploring, finding, searching, deciding, evaluating, observing, thinking critically, collaborating, cooperating, listening, personalizing, prudent risk taking.

109. **Special Interest Blogs**—Blogs (cf) can be used in many ways. Blogs

exist on an almost unlimited number of topics. Some are created by amateurs, but many are run by professionals, such as journalists. One good way for partnering students to use blogs in the classroom is for them to create their own special interest blog on a particular topic, such as what the class is studying, student activism, students' rights, or anything that they are passionate about. Another way to use special interest blogs is to follow topics of concern to the class or to individual students. This can be done by subscribing to each blog of interest as an **RSS** feed (**cf**), which can often be done just by clicking on a button somewhere on the blog. **VERBS supported by this tool**: exploring, finding, listening, reading, comparing, evaluating, questioning, reflecting, thinking critically, collaborating, connecting, dialoging, debating, prudent risk taking, writing.

110. **Speech-to-Text Tools**—These tools turn words recorded into a microphone into computer text. I used the speech-to-text tool Dragon NaturallySpeaking (Version 10) to write parts of this book. I spoke the text that I wanted into a microphone, and the program turned it into words on the screen. These tools can be very useful for partnering students, and partnering teachers should encourage their students to try them. A speech-to-text converter is built in to the latest versions of Microsoft Word. Speech-to-text is particularly useful for learning to

marshal one's thoughts before speaking and for partnering students with writing problems or disabilities. **VERBS supported by these tools**: writing, thinking critically, creating, personalizing.

111. **Speechwriting Tools**—An important skill for partnering students to learn is oral presentation. With so many things being automated, this is one that is unlikely to be and is likely to gain in importance. Schools in the United Kingdom already emphasize oral presentation much more than schools in the United States do. One way that partnering students can improve their oral presentation skills is by practicing writing and delivering speeches. A number of tools exist to help with this, and students should be encouraged to find and use them. In addition, special tools exist for putting speech text onto a teleprompter. **VERBS supported by these tools**: speaking, presenting, experimenting, reflecting, thinking logically, connecting, debating, leading, writing.

112. **Speed-Up Tools**—Tools to speed up the delivery of both audio and video have long existed, but for some reason they are not very widely used. They should be. Language teachers have long used tape machines that allow for speech to be slowed down or speeded up without changing the voice pitch. That same thing can now happen in audio software, and it works for video as well. (Included in Windows Media Player is a tool that

allows for speeding up or slowing down of any audio or video file played through that player. While watching or listening, you can hit Ctrl+F for speeding up, Ctrl+S for slowing down, and Ctrl+N to go back to normal speed. There is also a slider control hidden deep in the menus.) Partnering students who learn to use these tools can take in information from audio or video files much more quickly, and also slow those files down for better comprehension. **VERBS supported by these tools**: listening, watching, personalizing.

113. **Spelling and Grammar Tools**— The sophisticated spelling and grammar tools embedded in Microsoft Word and other word-processing programs are often taken for granted, and sometimes even ridiculed or disparaged. But they are powerful tools for better writing, and partnering students should be encouraged to use them. What is important, though, is that they be used thoughtfully and that students learn and understand how to use these tools to their best advantage. **VERBS supported by these tools**: verifying, writing, deciding, evaluating, observing, thinking critically.

114. **Spreadsheets**—These are an extremely powerful tool, with many uses for words (text) as well as numbers. Nonnumeric uses include making lists, ordering those lists, brainstorming, and support for other thought processes. Numeric uses include calculating, keeping

books, modeling, predicting, and many others. Spreadsheets can often be used as simple databases. Every partnering student should learn to use a spreadsheet effectively in both numeric and nonnumeric ways. **VERBS supported by this tool**: analyzing, exploring, finding, verifying, calculating, comparing, deciding, evaluating, experimenting, modeling, observing, predicting, questioning, problem solving, reflecting, thinking logically, cooperating, negotiating, innovating, simulating, prudent risk taking.

115. **Statistical Tools**—Statistics is one of the most widely used, most important mathematical applications there is. It is used in some way, or can be, in every subject we teach. And yet statistics is one of the least well-understood subjects by students, and often by teachers as well. A great many software tools exist to help rectify this deficiency, and partnering students should be encouraged to use them. Examples are Mathematica and SAS. **VERBS supported by these tools**: analyzing, verifying, calculating, comparing, deciding, predicting, problem solving.

116. **Survey Creation Tools**—These tools allow any partnering teacher or student to create and distribute an online survey and then collate the results. Survey Monkey is a well-known example. **VERBS supported by these tools**: analyzing, exploring, finding, listening, verifying, evaluating, experimenting, observing, questioning.

117. TED Talks—TED Talks are short videos, usually around 20 minutes in length that are edited versions of talks given at various TED (Technology, Design, Entertainment) conferences around the world. The range of subjects is quite broad, from economics to science, from art to language. The speakers are typically experts in particular fields who are encouraged to give especially provocative and engaging talks. It is well worth the time of partnering students and teachers to explore these talks, available at www.ted.com, and to share them with others. TED Talks can also be found using a video search engine. **VERBS supported by this tool**: listening, watching, ethical questioning, reflecting, thinking critically.

118. Text-to-Speech Tools—These computer programs read (aloud) electronic or printed text. Text-to-speech programs have existed for some time, although often with flat, unexpressive, robot-like intonation, and were used mainly by the blind and visually impaired for reading books aloud. Today, the intonation issues with text-to-speech are improving rapidly; already, one can choose from multiple voices and even accents. Text-to-speech can be expected to improve considerably in the coming years, to the point where it may not even be recognizable as being machine-read. Aside from serving the visually impaired, text-to-speech is useful for building listening skills and for students with poor reading skills. **VERBS supported by these tools**: listening, reading, reflecting.

119. Texting—Texting, as every teacher surely knows by now, is sending short messages from a cell phone or a computer to another electronic device. While texting is often seen as a distraction in class, there are also ways to use it as a tool for learning. Partnering students can text answers to questions or problems directly to the teacher (or to www.polleverywhere.com software that the teacher is using). One teacher, for example, has his students text lines from Shakespeare, as if they were living in, and using the language of, those times. I recommend asking your students, "In what ways could texting be used beneficially in class for learning?" I am sure that if all the positive, innovative answers to this question were shared among educators, we would all find ways to turn texting in class from a problem into a benefit. **VERBS supported by this tool**: collaborating, connecting, cooperating, dialoging, writing, personalizing, planning.

120. Textual Analysis—For those subjects that deal to a large degree with texts, such as English, foreign languages, and social studies, there exist numerous useful tools for analysis of those texts. Some tools, like those that measure word count and assess vocabulary level, are already built into word-processing or reading programs such as Microsoft Word. Textual analysis tools that come in separate programs include word frequency analysis, style analysis, grammar analysis, side-by-side comparison, version comparison, and others. **VERBS supported by this tool**: analyzing, exploring, finding, searching, verifying, evaluating, modeling, observing, predicting.

121. **Twitter**—Twitter, a brand-name tool highly in vogue as this is written, is a combination of texting and social networking. It offers the ability to receive and read constantly updated very short messages (with a limit of 140 characters) from all the people you "follow" on Twitter and to respond to any message. In addition, your messages are displayed to anyone who follows you. The number of followers a "Tweeter" has can range from only a few, to several hundred, to over a million for certain celebrities. Users of Twitter are still figuring out its benefits to their lives. I now use Twitter for the ability it gives me to follow the continuing thoughts and focus of people whose opinions I value. Educationally, Twitter can be a great tool for discussions on a particular topic, especially when those discussions include many participants from outside the classroom. (If Twitter adds a speech-to-text voice component, it will become a useful tool for sending short spoken messages to groups of followers, including students or staff, that they can read on their cell phones.) However, Twitter is almost certain to be supplanted by even better tools in the future. **VERBS supported by this tool**: searching, evaluating, observing, questioning, thinking critically, collaborating, connecting, listening, personalizing.

122. **Video**—Video has replaced movies and the earlier moving pictures as a way to describe images displayed serially at 30 or more frames per second. However, today the term typically refers to short clips rather than full-length movies. (It doesn't have to; video is basically digital storage of the images on film.) Because today's video is most often digital, it can be easily edited using software and it can be easily embedded in, and mashed up with, other applications by students. Video can be amateur or professional in quality, and, perhaps unexpectedly, with the popularity of sharing programs such as YouTube, the lower (or absent) production values of amateur video have actually become accepted as the norm. Because video is now so easy to create by partnering students using the video cameras in their cell phones or inexpensive video cameras such as the Flip, video creation, presentation, and online posting should be part of every partnering class. Posting videos allows easy sharing of student ideas and solutions as well as innovative and effective classroom practices. **VERBS supported by this tool**: creating, watching, comparing, deciding, evaluating, observing, reflecting, thinking critically, debating, dialoging, writing, combining, designing, innovating, making, finding your voice.

123. **Video Editing Tools**—Movie editing once required bulky equipment for cutting and splicing of film and

produced piles of outtakes on the cutting room floor. Digital video editing, on the other hand, is all done with software. The tools, which require a certain amount of computer memory but are easy to use, have moved quickly from dedicated machines, to portable computers, and even to some handheld devices and phones. All partnering students should get experience in digital video editing. All partnering teachers should be willing to accept video projects from students if they are well thought out, well shot, well edited, and well presented. Video editing products include Power Director, VideoStudio, Premiere, Windows Movie Maker, iMovie, and Final Cut. **VERBS supported by these tools**: watching, comparing, deciding, reflecting, adapting, combining, designing, writing, innovating.

124. **Video Search Engines**—Today, it is often the case that people must use a separate search engine to find all the videos on a topic that they are searching for. Examples of video search engines available today include Ramp, blinkx, podscope, TVEyes, Truveo, Yahoo! Video, and Google Videos. The need to use a separate video search engine, however, will almost certainly go away in the near future. **VERBS supported by these tools**: exploring, finding, searching, observing, comparing, reflecting, thinking critically, combining, designing, innovating, programming.

125. **Video cameras**—Also known as videocams, these have moved in a short time from being expensive and bulky equipment to being something that many students carry around in their pockets or have built into their cell phones. This enables many useful educational applications, such as microjournalism, documentation, creation, and sharing. It is important that partnering students learn the positive uses of videocams and be discouraged from using them inappropriately. **VERBS supported by this tool**: exploring, comparing, evaluating, experimenting, observing, thinking critically, collaborating, combining, designing, creating, innovating, personalizing.

126. **Videoconferencing Tools**—Videoconferencing can be a high-end affair, with strong "telepresence," used in corporate board rooms. But low-end, easy-to-use versions are available as well. For partnering purposes, there are lots of easy, often free (or initially free) tools, such as Adobe Acrobat Connect, that can be used with inexpensive video cameras and any computer to bring people in different places together via video. Partnering students should be encouraged to find and use these tools for bringing in and teaming up with outside experts and for connecting with peers in other places. **VERBS supported by these tools**: listening, watching, deciding, evaluating, questioning, thinking critically, briefing, collaborating, connecting, cooperating, dialoging.

127. **Virtual Labs**—Today, many of the same functions and experiments that

have traditionally been done in school laboratories using physical materials can be done virtually on computers. This includes biology activities such as dissecting frogs and fetal pigs or chemistry experiments such as titration. In fact, it is often the case that the physical laboratory is no longer necessary at all to achieve many learning goals. While some bemoan the loss of hands-on experience, virtual experience, in many situations, can be equally good or even better as well as considerably less expensive and faster. While partnering teachers may still want to give their students some hands-on experience for some topics, it is also important that they give students opportunities to conduct experiments virtually. **VERBS supported by these tools**: analyzing, exploring, finding, verifying, calculating, comparing, deciding, evaluating, experimenting, observing, predicting, questioning, thinking logically, cooperating, innovating, prudent risk taking.

128. **VoIP**—Voice over Internet Protocol. See **Skype.**

129. **Voting Tools**—See **Clickers.**

130. **Wikis**—These are simple web pages that anyone who has permission can edit or change. If you go to Wikipedia, for example (which is probably the biggest wiki in existence), you will see that every entry page contains an "edit this page" tab. The same ability to edit is built into, and defines, every wiki. To prevent damage as the various users add to and change the wiki's content, an electronic record is kept of each previous version. This allows a wiki's administrator to go back to a previous version if any changes made by users are unacceptable, unwanted, or incorrect. Wikis are the collaborative tools that are probably the easiest to set up and use (the term *wiki* comes from the Hawaiian wiki-wiki, meaning "quick quick"), and they have many potential uses for learning and partnering that are described in a variety of books. **VERBS supported by this tool**: finding, reading, searching, comparing, deciding, evaluating, observing, reflecting, thinking critically, collaborating, combining, connecting, debating, dialoging, networking, writing, innovating, personalizing.

131. **Writing Tools**—Some may think that the only tools necessary for writing are a surface (e.g., paper) and an implement (e.g., pencil, pen). But there are many digital tools that can help students in the writing process. A number of these have been listed previously, such as **outlining tools, brainstorming tools, Intuition,** and **screenwriting tools (cf)**. If one expands the idea of writing to include any form of authorship, one can add such tools as those for storyboarding, video making, digital storytelling,

and others. **VERBS supported by these tools**: writing, collaborating, combining, connecting, cooperating, thinking critically, thinking logically, reflecting, innovating, personalizing.

132. **YouTube**—This web site, which every teacher has at least heard about, if not actually used, is the world's largest online repository for short videos, with several hundred million already posted and several thousand more posted every day. Although there are many other good video sites such as TeacherTube, SchoolTube, Big Think, TED Talks, and others, YouTube is, for many reasons, the most important. What YouTube has done is make video into an important form of two-way communication. (It is two-way because viewers can respond to videos either in text or with videos of their own, and this is often done in both trivial and highly sophisticated discussions.) For this and other reasons, banning or restricting access to YouTube, as many schools and districts do, is a strategy that is antithetical to the teaching objectives of partnering. Students should instead be taught and encouraged to use YouTube wisely, to find all the existing video that is related to what they are studying, to evaluate its quality, and to create responses and new videos of their own that improve the quality of YouTube's material. **VERBS supported by this tool**: exploring, finding, listening, searching, watching, comparing, evaluating, observing, reflecting, thinking critically, collaborating, debating, dialoging, designing, innovating, making, personalizing, prudent risk taking.

PARTNERING TIP

Share this list of tools with your students. Discuss the list to both learn more about tools and to see which tools your students are interested in using. Decide which tools match best with the verbs students are using and practicing.

Ask your school's tech coordinator about which licensed tools are available to your students, such as CAD, Intuition, Flash, and others.

Thank you for bearing with me and this long list. I hope you have found it useful and that you will return to it as a reference. Again, please note that if you want more information on any noun, the best way to get it is to look that noun up on Wikipedia or put it into a search engine. Keep in mind that tools change so quickly that specific names, in many cases, will be outdated even before this book gets published.

Of course, now that you, as a partnering teacher, are aware of all these tools, what do you (or rather your partnering students) use them for? The answer is to create—in as many ways and for as many learning purposes as possible. That is what today's students want to do. In the next chapter, we will look at *creating* in more detail.

8

Let Your Students Create

Guiding Questions

1. How can I elicit maximum creation from my students related to their learning?

2. How can I help my students engage in world conversations?

3. How can I continually raise the bar for my students' creations?

Today's students are incredibly eager to create, and don't get nearly enough opportunities to do so—just ask them.

Given all the tools listed in Chapter 7, it makes sense that today's students—who have access to many of these technologies—would want to use them to create things far beyond the scope of student projects of the past. They do want to, and many of them already are creating projects ranging from multimedia presentations, machinima, and mashups to graphic novels, web sites and blogs, and games. (The list could go on and on.) But not enough of them are doing this in school, as part of their class work.

"Let us create," said a student on one of my panels to the audience of teachers. "Let us show you how much of ourselves we can put into it." The partnering teacher's role is to give students this opportunity, to help and encourage them to do as much of this creation as possible, as part of their formal learning.

There has always been, of course, creation by students, but what I am talking about here is different. Formerly, for the most part, students were told precisely what form their work should take—"Write an essay of x pages or y words," "Cut out pictures, or create a cartoon or illustration." The difference is that now students have many more vehicles to express both their learning and their creativity. Take writing, for example (an obviously important verb). A good logical paragraph or essay can now be created in so many more ways and places than in the past, including a post to a public blog, a response on Facebook or YouTube, and even a video script (all of which are new nouns). A student I know, not known among his teachers as a writer, got passionate as a high school senior about some issues in the college admissions process. He wrote an essay on his web site that got forwarded around the country.

Illustrating something graphically (another verb) is still important. But students now have easily accessible video, multimedia, game tools, comic creation tools, and many other new nouns to accomplish this. Communicating (the verb) is still key, but now students have e-mail, texting, Facebook, Twitter, and many more ways to do it, with many more tools yet to come.

So it is important for partnering teachers to understand that what today's students want to create, and can create, is not the stuff of the past, not the same old homework essays, science projects, and construction paper assignments that have been used for ages and were the basis of their teachers' education. A fifth grader I know was assigned as homework—in the 21st century—to make a Pilgrim costume out of paper, cloth, and so forth. This is a kid who can create any number of intricate characters, avatars, and costumes in any number of complex games. Usually a "good" and willing student, in this case he totally rebelled and refused. His mother, fearing for his grade (and, of course, having done this herself when she was a fifth grader), did the assignment for him.

Why shouldn't this student have had the opportunity to do the same activity *his* way, such as to make a pilgrim in one of his games (and in so doing perhaps rethink the concept of "pilgrim" in a broader context)?

As we have seen, it doesn't matter whether his teacher knows how to use the all tools that the student does. Chances are the teacher won't, not being a game-playing fifth grader. What *is* important is that the partnering teacher give all students the opportunity to create at the maximum level of which they are capable, and that the teacher be open to accepting that the same objective, or assignment, might be accomplished by different students, or different groups of students, in different ways.

Remember science fairs, where kids get to create in any way they want? Each of today's partnering classes can and should be like a science (or English or math or social studies or foreign language) fair, on steroids. (And when they are, parents can't do the projects for the students, because they don't know the tools!)

I recently had the privilege of conducting a workshop for about 50 students who were attending a conference with their teachers (something I often advocate, and highly recommend). The setting was a technologically favorable one, in that the kids all had access to a well-stocked computer lab, but the students were an ordinary high school mix, representing high, low, and medium GPAs. We began by working as partners to come up with this guiding question: "What could we make to show our teachers what we are capable of creating?" Next we spent some time listing all the things that at least some of the students knew how to create—videos, podcasts, games, computer programs, Facebook pages, competitions, and more. Each student then chose his or her preference, and the group divided up into teams. There were, in the end, 10 different tools used, some by more than one team.

Even though the students had a total of only three hours to complete the projects (as a model of a weekend homework assignment), the results were extraordinary. One team of a girl and a boy made a podcast in which they did radio interviews with each other, using audio speed-up and slow-down software to reverse their genders! Two teams wrote and shot YouTube-style videos, complete with titles. Two teams created original games, using existing templates. One student wrote a specialized search program. One team made a Facebook page. During the work, students pointed each other to the best tools to use.

The groups then presented their projects to the audience of teachers and peers. The project ultimately judged the best by the audience was a geography competition, set up by the students between a teacher team (using as tools an atlas and a ruler) and a student team (using Google Earth). On some of the questions, the teams were roughly equal. But when asked the distance from Toronto to Vancouver, the student team simply clicked and got the precise answer, while in the same amount of time the teachers could only answer "five inches."

The point worth taking away is not just the fact that the projects were all great, but also the variety of the projects and the tools the students were able, and preferred, to use.

For any guiding question, in any subject, there currently exist many ways of creatively answering it and creatively presenting that answer. The more students are encouraged to do this, the better prepared they will be for their future. Of course, some students "get" this more than others. Some may prefer, at first blush, to do as little as possible or even to do things the old way (whereby they don't have to think and can often sleep). If you find, at first, that not all of your students are proactive and excited about creating, seek out the ones who are and get them, through teamwork and peer-to-peer interaction, to pull the others along. Seeing the accomplishments of their peers should also help.

PARTNERING TIP

As you find out more and more about your students' passions, also find out (by asking) what they like to create and have created in the past (much or most of this will have been done outside of school). Make and post a list of possible creations, that students can choose from or add to. Encourage students to try their hand at all of these over the course of the semester or year. To help students who are unfamiliar with some of the tools learn, create teams combining experienced people with newbies.

A REAL, WORLD AUDIENCE

One of the great differences between today and times past is that, formerly, students created whatever they did for an audience of one—their teacher. But today's students can create for, and share their work with, a world audience. And, happily, the world can, and in most cases is eager to, give them feedback. So early on young people get the kinds of feedback that used to be available only to professionals, and only rarely to students. This is enormously appealing to today's young people, who are used to a world of multiple reviews of movies, games, products, and more. Students who get hundreds or thousands of hits on their video, or hundreds of comments (or none) on a web post, truly know where they stand—not just in school, but in the real world.

Having a real audience is, many teachers report, an incentive for students to do better work. "Persuasive writing assignments are surprisingly popular," wrote a teacher online, "especially in the form of letters to politicians and lobbyists, who always have someone to answer their mail."[23] Of course, this should not surprise any partnering teacher. It goes right back to the "make it *real*" idea discussed in Chapter 4.

Ted Nellin, twice honored as a New York City Teacher of the Year, has been doing this for years—long enough to know that it works—with his English classes, developing and using a partnering method that he calls CyberEnglish. In his classes, everything students write gets published online for the world to see. In order to present their work to maximum advantage, all students in his classes are required to learn HTML, the programming language of the Internet.

Student reports done as text, audio podcasts, or video can all be uploaded (in or out of class) to public sites such as YouTube. For example, many language students, on their own, put examples of their speaking on YouTube and solicit feedback from native speakers. Partnering teachers should encourage this behavior. If using real names or images is an issue, ask students to use a "handle" of their own choosing and alter (or "morph") their faces.

PARTNERING TIP

Ask yourself: What could my students create and share with the world that would enhance their learning? Now go ask your students the same question. Are there differences between their ideas and yours? Encourage your students to create and share those things, and jointly review whatever feedback arrives.

World Conversations

Large numbers of "world conversations" are going on all the time in online editorials, op-eds, blogs, Listservs, and more. Partnering teachers should encourage their students to seek out and join these conversations, contributing whatever, wherever, and whenever their passions lead them to. Here are some world conversations in standard subjects:

- Social studies students can join world conversations on disarmament, eliminating land mines, eliminating hunger, and world education.
- English students can join world conversations on the effects of the Web on writing, the meaning of words, whether China or India will become the largest English-speaking country, whether a "standard" English exists, and whether all people will eventually speak a common language (English or something else).

- Math students can join world conversations on metrics and standardization, on teaching math in different ways, and on "crowd solving" difficult problems.
- Science students can join world conversations on real versus imagined dangers of atomic energy, cell phone radiation, evolution versus creationism, and the ethics of new scientific fields and developments.
- Foreign language students can join world conversations on all of the above topics in different countries. Local perspectives on world conversations often tend to be parochial and one-sided, and it is very helpful to partnering students to see a number of different perspectives.

PARTNERING TIP

Why not have your students join a world conversation on some of the things you are studying? This involves collecting opinions from many different places, using the Web, Really Simple Syndication, Google translation, and other tools, and then sharing student opinions in return, via a class blog or postings directly to the various sources. If security is an issue for some communications, secure sites such as ePals can be used.

AIM HIGH, RAISE THE BAR

My experience is that today's educators almost universally underestimate what students are capable of creating in the early 21st century. When students are truly allowed to create and when, given the opportunity, they come up with works of high quality (as very often happens), many educators declare themselves surprised by what their students accomplish. An example of this is the exceptional movie-making program/competition at Mabry Middle School, in Georgia, started by ex-principal Tim Tyson. The program resulted in a series of excellent short videos, created entirely by students in Grades 6–8 on such global topics as genetically modified food, immigration, adoption, and fighting malaria.

When I first heard Tim Tyson introduce these videos at a conference, he declared himself "blown away" by what the students had done. And, it should be noted, the videos are really excellent. But I think Tim, just like many of us, had set his initial expectations of what his middle schoolers could acoomplish far too low. We all need to raise our expectations bar and say to our students, "We want work that is your creative best and that pushes the boundaries of what you and we think is possible. If your work doesn't go beyond our (higher and higher) expectations and blow even your peers away, it's just not what we are expecting from you, and possibly not even acceptable."

At the same time, we need to be careful not to praise work, or evaluate it highly, just because it uses technology. I have seen many videos made by elementary school kids, where the adults exhibiting them were so totally awed by the fact that the kids could use the technology ("Oh my god, they're using green screen") that they ignored the poor or nonexistent quality of the content. Kids learn the technical stuff early and easily—my four-year-old can take videos—so it is the content that we should be focusing them on. We need to expect our students to do exactly what the student quoted earlier said: show us how much of themselves they can put into it.

As many keep rediscovering, our students are generally given too little rather than too much challenge, and students far prefer the stimulation of being challenged more. Remember, they are rockets, and will, if we do our job well, take off and rise to the challenge. But for students to *want* to rise to such challenges they have to have the freedom to do it in their own way.

Allow Choice

To set the bar truly high and to seek and demand an exceptional level of creativity from students, partnering teachers have to find ways to set students free to do things "their (i.e., the students') way" much more than we have ever done in the past. Our partnering students will only be truly inspired, and will only produce at their creative best, when they are doing something that they have chosen to do.

That doesn't mean we can't, or shouldn't, "assign" things. We can and should. But what we have to give students is the option to complete our assignments in whatever way most inspires them. When asked to communicate something, express an opinion, or give a logical explanation, it is fine if students want to write a traditional essay. But a blog post, video, animation, game, game design, or even a rap song might demonstrate equally well that they know and understand the material. Even when "learning to write" is the goal and the assignment (the verb), we should remember and remind students that there are so many more potential products of this assignment (nouns) than an essay submitted on paper. Most are already aware of this. "Just tell us where you want us to go," I've heard many students say, "and let us figure out how to get there."

Another example of providing choices to motivate partnering students is that we are long past the need to have all students in a class read the same book at the same time. (I still remember having to slog though a book called *The Mill on the Floss*, although I couldn't tell you the first thing about it.) The reasoning used to be that this was a book, or text, to which every student had access. The pedagogy was to assign this book to everyone, chapter by chapter, and then discuss it, point by point. But in this century, when every kid has a different collection of songs on his or her iPod, and access to materials is so much easier, does this still make any sense? Can't we allow students to be more individual and creative in their reading choices and still accomplish the same goals?

Partnering teachers need to think about which we are more interested in: that every kid reads the same book, or that the lessons in that book (be they stylistic, such as suspense or irony, or thematic, such as the consequences of jealousy) be learned by all. In the latter case, we can let each student choose his or her own work to analyze and tell us where and how it contains the elements we are looking for. The work that they analyze in this way might just be a movie, a song, or a game, rather than a novel, a short story, or a poem.

One of the most important tenets of partnering is carefully listening to students and letting them act on their likes and desires, balancing those with our own needs and requirements as teachers. We still want, of course, to open kids' minds to new things and experiences, in the hope that they will grow to appreciate and love them as we do. But we also want to encourage them to go in their own directions.

And they can influence us as well. I recently heard a fifth-grade student describe how she had introduced her teacher to one of her favorite books—which the teacher enjoyed—and how this had helped her bond with that teacher.

PARTNERING TIP

Ask yourself: Where could I give my students more choice in what they use, do, or study, and still achieve the learning I am looking for? Then ask your students the same thing. Implement the best ideas. Collect feedback on how they work. Share the best results.

Engage Slackers

No matter what the task, it is never the case that every student approaches it with equal enthusiasm and effort. What about the "slackers"? What about the tune-outs, the students who never seem interested in anything we do or offer?

If you talk to a few, you'll probably find out, as I have, that in many cases their lack of interest is due more to their not wanting to do the precise thing we offer, rather than not wanting to do anything at all. So we can motivate many of them by allowing them, in pretty much every case, to follow their own interests. If that's what we ask and expect of them, they have a lot less chance of not doing it.

PARTNERING TIP

Try putting all of the slackers in your class into the same group for a particular time or project, challenging them to create, in their own way, "the best project the class has seen." You may be quite surprised by the result (as other teachers who have done this have been).

One such group of potentially misunderstood students in Arizona is being catered to by Barnaby Wasson, who teaches and partners with students who are children of migrant workers in a program called Conexiones. He has turned many previously passive, apathetic kids into excited journalists by letting them interview people (relatives and others) and create podcasts and videos, which they post online. The students have even attended conferences as documenters.

Another potential way to deal with slackers is to emphasize quality over quantity. Make a wonderfully written paragraph worth as much as or more than a middling five-page paper, and let students know they can do shorter or smaller pieces—as long as they are excellent. The combination of their own interests and "less" work (nominally: shorter is actually harder) may motivate some.

A partnering teacher in England lets primary school students submit video book reports, imitating the style of TV film critics. Another lets students watch video games and create verbal and written descriptions of their favorite parts. In this class, writing skills have risen dramatically, especially among boys.

Students who are seen as slackers always have a reason for their behavior, and they typically have something else they would rather be doing—usually whatever it is that they are passionate about—than the work they are assigned. It is the partnering teacher's job to connect the work with those passions, whatever they may be. In a class without lectures, there should typically be much more time for this.

Bring in the Pros

One of the most inspiring things you can do for students who are trying to learn to express themselves and create in new media (or in any media for that matter) is to bring in professionals to help teach kids the tricks of their trade. Tim Tyson did this at Mabry Middle School for his video creation project, inviting local volunteer documentary filmmakers to teach and help the students. Other teachers have brought in local writers, broadcasters, bloggers, and multimedia creators to help kids on a volunteer basis. Another good source of help is available online—YouTube has tutorials for almost any piece of software you can think of, plus videos of people from many professions talking about technical aspects of their craft. There exist several sites and programs for "telementoring," where adult professionals (sometimes, but not always, older or retired) can provide help to students and teachers. Students generally appreciate being treated as budding professionals in this way. For the teacher, of course, it is also a learning experience.

> **Check It Out!**
>
> For more information on telementoring, go to www.december.com/cmc/mag/1996/oct/nellen.html.

PARTNERING TIP

Have your students find out who the creative professionals are in your town, city, or neighborhood and among the parents of your student body. You or the students should ask those people if they will volunteer time to coach students (individually or in groups) who are doing creative projects in their field (which could be advertising, filmmaking, music production, broadcasting, game making, and even science or engineering).

Consider hooking yourself and your students up with creative projects already out there, such as FIRST Robotics, humanoid robotics competitions, or Odyssey of the Mind.

Ask Students for Technologies to Use

When it comes to introducing particular technologies (nouns) into your teaching and classroom, you'll have a much better chance of success if you are not the one who chooses them, at least not on your own.

Take PowerPoint, for example. Many teachers have learned to use this noun, and they typically use it as a tool for telling, using only its most simple capabilities. Many students dislike and resent this.

If the teacher's objective, though, is to have multimedia presentations that can be stored online for students to use on their own to learn from, a partnering teacher would do best to consult his or her students first on the best way to do this. Students might prefer to make these in partnership with the teacher—with the teacher providing the context and the students using the technology.

Or you might find that your students prefer to use a different tool for this altogether. What if, for example, they said they preferred Flash presentations? (Which, in many cases, teachers don't know how to make.) Working together as partners, you and your students might be able to create learning animations that are good enough to post on YouTube or TeacherTube and share with colleagues around the world. In some cases, your students may prefer that you not even participate in the creation, but take the role only of reviewer and quality assurer.

PARTNERING TIP

Before you introduce any technology into your classroom, either attempting to use it yourself (not recommended, as you know) or suggesting it for student use, talk it over with your students. Ask for their preferences and suggestions for whether and how it should be used, how they can use it, and what else they might like to see or have in order to enhance its effectiveness.

A great opportunity for this type of interaction might be if you, as a partnering teacher, are provided with an interactive whiteboard in your classroom. According to administrators, many of these expensive tools actually sit idle, while the teacher gets comfortable (or waits to get trained) regarding their use. But in most classes, many students, if asked, could immediately, on their own, set them up, connect any computers they may have, and use them for presentations. Partnering teachers should reach out to their students for help in understanding the best ways for the teacher and students to use such tools together and to research what software—such as games and interactive tools that would make its use even better for students—might be available.

Balance Cooperation and Competition

As students create, is it best to have them cooperating or competing? Many teachers introduce and use group work, team work, and other activities that promote cooperation among students in the class. And many teachers introduce games and other forms of competition among students. But it is much less frequent for teachers to try to carefully balance these two things in their designs and planning. Such careful balancing of cooperation and competition is, in the world of video and computer games, an important and often crucial part of good design. A good balance is a real key to a game's being engaging.

That same balance between cooperation and competition is important in terms of designing partnering classes and student creation as well. The reason for this is that many students prefer, and thrive on, only one of the two and dislike the other. In many cases, those who are motivated by competition and those motivated by cooperation form very distinct sets, sometimes with little overlap.

Inquiring about who in your class likes which, and then carefully planning around this, can result in a great deal more motivation on the part of students. This comes from no student being pushed or forced into doing something he or she seriously dislikes. (You can, however, ask students to go "cross-type" for learning and "stretching" purposes, but this is best done with students' knowledge and permission.)

PARTNERING TIP

Ask all of your students whether they prefer to cooperate or compete (or whether they like both) and under what conditions. Keep a record of the preferences of each student. Based on those preferences, create or suggest different types of tasks and tools for each of the groups to use. And balance the two by having teams that cooperate internally but compete externally.

Students who know they have the freedom to create in whatever (appropriate) ways they want to as part of their school work (and who know they have the help and support of their teachers and, when possible, professionals) are far more motivated than those who don't. Partnering teachers are encouraged to talk with their students about this, and to give students as much latitude and support as possible for their creative efforts, continuously setting the bar higher and higher and making sure all efforts (not just the "best" ones) get shared with a world audience. The pleasure of seeing, evaluating, sharing, and getting feedback on these efforts should be extremely rewarding for any partnering student, teacher, and class.

9

Continuous Improvement Through Practice and Sharing

Guiding Questions

1. How can I (and my students) continuously improve through iteration, practice, and sharing?

2. How can I (and my students) move to higher levels of partnering?

3. How can I (and my students) eliminate boredom?

There are very few principles more important to learning and doing anything than continuous improvement. No one starts out at something new as perfect, or even very good. Anyone who wants to succeed needs to devote him- or herself to continually getting better. Even the very best at whatever they do—whether Fred Astaire, Tiger Woods, or Will Wright—are (or were) continuously trying to improve their performance every day of their careers. Will Smith, who became enormously successful sequentially in music, on TV, and in movies, has spoken about how much hard work he needs to put in to everything he does.

Partnering is no exception. It requires, as I have explained, a wide mix of skills, some of which are almost totally new to nonpartnering teachers. Each of these skills—coaching, guiding, goal setting, questioning, designing, and so on—has its own improvement curve, especially in the new context of partnering. The good news, though, is that the various skills all reinforce each other, and partnering quickly gets easier. This is true for teachers as well as students, who are often new to this way of teaching and learning as well.

It is not just teachers who need to continuously improve at partnering. Students do too. Most current students have been schooled, up till now, under the old paradigm of being told and asked to regurgitate. Learning on their own, with their teacher as a coach and guide, is a new experience for most of them. Students need to get better and better at learning this way—taking initiative, answering guiding questions fully and accurately, practicing and mastering skills, and using all the tools available to them to their fullest advantage.

One of the best things about continuous improvement is that it is measurable. And if you set up markers, and reflect and measure yourself against them on a regular basis, as I will show you how to do, you are likely to see yourself and your students improving rapidly.

There are three main routes to continuous improvement: iteration, practice, and sharing. To improve the fastest, you can and should take all of these routes simultaneously. To simplify, though, I will discuss each of them in turn.

IMPROVING THROUGH ITERATION

To do it really well, partnering takes a great deal of practice, as I will discuss in the next section. But it is crucial to recognize that practice alone does not make perfect—one has to be practicing the right things. (This is, of course, useful information for students as well.) What practice does is make things permanent, easier, and, in many cases, automatic. And it is precisely because of the permanence—that things long practiced are hard to undo—that one has to always be practicing the *right* things.

How do we find the right things to practice in our own specific teaching? The best way is through iteration. Iteration is extremely important because it is almost impossible to get anything that is both complex and highly people dependent right the first time. And partnering is both. So it is important that partnering teachers and their students start somewhere and iterate, removing things that don't work, trying new things, taking the inevitable ups and downs that come with any complex task such as partnering in stride, always reviewing whatever happens, and working to continuously improve.

An excellent way to do this is to keep a journal. (The modern version of a journal is, of course, a blog, which can be either private or public.) Many teachers keep journals online, and some as we shall see, even share them.

PARTNERING TIP

At the end of every class (or at least every couple of classes), iterate by asking your students, "How did our partnering go today? How could we make it better?" You can ask students to answer these questions either live, online, or on paper.

Follow up and act on as many of their suggestions as possible. (Of course, not all student suggestions will work, or work perfectly, but trying them at least lets students know that their ideas are listened to and not just rejected out of hand.)

Ask your students to keep their own partnering or learning journals as well. This will help them reflect and learn what works best for them.

Iteration and Variety

There is yet another benefit of iteration for students: variety. Today's students generally crave variety and change, and the more ways their teachers try things, the more interested they are likely to be (and the more likely teachers are to find the best solutions for their particular students). A very important time to remember to iterate is at the start of any new year or class. No matter what you have learned worked best with previous students you taught, you will almost certainly have to make adjustments in your partnering for your current students—if for no other reason than the technology that they will have been exposed to each year will have changed, in many cases dramatically. Iteration is the way to do this.

Iterating Students' Work

Iteration also applies to student work in a very important way. Students should be encouraged by the partnering teacher to see all of their work—whether research, presentations, or other types of projects—not as a series of unconnected tasks or assignments, but rather as a series of continuous improvements to their skills at doing the various verbs and using the various nouns. Thus students should be asked often to reprise something they have done (an essay, a video, a posting, a podcast), perhaps in a new lesson or context, and to iterate, making it a better effort than before. Doing this involves specific, upfront considerations by each student and the teacher of what the issues were with the previous effort, what needs to be improved, and how it will be done. Over the course of the semester or year, students who do this should see their skills improve dramatically.

IMPROVING THROUGH PRACTICE

Once you have started with the basic partnering concept, that is, that you and your students are learning partners, each with specific roles to play, and once you have iterated as much as possible to find out what works best in your situation and to be sure you are doing nothing wrong or counterproductive, then—pretty much automatically—the more you practice, the better you get. This is true for both teachers and students. In terms of getting better at something, there is no substitute for doing the right things, over and over, and integrating them into automatic practice. This goes for all things, from the simplest (such as, if you are a student, automatically checking your daily assignment and getting started) to the most complex (such as, if you are a teacher, creating exciting, interesting, and meaningful guiding questions).

The remainder of this section on practice describes some of the things that students and teachers should be practicing, daily, to get better at the process of learning through partnering.

Practice for Students

Above all, students need to practice the self-motivation and self-discipline required for successful partnering. This is clearly not something that comes automatically or immediately for every student. But each student is capable of getting better at these skills and should be helped and encouraged by their partnering teachers to do so. (In doing this, teachers get to live out and practice their coaching role.)

Second, students need to practice the required verbs (skills) once the teacher has made clear, in each case, what those are.

Third, students need to practice making the connection between their personal passions and interests and the work they are doing in school. As I've said, students are best motivated by a connection between what they are learning and what they like and are interested in. Partnering makes it easier to find and use that connection to help students learn. But another thing students need to practice is finding and refining their passions, and applying those passions to their learning.

In partnering, the principal way teachers encourage students to practice skills is by inciting their personal passions around those skills. The goal is to give every one of our students the opportunity to be good at (or even the best at) something they choose and are passionate about.

How can this happen? A great strength of the partnering pedagogy is that not every student has to do things the same way. When that is the case, some students will obviously be better at some ways of doing things than others. In partnering, as long as he or she gets there, each student can choose his or her own path to answering the guiding questions and presenting his or her findings. And since each student's own way is unique, he or she can be the best at it.

But doing that does take practice. The broader the opportunities and options students have, the more they can find and practice their own fit. One partnering class, for example, created a Spanish-language guidebook to New York City, based partially on the guiding question "What would be different in a Spanish guidebook?" Each student in the class needed to find and practice, with the teacher's coaching, a role in that project that suited him or her best.

It is the thesis of this book—and of the partnering pedagogy—that by asking interesting guiding questions and letting each student relate to them and answer them in his or her own way, individually and working with peers, and then by allowing each student to discuss and refine the work in his or her own way with the teacher's guidance, each student will be able to relate much of the curriculum to his or her own interests and passions. By doing so, students will be much more motivated to work and practice than they are by a telling-and-worksheet pedagogy.

But What About Students Who Say They Prefer Being Told?

Of course, there will always be some students who prefer the old telling way. Some just prefer sleeping through the lectures to doing the work it takes to get motivated in the partnering pedagogy. The best way to get to these students is through finding and stimulating their passions.

But sometimes the students who prefer the old way are "good" students—those who have mastered the old system, figured out how to succeed at it, get high grades, and just don't want to be bothered learning a new way. They may argue, with some justification, that the old skills, if learned and executed well, will likely get them into a good college. So should we maintain the old system, in parallel with partnering, for them?

I don't think so, for two reasons. First, even these students would be much better off learning through a partnering pedagogy. The reason is—and most of them are smart enough to understand this—because the kind of on-their-own learning they learn to do in partnering will last them a lifetime, as opposed to what they learn in the telling pedagogy, which they typically forget as soon as it is no longer required for a grade or test. Partnering is a longer-term strategy.

The second reason is that colleges are changing too. I'm invited to give the same talks at colleges and universities that I give to K–12 schools. Colleges too are seeking to replace lectures with more partnering and are, in more and more cases, succeeding. Just as in the K–12 world, where schools are moving forward (at different speeds), colleges too are beginning to look for characteristics from their applicants other than high grades, good SAT or ACT scores, and the ability to take notes. Institutions of higher learning are starting to look for, in their applicants, the skills acquired through partnering. So it is important for all students to be practicing those skills.

Practice for Teachers

Often, particularly at the start, what teachers need to practice the most in order to be successful at partnering is just "letting go." That is, becoming comfortable with not always being on stage and with students working on their own. Tolerating a somewhat noisier, less rigidly structured classroom and accepting that students will use tools and technology that teachers are not completely (or at all) familiar with.

Many teachers are used to judging themselves on their ability to control their class and be the expert. The first time that a teacher who has taught only by lecturing attempts to partner, the chances are it will feel very chaotic and not everything will go exactly as planned or hoped. As I said before, this is not bad; it is normal, and it should never be an excuse to give up. Partnering is a complex skill (or rather, set of skills) that, from the teachers' as well as the students' side, not only must be learned and iterated, but requires a good deal of practice to get really good at and master. It does not take long, however, for dedicated teachers to get over their initial fears of giving up or losing control. The report on a recent partnering project sponsored by Apple and the New Media Consortium notes,[24]

> At the outset the teachers were very concerned about how the process would unfold. They were apprehensive about giving up control and worried that the students would not pick up the reins and do the work. By the end of the project, however, those concerns had virtually evaporated.

Practicing the Roles

Aside from learning to let go, what should teachers practice? They should practice, in turn and in parallel, all of their various roles in partnering. They need to practice coaching, guiding, goal setting, questioning, designing, and assuring quality, as discussed in earlier chapters.

Taking Motivating Strategies From Video Games

Interestingly, there is a lot about these roles (and other useful things) that partnering teachers can learn from the video and computer games their students play. Although these games are often disdained by educators, few would disagree that they are great at motivating kids to put in lots of practice and effort, or that motivating their students to practice and put in effort is one of the big goals of partnering teachers.

The motivational power of games, however, is not a random effect or by-product, but rather the result of several strategies employed more or less systematically by game designers. The designers of the best games manage to accomplish many of the things we, as partnering teachers, are looking to do to motivate our students, so we can and should use many of the same motivational techniques that game designers use.

For example, one of the things good video games do extremely well is to make the same game (which, in our case, would be the same class or task) feel different for each player, that is, customized to their individual preferences and abilities. Games do this through artificial intelligence programming that automatically assigns any player extra help (or resources, or buddies) whenever he or she needs it and, at the same time, gives a player who is doing well extra challenge by removing resources or adding difficulty. A teacher's human intelligence, when applied individually and consistently, is even better at being adaptive than the artificial intelligence of games. So this same fine-tuned "adaptivity" to each player that makes games so compelling is something partnering teachers need to strive for and practice with students.

A second thing that we, as partnering teachers, can learn from games is that, in any good video or computer game, all the goals—immediate, medium, and long term—for the player are always crystal clear. But, at the same time, there are many—often hundreds of—possible paths to reach those goals. And feedback about whether one is on a path toward reaching those goals is always frequent and immediate. Partnering teachers need to strive for these same characteristics in the classroom.

So while, as I have discussed here and elsewhere (see *"Don't Bother Me Mom—I'm Learning"*), computer games are very good for learning and are likely to be nouns that we should consider using with our students, we can also get many of their motivational benefits without games because partnering can incorporate many of them.

IMPROVING THROUGH SHARING

It is impossible to understate the importance of avidy sharing with one's colleagues for improving one's skills at partnering. And to be effective, this sharing must happen in two directions: partnering teachers must always be looking for good examples and practices from others, but they must also be generous and timely about sharing their own.

There Is So Much to Share

One thing I have learned in my travels is that there is a lot of really good partnering—a huge amount, in fact—going on right now in schools all over America and the world. But unfortunately for a teacher looking to start partnering, much of it is going on without anyone knowing about it, except for the teachers and students involved. This is, as I'm sure you understand, a most frustrating and unhelpful state of affairs. What it means is that you, as a learning partnering teacher, cannot use and do not benefit from the successful ideas and practices of thousands of your colleagues, and this slows down your own progress considerably.

One of the biggest ironies in the digital age is that the older, predigital generation (which includes many of today's teachers) was raised not to share—their motto was "knowledge is power; keep it close to the vest"—while the generation of digital natives (which includes most of our students) has grown up thinking that sharing information (by posting, blogging, texting, tweeting, etc.) is precisely *how* you get recognition and power. The motto of the younger generation, if it had one, would be "sharing is power." Since sharing leads to faster learning, the unfortunate result of this situation is that the older generation learns much more slowly. While teachers generally pride themselves on their own understanding, they often lack essential information about what others are doing. As a result, teachers all over the world are continuously reinventing the wheel. This is particularly true in partnering.

While this state of affairs may have been acceptable when sharing was difficult (to do it you had to write and publish an article or a book, or get accepted to speak at a conference), it is no longer acceptable now that sharing has become so easy that it can be done just by talking into a cell phone or video camera, typing a quick entry on a blog, or taking any number of other enormously easy actions. So partnering teachers need to learn to share more.

The Best Way to Share: Short Video

Today, there are a great many tools available for sharing ideas and successes. Many teachers have their own blogs on which they share, and many subscribe to and read the blogs of others. But in my opinion the best way (and one of the easiest) for teachers to share their successes, in terms of both giving and getting, is through short videos posted on YouTube, SchoolTube, TeacherTube, or an equivalent. To see the power of this (if you have not already done so), go to these web sites and browse for a topic that interests you. Already, there is much to find, but there could be so much more. Your and your colleagues' successes could and should be there as well, as should those of every teacher in the world.

Brian Scully, a teacher in Massachusetts, is using texting to teach ninth-grade English students *Romeo and Juliet*—what an interesting idea! I heard about it through the grapevine of asking, in my talks, for innovative ideas. But wouldn't it be great if there were a video online so that any teacher searching "Romeo and Juliet, 9th grade" could find this unusual example, hear Brian talk about the what and why and results of it, see some examples, and maybe even hear a student comment? So many of the wonderful things people share with me after my talks could be so easily put online and shared with teachers everywhere.

This Is So Easy to Do

All a teacher has to do to create such sharing videos is ask a student with a video camera (or even a cell phone that takes video) to point it at the teacher while the teacher talks for literally 30 seconds. Or the teacher can hold the phone at arm's length or put it on a tripod and talk. Period. That's it. The video can then be metatagged with useful search information (e.g., teaching, fifth-grade math, multiplying fractions) and uploaded and posted. Uploading, in new cameras and phones, consists of nothing more than pushing a button.

One hurdle is accepting that it is OK for these videos to be what many of us used to consider "amateur" in quality (and it *is* OK; YouTube video is a different animal than professional video, even though some of the latter is still posted). But once one accepts this, making these sharing videos is easy, even trivial. The whole process takes five minutes at most.

What I tell people who make good comments (or share good things they are doing) at my talks is that, had they made the same comment in front of a cell phone and posted it as a YouTube video, hundreds of thousands of people could find it and hear it.

If more detail is desired, or required, one can add shots of one or two students talking and perhaps a shot of the class at work (taking and adding these is also trivial for many of our students). When uploaded, the record of a teacher's innovation is permanently on the Web, shared for all other teachers to see. With the addition of a few metatags, it becomes something that any partnering teacher can easily find and watch.

It bears reemphasizing that, with practice, creating and posting a YouTube video of a successful idea can be a five-minute exercise from start to finish. (So much for "not having time.") Of course, longer and more "professional" videos can be created as well, but the point is that it is better to share right away, rather than wait until everything is "right"—either it never is, or you've wasted valuable time waiting.

Until this posting and sharing begins to happen in a regular and systematic way by partnering teachers, we are, sadly, re-creating almost everything on our own, time after time, which is a terribly inefficient way to do things and a huge waste of our time and effort. So please, as you succeed in partnering, become a sharer!

Learning From Colleagues

Other than from your own imagination or the minds of your students, the very best source of good ideas—ideas that will almost certainly work in your context—is your colleagues. Colleagues in your department, your school, your district, around your state and the country, and even in other countries around the world. Every success that one of your partnering colleagues has is a potential success for you, and your successes are potential successes for all your colleagues. Be sure to talk to them about partnering.

Sharing as a Normal Part of the Job

In my view, the kind of sharing I have been talking about here should be a normal, required function of every teaching professional, especially in our age of easy-to-use technology tools. Too often, rather than finding out what the person in the next room is doing that is innovative, or searching around the school or district for good ideas, teachers travel hundreds or even thousands of miles to professional conferences. These are enjoyable and often fabulous sources of new ideas, but subsidies to attend them are diminishing, and in many ways this way of sharing no longer makes as much sense in the age of the Internet. For the purpose purely of learning about something new that works, watching a video on the computer will often do just as well, especially if it can be followed up with questions and answers with the presenter right there or separately by e-mail.

PARTNERING TIP

Make it a personal goal to share, via online video, at least one good idea a week (or month) with your colleagues. If you can't do this by yourself with your own cell phone or video camera (the Flip is probably the easiest video camera to use), ask your students for volunteer partners.

Of course, in-person conversations, personal friendships, and collegial relationships are important, too, and if it is possible, it may make good sense for a teacher getting started in partnering to attend a partnering conference. Should you attend these conferences, wouldn't it be great to have strangers coming up to you saying, "I loved your YouTube video on teaching Shakespeare with texting. Please tell me more!" Remember: the group that shares the most, learns the fastest.

PARTNERING TIPS IN REVIEW

1. Talk with your students, as much and as often as possible, about their learning and about partnering. Take some time to explain what you are going to try to do and why. Get students' reactions and suggestions. Ask for their help in the partnering process, and work with them to define their roles as well as yours.

2. Find and consult with colleagues who teach in your subject and grade level who have tried this before and have been successful. You can often find these colleagues in your own school, but you can also find them through professional groups you belong to and online.

3. Search the Web for good examples of partnering. The best places to start are probably YouTube, SchoolTube, and TeacherTube. But Google and other search engines are good sources of information as well. You many need to use some of the "brand name" terms as search terms, for example, "question-based learning," "problem-based learning," "inquiry-based learning," "student-centered learning," "challenge-based learning," and "constructivism."

4. Pick a particular topic or lesson that you have to teach, and create a good set of guiding questions. The criterion for the questions is this: if a student can answer all of these, they have a sufficient understanding of the topic and should succeed on any test. While some of your questions may be factual, keep in mind that they are better when they are more open ended and idea based. For example, rather than asking, "In what year did Columbus first land in America?" you might ask, "Was Columbus the only one searching the world in the 15th century? Who else was searching? Why were they doing it? What did they find?"

5. Reflect (preferably with your students) on what verbs (skills) you will want students to employ as part of their finding the answers to the guiding questions. How will you recommend they go about answering the questions?

6. Think about the tools (nouns) associated with those verbs. How many of the tools do your students have access to?

7. How will you have (or let) students share their answers with you and the class? What kinds of feedback, critiques, and discussions will you have?

Thinking about these things over and over, before and after your classes, and refining each future class based on what did and didn't work in your context will, over time, provide all the practice you need to become expert at the partnering pedagogy.

BECOMING AN EXPERT "PARTNERER": GETTING TO LEVEL 5

How will you know you are getting better and gaining expertise? It is useful to have a metric or rubric to help you judge, in a relatively objective way, how you and your students are doing in moving along the continuum from the old telling pedagogy to the new partnering pedagogy (see figure 9.1).

Figure 9.1   Pedagogy Continuum

Do you know where you and each of your colleagues are along this continuum?					
Lecturing to and controlling your students				**Coaching, guiding, and partnering with your students**	
0	1	2	3	4	5

Below are definitions of six levels, one set each for teachers and students, that you can use to measure where you stand and how much you and your students have moved over time toward partnering.

Partnering Levels for Teachers	
Level 0	All teaching is done by lecturing (i.e., telling, direct instruction), and all student practice is done using worksheets.
Level 1	In addition to lectures, other presentation modes, such as DVDs or videos, are introduced periodically. Worksheets are still the primary mode of in-class practice for students.
Level 2	The teacher lectures while using interactive whiteboards and showing PowerPoint presentations and videos. In addition to worksheets, some computer and search-based student activities are introduced in class or in computer labs.
Level 3	The teacher tries to keep lectures short, using a rule of no more minutes per lecture than the grade level. Students do a variety of in-class activities, many on the computer.
Level 4	Partnering (i.e., guiding questions given, students work on their own, followed by presentation and discussion) is done on some days, with some topics. Lectures, explanations, and worksheets are still used for some material.
Level 5	All teaching is done through partnering. The teacher never tells or lectures, even when giving instructions. Students always work on their own or in groups, always have clear goals that they know where to find, and accomplish the goals regularly using a variety of tools. Discussions and critiques are student led, fully participative, and lively.

Partnering Levels for Students	
Level 0	Students are expected to listen, take notes, hand in assignments and homework on time, and pass frequent tests.
Level 1	Students engage in some active doing, non-listening-only activities in addition to those from Level 0.

(Continued)

(Continued)

Partnering Levels for Students	
Level 2	Students spend at least half their time doing partnering activities, finding their guiding questions and goals on their own, and selecting activities from a teacher-provided menu.
Level 3	In addition to the activities from Level 2, students discuss upcoming lessons with the teacher, help create guiding questions, suggest activities and tools, and do their own research. There is still some listening and note taking.
Level 4	Students are expected to, and do, find or create guiding questions, do research, make presentations, self-form into groups when necessary, complete self-designed projects, and lead and participate in critiques and discussions.
Level 5	Students do everything from Level 4 and also help the teacher design classes for maximum engagement and teach their peers whenever necessary.

Moving Through the Levels

As you work to change your pedagogy, it is important to assess periodically (say, every month or two) what progress you are making. A good way to do this is by having a discussion with your class. The key things for you and the students to look for and monitor (and maybe even graph) are the amount of lecturing, telling, or direct instruction the teacher does in each class and the students' comfort with and ability for working and learning independently.

As you and your students move up the levels, you should acknowledge this progress. A good way to do this is to share by making and uploading to the Web a short video describing and documenting your progress and any specific skills or milestones reached. Post these for your colleagues to see.

The Need for Continuous Improvement

While on the previous charts there is a Level 5 (i.e., a "top" level) to get to, most professionals understand that mastering skills that are really important—whether it be any of the verbs we have talked about or even the art of teaching itself—takes time, frequently an entire career and sometimes an entire lifetime. Great musicians, for example, never stop trying to improve. They do it throughout their lives by practicing, performing alone and with others, and taking lessons with master players and teachers. Great athletes are the same; look at Tiger Woods, the unquestioned best golfer in the world, who totally reworked his swing to eliminate a flaw that bothered him. In fact, in any field the best are never convinced they have learned all there is, and they never stop trying to get better. "Ancora imparo," wrote Michelangelo on a drawing near the end of his life: "I am still learning."

Teaching is, or should be, the same. Teaching is not something one can just pick up in a year or two and then coast through for the rest of one's career. Partnering, especially, is a career-long skill to be learned. A partnering teacher constantly needs to try to improve—minute to minute, class to class, year to year.

Some may think the best way to do this is by going to classes or attending inservice training, when available. That may certainly help, although the quality of what is offered varies widely. But it is wrong to depend only on others to help you—there are many steps that any partnering teacher can take on his or her own to improve.

PARTNERING TIP

Whenever you attend a professional development conference (especially one that involves any kind of technology), try to bring a student with you—preferably the smartest kid you know. (It may be your own.) Having a student at your side gives you enormous opportunities to ask the student questions, let him or her help you, see his or her point of view, and so forth, giving you a perspective you wouldn't have if you spent the time alone or only with your colleagues.

If you can't do this in real time, try to do it virtually, staying in touch with an individual (or even a class) via various kinds of communication software. To find out how to do this, ask your students and your school's tech coordinator. These people can also help you capture what you learn at the conference on video, on a blog, or in other ways and later share it with your colleagues who did not attend and with your class for their suggestions.

MORE WAYS TO HELP YOURSELF IMPROVE

There are many things to do to improve at being a partnering teacher, and you should try all of them, always looking for the ways that work best for you. Here are some additional suggestions:

Let Yourself Be Surprised

As teachers we often have an internal motto of "No surprises!" in the classroom. It is easier and things tend to go more smoothly when we prepare and control everything in advance as much as possible. Unfortunately, this is not necessarily the best learning strategy because we typically learn the most, not when we control things, but when we don't, and are surprised.

Do not be afraid to say to your students "Surprise me!" It can be by the tools they choose to use, the way they approach answering the guiding questions, the feedback they give, or anything else. Once your students find that you are seriously delighted by their creativity and inventiveness in answering the guiding questions, they will want to show you more of it.

Set Goals for Yourself

People typically make the most progress in changing when they set goals for themselves to achieve. Over 20 years ago, Stephen Covey set out to find out what makes people effective.

His methodology then was the same as the one I use with students now: talk to many of them, and look for commonalities in what they say. In his now famous (and highly recommended) book *The 7 Habits of Highly Effective People,* one of the first habits is to "begin with the end in mind." By this he means having, and visualizing, a goal whenever you start something. One way to set your goal for improving as a partnering teacher is to try to continually move along the 0–5 spectrum listed earlier, toward being a Level 5 partnering teacher. Since going from Level 0 (or wherever you are currently) to Level 5 is not something that can happen at once, setting an intermediate goal of perhaps one level per semester or year many be appropriate. Your goals, if they are to be reached, have to be realistic and doable.

Get Feedback From Students and Colleagues

There is no surer way to improve than by getting honest, constructive feedback on how you are actually doing. There are a number of ways to do this:

1. Ask your students. You are best off asking them specific questions such as these:
   - Do you think I talk too much when I teach?
   - What are your favorite things that I do? Your least favorite?
   - What are your pet peeves about my teaching?

2. Have colleagues you like and trust observe your class and give you feedback. Ask them questions like these:
   - What do I do that you think I'm unaware of?
   - What specifically could I do to improve?

3. Discreetly video your classes (e.g., by having someone set up a wireless video camera on the ceiling of your classroom or a tripod in the back). This has to happen often enough that you forget the camera is there and teach normally. Watch (preferably with a colleague) and learn! (We are all embarrassed when we see ourselves on video, especially the first time; the smart folks get over it.)

4. Have your students video you. They are likely doing it anyway—ask them if you can see it.

Strive to Eliminate Boredom

All the students I talk to report that they are bored in class some of the time—most report that they are bored more than half the time. But not in all classes or with all teachers. So I recommend striving to make your classes boredom-free zones.

Making your classes less boring rarely means becoming a better "performer" in front of the class. "I could turn cartwheels in front of my students and it wouldn't help," laments one teacher. But being more engaging almost certainly involves partnering well and having more student participation, more differentiation, and maximum student use of the technology available.

As always, I recommend first talking to your students about making your classroom boredom free. Solicit suggestions about what they find boring and other, less boring (to them) ways to accomplish your desired goals. Make sure you get everyone's opinion.

Second, do some research on your own online. Search for "boring" or "boring class," and see what videos you find. It should be enlightening.

Third, go back and review your students' passions. Think continually about ways to engage individuals and clusters of students around these passions. Get feedback from them about whether what you try works.

Fourth, think again about how to make your students' learning real, not just relevant.

Fifth, especially at first, frequently "take the class's temperature," that is, find out whether they are bored or not—during every class. As I have said, this can be as easy as having them hold up a red or green card.

Finally, iterate. Not everything you try will work, and you (and your students) will constantly have new ideas.

As teachers and students make progress in adopting and adapting to the partnering pedagogy, the improved results will almost certainly speak for themselves. But of course, we live in a world obsessed with numbers and formal assessments. And being able to demonstrate progress toward our goal of better educated students, when done reasonably, is no bad thing. In the final chapter of this book I discuss assessment—of students, teachers, administrators, and even parents—and what it means in, and for, partnering.

10

Assessment in the Partnering Pedagogy

Guiding Questions

1. What are the roles of assessment, in general and in partnering?

2. What types of assessment are most useful for partnering students?

3. How can we assess the progress of all participants in the educational process?

As we look to assess our partnering students, let's begin by stepping back and thinking for a minute about what assessment is for. Most of the assessment we do these days is for sorting and comparing. That is, tests allow us to rank individuals, schools, and even countries by who is "ahead" and who is "behind." Almost all of it is based on average scores, across a class, social group, city, and so on.

This comparison is great for managers and politicians. They want to see averages rise. They want to see schools that had ranked lower rank higher. They want to see adequate yearly progress. It is also great for admissions officers, whether we are talking about admission to college, the military, or jobs. In fact, standardized testing started in the military in World War I.

But does any of this really help individual students? In my judgment it does not—at least not directly. What an individual student is (or should be) interested in is not whether his or her class is improving, or even whether he or she has moved up or down in relation to the rest of the class. An individual student should be interested in the answers to these questions: Am I improving? Am I learning? Are my skills getting better? Am I well prepared to face my future? What should I be working on?

USEFUL ASSESSMENT

Beyond Just Summative and Formative

The usual types of assessment we talk about are summative and formative. Summative is the single mark or score on a test, with no other feedback. This is what is used for ranking and comparison. Although perhaps useful for some purposes, it is of little use to a student other than as either an ego booster (or, too often, an ego deflator).

A more useful type of assessment is formative. This is assessment with feedback, the purpose of which is to help a student improve. Formative assessment includes papers and tests marked with comments. The trouble with most formative assessment in our schools is that the feedback comes too late and is too far removed from the creation of the work and the decisions students made to be useful. So despite teachers' often herculean efforts to mark and return homework or tests, the feedback does little to actually help students improve. Because assessment is only truly formative if feedback is actually read, thought about, and acted upon.

Ipsative Assessment

There are, however, other types of useful assessment. One is ipsative, which refers to beating your personal best.[25] Ipsative is the kind of assessment used, for example, in sports. No one gives you a number or letter grade (except in a few types of competition); it is your results that matter. Improvement is just that: doing better—going faster, scoring more points, or whatever the sport requires. Increments are carefully measured. People work hard to shave a tenth or even a hundredth of a second off their best time. Careful statistics and records are kept on individual performances (such as the baseball batting average, or the pitcher's earned run average.)

We do have some ipsative assessments in our schools; they go by the phrases "raising your grade" and "doing better on the next test." Unfortunately, we rarely break performance down into individual skills, although some teachers, schools, and report cards have taken to doing this. It would be useful for partnering teachers to do even more of this, in the same way a complex video game shows players all the different skills they need to get better at, and lets them know exactly where they stand on each one as they strive to move up through the levels of the game.

Peer Assessment

Another kind of useful assessment is peer assessment, which involves having students' work assessed by a group of their classmates or peers in other places. The value of peer assessment is twofold. On the one hand, if done well it can give students a feeling that their work truly has an audience and that that audience (i.e., their peers) cares about their work. And it can also give students some appreciation of the work of their peers and classmates, and where their own work stands in relation.

Peer assessment is easily facilitated by digital technology. For today's students, peer assessment works particularly well with work posted online and online portfolios. Students can see the work of their classmates (or peers in other places) and give feedback. By posting their work online—on blogs, YouTube, or other sharing sites—it becomes easy for students to invite comments from other students. Since comments can be made public, this extends the value of peer evaluation far beyond the traditional "exchange papers with your neighbor."

> **Check It Out!**
>
> Here are some resources for peer assessment:
>
> www.tnellen.com/cybereng/38.html
>
> www.tnellen.com/cybereng/peer.html

Real-World Assessment

Feedback and assessment become "real world" as we extend the meaning of *peer* around the globe, and as students in different schools, cities, and countries give feedback on our partnering classes' online work. Students often welcome this world feedback and seek it out on their own. Blog posts can often be commented on by people anywhere, and students can see the number of comments each post gets. When a student makes a how-to video and then posts it online, getting feedback is a great assessment of their learning. And equally important, doing so adds to the pool of videos available to others. Many students offer up their budding language skills on YouTube for public feedback.

> **Check It Out!**
>
> Here are some language students who have put themselves online in order to get feedback:
>
> www.youtube.com/watch?v=G8RCVg E1CjQ
>
> www.youtube.com/watch?v=VYbUjg bjzCE

A type of real-world assessment often used in business is "360-degree" assessment, whereby a person's work is assessed not only by his or her bosses and peers but also by the people who work for him or her. An equivalent for teachers would be if you were assessed each year not only by your administrators, but also by your fellow teachers and your students.

Two fields that have long used real-world peer evaluation with great success are studio art and architecture. Education programs in these fields typically hold regular critiques (sometimes known as charettes) during which everyone, students and teachers alike, gets to give an opinion of each student's work, with the emphasis on constructive feedback. By doing such critiquing on a regular basis (and having it done to their work), students learn to be better critics of others, as well as to accept criticism of their own efforts offered in the spirit of mutual respect and making work better. It would benefit both students and teachers to use this type of assessment more in all classrooms.

Check It Out!

Guidelines for student critiques can be found at http://artsedge.kennedy-center .org/content/3338/.

Many teachers have found that just knowing they are writing or creating for a real audience (and will receive real feedback and assessment) motivates students to increase the quality of their work.

Self-Assessment

The final kind of useful assessment I will discuss—self-assessment—is by far, I think, the most important. Unfortunately, it is the least used in our classrooms. Self-assessment is critical because it is what today's students will need and use for the rest of their lives in order to control their actions. While in the future they may get some assessments annually at work, most of what they need will be to say to themselves (just as we do, or should), "This is an area where I'm weak. How can I get better?" The more we help our students understand when and how to do this self-assessment on their own, the better off they will be. If they rely only on their teachers, or others, as outside arbiters of their progress, they will be at a loss for how to assess themselves and improve for the rest of their lives.

Assessing Students With Their Tools

There is one more thing that needs to be mentioned in any discussion of assessment in partnering. More and more, partnering students should be evaluated with their tools. This means that they should be evaluated while using the same tools that they carry with them and, hopefully, use daily in their work: calculators, computers, and cell phones. In the 21st century, when students have increasing access to these digital tools and are increasingly integrating those tools into the learning process, it makes little sense, when evaluating students, to take those tools away. Can you imagine a doctor being asked to make a heart evaluation but being told not to use his or her stethoscope?

Most math educators have finally realized that calculators and computers—once students have learned to use them properly—actually enhance students' mathematical capabilities. What is positive about allowing these tools in assessment is that it forces both students and teachers to focus on the true fundamentals of why and how we calculate, rather than on just memorization and mechanical algorithms. Although there are still some tests in which these tools are not allowed, the direction of change is clear.

Similar attitude changes with regard to tools are happening in all other subjects. Teachers are increasingly allowing students to use their computers and/or cell phones during tests and exams. Although this may seem odd or make little sense if the tests are about facts students can easily look up (unless everyone has equal access, and the test is about speed or efficiency), if the tests involve gathering facts and evidence from the Web and drawing and supporting conclusions, digital tools should enhance students' ability to demonstrate their understanding (which is, hopefully, what we are testing).

Obviously, as such changes take place, current definitions of "cheating" will need to be changed to accommodate these tools and define their acceptable use. But that is not a bad thing, or even a new phenomenon. In many colleges and universities, and some high schools, the use of tools during certain exams has been going on for years—giving so-called open-book tests is standard operating procedure. So why not give "open-phone tests," as some schools are already doing?

PARTNERING TIP

Think about the situations in which evaluating students with their tools might be a good idea. Ask your students about this. Are they in favor of it? How would they deal with the various issues that might arise?

What do you and your students think of open-phone tests? (Remember the student mentioned on page 105? During one of my presentations, the high school senior told me, "Most of our tests already are open-phone tests—you guys just don't know it!") Think of experiments you and your partnering students might do in this area. Try creating and giving an open-phone test in each of your classes. Discuss the results with your students, and then iterate to make it more effective.

ASSESSING STUDENTS' PROGRESS

In partnering, therefore, the best ways to assess students are to

- give students necessary and helpful feedback (formative),
- encourage them to do better and better (ipsative),
- provide them with feedback from fellow students (peer),
- include evaluations from a global audience (real-world),
- get them to understand their own progress (self-assessment),
- allow them to use their tools (21st century), and
- because we have to, satisfy the outside world by using standardized tests (summative).

Addressing Assessment Fears

The number-one fear that teachers and administrators (as well as parents) often express about partnering and assessment is that students learning in this new way will not do as well on current standardized exams. The second, related fear is that all the new and different things that students are doing, and the skills (verbs) they are learning through partnering will some-how not count, because they are not tested.

The first of these fears is unjustified; the second is at least partially real, and is a concern that we can and should do something about.

The reason I say that the fear that students will not do as well is unjustified is that everyone I have talked to who is in a position to know says the opposite. I have heard a great many teachers and principals (mostly from charter schools, where partnering is more widely practiced) express that partnering students in fact do better on exams, because they are more engaged in their learning. I don't know that anyone has collected data on this in a systematic, quantitative way as yet, but it is something that should be attempted (with the caveat—usually ignored—that quantitative data are easily manipulable to support one's point).

The fear that important skills go unmeasured is, however, justified, because they do. We need to upgrade and expand almost all our assessments to include more skills-based learning around all the partnering verbs. Organizations such as the Partnership for 21st Century Skills (www.21stcenturyskills.org) are working on ways to measure and assess a variety of these skills, and partnering teachers should be aware of their, and others', efforts.

ASSESSING TEACHERS' PROGRESS

I have already referred to teachers self-assessing their own partnering skills, that is, figuring out where they are along the partnering continuum (or progress line) and setting goals to move ahead. Believing as I do that self-assessment is the best and most important kind of assessment, we could just leave it there: every partnering teacher can and should self-assess, at least annually, on the partnering criteria. But it is also important to make that self-assessment known, certainly to administrators and probably to students and parents as well, and to see if it jibes with the assessments of others, particularly of the partnering students.

One could conceivably do this sharing of where people stand through a system of colors (preferably noncontroversial ones with no other meanings) or other symbols. So one might call the six partnering levels Red, Orange, Yellow, Green, Blue, and Indigo, where teachers and students are striving "across the rainbow" toward the "unattainable violet." Both teachers and students could somehow display the colors and be recognized when they move up to another level.

Another function of the colors, and the public knowledge, would be that those who are further along down the road to partnering could more easily find and help those who aren't as far along to help them move forward. Such a buddy system is best if voluntary, but it could also be imposed if progress is unacceptably slow.

It is, of course, important that progress along the partnering scale not be wholly conflated with being a "good" teacher. There are many qualities that make a teacher good, and the ability to partner—important as it is—is only one of them. There are many other key qualities, including empathy for students (i.e., liking kids); knowledge of, enthusiasm for, and being up-to-date in one's subject area; and ability to relate to and deal with all the interested parties (including colleagues, administrators, and parents). A teacher may have many of these qualities, but to have them all requires dedication and effort. It's a lot like golf—for a professional golfer to win even a couple of major tournaments requires many different skills (driving, chipping, putting, concentrating, decision making under pressure, etc.). Most professional teachers are, like most professional golfers, "journeymen" or "journeywomen" (in golf terms), that is, far better than any nonprofessional, but always striving to do what they do better.

Because the skills of partnering are enormously important to students, all teachers should be motivated to get better at them. It has been suggested by some that progress along the partnering continuum be made part of teachers' annual assessment, with expectations for progress set and actual progress reviewed. Whether this is done formally or not depends on each individual school and district, but it is certainly something that is worth thinking about.

ASSESSING ADMINISTRATORS' PROGRESS

Given the way the U.S. education system works, school administrators are, as I write, all over the board in their support of partnering as a pedagogical goal. I speak often to groups of "converted" administrators—those who listen to kids, see the future, and are willing and even eager to move toward it. But I also hear often from teachers trying to accomplish many of the things outlined in this book that they feel unsupported, or held back by their administrators, as they try to move forward on their own toward partnering.

Thus it is worth having some form of assessment for administrators as supporters of the partnering pedagogy. One could certainly ask the following questions:

- Do administrators (in a school or district) believe partnering is the way to go?
- Is there consensus? If not, where is the discord?
- Do administrators know where each of their teachers stands on the partnering continuum?
- In what ways do administrators support partnering?
- In what ways do administrators support teachers who are looking to partner more?
- In what ways do administrators help recalcitrant teachers change?
- In what ways do administrators support partnering students and their parents?

Based on the answers to these questions, one could certainly rate administrators on their propensity toward, and support of, partnering. But who would do this? It needs to be done throughout the administrative hierarchy, from the school board on down.

ASSESSING PARENTS' PROGRESS

Parents, as everyone knows, are crucial to their kids' education. Today most parents are caught, just as we all are, in the great changes of our times, and most are as perplexed as the rest of us about what to do. Parents all want the best for their children, including the best education possible. Yet today it is far from clear what that means. Parents hear of and see a number of often-controversial educational changes being undertaken in their children's classrooms, and it is not surprising that a number of them should ask, "Why all the changes? Is partnering really what my kid needs to succeed and get to college? Why can't my kid be educated in the same way I was?"

It is part of the partnering teacher's job to help parents recognize just how much the world has changed, and with it their children. Partnering teachers need to help parents understand that to meet the needs of the future (both society's and their children's), 21st century students require a different type of education than their parents got—even if the parents think they got a good one.

Both partnering students and partnering teachers need strong parental support in order to get the job done. Here, therefore, are my recommendations to partnering teachers regarding parents:

- Involve your students' parents as much as you can. Try thinking of them as your students as well, that is, as people you are educating. It would be great for the school to hold an open house where the partnering work can be discussed; perhaps you can hold one for your students' parents. When you do this, have teachers, students, administrators, and parents around for a question-and-answer session with the audience.
- Use as much technology as you can to communicate to parents what you are doing, in whatever language(s) they speak. Partnering students can help make short videos to explain what you are doing, which you can share online (if parents have access), via CD, or even via students' cell phones. Your students can set up a multimedia blog or newsletter of their work and show it to their parents at home (if there is a computer) or at the library. As digital TVs achieve higher penetration, they can be used to play these as well.
- Feel free to share parts of this book (and other books supporting partnering) with your students' parents, and try to get copies put in the school and local public libraries. Encourage parents to read about partnering and the changes in 21st century students and learning.
- Encourage your students to share their positive classroom experiences frequently with their parents, and their enthusiasm, once it emerges. You can even, as a project, have simulated conversations with parents and talk with your students about how they might answer their parents' objections, if they have any. It is their children's enthusiasm for school that will ultimately be the strongest persuader.
- Invite parents, as appropriate, to come into your classroom, either in person or virtually, and to participate on student teams.

A Checklist for Parents of Partnering Students

Finally, consider handing out to parents a checklist of what they can do to help their children and letting them self-assess how well they are helping their children learn. This checklist might consist of an overall self-assessed grade, plus separate grades in the following areas:

- Listening to their children
- Helping their children
- Encouraging their children

- Participating in parent-teacher meetings and other parent events
- Sharing their knowledge by coming to school and talking with students

There might also be a place in such an evaluation (or as a separate exercise) for students to write or say, "Here's what I wish I got more of/less of from my parent."

ASSESSING SCHOOLS' PROGRESS

How do we evaluate a partnering school? First, of course, we have to acknowledge that the standard (and increasingly standardized) ways of evaluating schools aren't going to go away and that partnering schools will be evaluated using the same criteria as all others. But that, in fact, is good news because we can expect to see a number of positive results as a school moves more and more toward partnering as a full-time pedagogy. These include the following:

1. Rising test scores—when partnering is done correctly, students will be (1) happier with what they are doing; (2) more engaged in their own learning; (3) clearer, through the guided questions, about what they need to know; and (4) practicing many more skills on their own and with their peers, and therefore will be more effective learners

2. Much more quality student work to post and be proud of—online and off

3. Teachers sharing successes and working together much more than in a traditional school

4. Much better teacher-student relations—essentially those of partners

When implemented well, partnering schools and classrooms should consistently be among the very best.

ASSESSING OUR NATION'S PROGRESS, AND THE WORLD'S

Much has been made recently about America "falling behind" other countries in education. I am not sure I totally agree, either with the diagnosis or with some of the proposed solutions. The comparisons seem to depend on rankings on supposedly comparative tests and on less than desirable graduation rates in U.S. high schools and colleges.

While both of these measures are useful data, they do not tell the whole story and—much worse—they lead to wrong prescriptions about what to do about education. To understand why, ask yourself the following questions:

- Will the United States (or any country) be better off in 2050 with a population that is confident that it can compete on international tests, or a population well versed in 21st century tools for problem solving—a population that knows that it can, in any situation, figure out the right thing to do, get it done, do it with others, do it creatively, and continually get better?

- Will the United States (or any country) be better off in 2050 with a population that can read and write at a ninth-grade level (assuming we could ever attain that, which is highly unlikely) and in which every person has at least an associate's degree (ditto), or with a population that is confident that it can make our increasingly complex digital machines do what they need (i.e., can program at some level) and is highly entrepreneurial?

Being "behind" truly depends on what you measure. As Steven Johnson pointed out recently in an article in *Time,* the United States is responsible for just about all of the Internet innovations in recent years.[26] So in some important areas, we have been and continue to be ahead, and being behind in other areas, such as learning the old-fashioned "school" stuff, may not matter. That depends, of course, what students do instead of learning it, but it is very important that we come to grips with the fact that the things we are required to teach today may not be the things our students need for the future at all, and most of it (likely 80 percent by the Pareto rule) almost certainly isn't.

And finally, why do we insist on measuring learning nation by nation, rather than measuring the world as a whole? Such an approach only encourages competition and fighting, and neglects and discourages the "world" learning that the technologies of the 21st century are so quickly enabling. Education is an area in which we should all be cooperating, trying hard to raise the level not just for Americans, but for every child in the world.

Conclusion

The (Not Too Distant) Future of Education

> ### Guiding Questions
>
> 1. How can we create a better curriculum for 21st century students?
> 2. What are the essential skills our students need to learn in order to be successful?
> 3. What should future schools and education look like?

Painted with a very broad brush, education, in the period up though the Renaissance, was done mainly through home teaching, apprenticeship, and, for the lucky, tutoring. The Enlightenment brought public schooling and the idea of education for all (in some places). The Industrial Revolution brought standardization. The 20th century added standardized measurement and testing. And the 21st century is bringing us partnership. The future will no doubt bring something new, including, perhaps, students learning totally on their own and in virtual groups of their own choosing.

This arc is in line with the gradual emancipation of young people, comparable in some sense to the great emancipation of women, particularly in the West. Until not too long ago, the opinions of half the world (i.e., women) were not given much weight or even considered in many areas. That has now, at least in the West, changed immensely. (In the world as a whole, however, there is still more work to be done.)

Today, the opinions of a different half of the world (i.e., those under the age of 25) are often given short shrift. But that too is changing rapidly. With the advent of digital technology, and the realization that, in the modern world, young people have a very real and equal contribution to make to their elders—at the same time that they learn from them—new forms of social organization, such as teaching through partnering, have emerged. This newfound mutual respect between young and old is clearly the way of the future.

Once we accept this, however, two large issues remain:

1. What our students need to learn for the future is, to an enormous degree, different than what we are teaching now.

2. Future education is a worldwide issue, not just a state or national one.

Given that, let me conclude with some future-oriented observations.

WHAT SHOULD A NEW CURRICULUM BE?

Essential 21st Century Skills

We have seen how important individual passions are, particularly as we move out of an industrial era into a much more individualized one. But it is not enough, of course, for students to merely find or recognize their passions, or even to have them recognized by a teacher. Students need to be able to use their passions to motivate themselves to achieve 21st century success. To do that they need skills that will be relevant and helpful in the 21st century.

What are these skills? Do we currently teach them?

My own take on 21st century skills is to focus more on verbs, as mentioned in previous chapters, in the following way:

The Five Essential Metaskills for the 21st Century

The Goal: To Be Able to Follow One's Passions as Far as One's Abilities Allow

In order to do this, no matter what the future brings, individuals must master the following skills and subskills:

1. Figuring out the right thing to do
   a. Behaving ethically
   b. Thinking critically
   c. Setting goals
   d. Having good judgment
   e. Making good decisions

2. Getting it done
   a. Planning
   b. Solving problems
   c. Self-directing

    d. Self-assessing
    e. Iterating

3. Doing it with others
    a. Taking leadership
    b. Communicating/interacting with individuals and groups (especially using technology)
    c. Communicating/interacting with machines (i.e., programming)
    d. Communicating/interacting with a world audience
    e. Communicating/interacting across cultures

4. Doing it creatively
    a. Adapting
    b. Thinking creatively
    c. Tinkering and designing
    d. Playing
    e. Finding your voice

5. Constantly doing it better
    a. Reflecting
    b. Being proactive
    c. Taking prudent risks
    d. Thinking long term
    e. Continually improving through learning

Were we to incorporate all of these skills in every subject, starting from elementary school, having our students, over and over, figure out the right thing to do, get it done, do it with others, do it creatively, and continuously do it better—then by the time they left us, students would have practiced these essential skills hundreds or even thousands of times and would likely have internalized them as an effective way of doing things.

There is no better preparation I can think of for the uncertainties our students will face in their 21st century lives.

USING THE PARTNERING PEDAGOGY WITH NEW CURRICULA

Whatever their final form, because many people are thinking about and working on them, new 21st century curricula will eventually emerge. The first stage of curricular change—the one that we're in as I write this—is to graft new skills, particularly technology fluency and multimedia literacy (and occasionally other useful things such as financial literacy), onto the curriculum that we currently teach.

The problem with this is that we already teach too much (or try to). Most teachers have had the experience of reaching the end of a semester or school year when only partway through the curriculum and textbook. We really do have to form "deletion committees" to see what we can omit, or stick into "reference." Latin, for example, has finally disappeared from most public school curricula. Not that it's not important—particularly to some—but there are other things that are more important for all. (Plus, as I understand it, we just ran out of teachers.) There are many other things that, albeit controversially, we can delete from the curriculum or teach only in special ways or cases. Prime candidates include cursive handwriting, the long division algorithm, and most controversially, memorizing the multiplication tables. Eliminating just those three would literally give us years of time to teach kids more future-oriented things such as the *why* and *when* of math (rather than just the *how*), programming, and the metaskills listed in the previous section.

I often remind people who think kids will always need the multiplication tables "in their heads" that we once made kids memorize the positions of the sun in the sky in order to tell the time. Then someone invented the watch, and we all just strapped them to our wrists. Today, we no longer teach kids to "tell time," we teach them to *read the machine*, with, of course, huge gains in accuracy. Our kids now have continuous access to "free" calculators in their phones and other gadgets—these have become give-away devices and are ubiquitous. We need to teach students to use those machines properly and effectively. Partnering teachers should support such forward movements and not get stuck forever teaching a "backup" curriculum (see www.marcprensky.com/writing/Prensky-Backup_Education-EdTech-1-08.pdf), spending too much time teaching skills that will rarely if ever be useful in the future world that today's students will live in.

As new and more appropriate curricula emerge (and, I hope, groups with some financial and political clout, such as the Gates Foundation, will lead the way), those curricula will almost certainly be more skills (i.e., verb) oriented and less method (i.e., noun) oriented. This is great news for the partnering pedagogy, which, as we have seen, focuses more on the verbs than on the nouns and expects the best nouns to continually change.

I hope and expect that there will be many experiments over the coming years in using the partnering pedagogy with new additions to the curriculum, such as programming and game-related skills. At the same time, I hope and expect that the partnering pedagogy will help educators put the emphasis back on some of the basic skills (verbs) that have been neglected or put aside for lack of time to teach them. You can go back to the list of verbs in Table 2.1 and decide for yourself what some of these should be.

CREATING SCHOOLS WITH PARTNERING IN MIND

Many places are thinking about building or creating new schools as younger populations grow, old schools wear out, and new technologies and ideas come into prominence in education. What should the builders be thinking about, particularly with the partnering pedagogy in mind?

The most radical thought of all, of course, is to ask whether school buildings will even be necessary in the future. In the coming technological age, they almost certainly are not for some types of learning, but they still may be for others. To the extent that schools exist to keep kids safe so parents can work, we need buildings to house kids (until we figure out other, technological solutions to this, which, in time, we will).

And to the extent that we want our kids to participate in drama, filmmaking, art, sports, and, in fact, any physical group activities, they will need places to do this. Note, however, that many "group" things formerly only done face-to-face can now be done as well—or even better—remotely. Examples include software development, report writing, and many types of collaboration.

Another argument often advanced for having schools—socialization—may in fact be an argument against them. While some students clearly enjoy and thrive on school, many students report that the social experience of school, particularly high school, is a difficult and terrible one and that socialization is best left for after school.

Do We Need Classrooms?

But if we assume that, for the immediate future at least, school buildings are in fact necessary, what kinds do we build? The most immediate question, I think, is, Do we build classrooms in them?

This is much less radical a thought than the idea of not building schools at all because as far as I can see—especially with partnering and all the new technology of the 21st century—the classroom has been a dying educational organizational format for many years. Most educators have recognized that 21st century education requires much more flexibility than an arrangement of fixed classrooms can provide. In addition, the idea of the classroom as a walled city, where no one but the teacher and the students (and an occasional visitor) ever really know what goes on inside, is coming to an end, with glass walls and increasing numbers of video cameras replacing secrecy in many classrooms. This is clearly the wave of the future. So building more fixed classrooms only keeps the old system on life support and prolongs its agony.

But what might be an alternative to classrooms? For a clue, we should look to the hotel/convention center/conference industry. People in that industry realized some time ago that the very same meetings or conferences may require, at various times, places for groups of thousands, hundreds, tens, and sometimes only two to four people, as well as some places for people to work individually. They also realized that these needs might change every day or even every hour. So they created the flexible, soundproof partitions, allowing most spaces to be reconfigured radically, typically in under 10 minutes. Why don't our schools have a similar arrangement?

And if our schools do become this flexible, who will design and decide on the day-to-day and minute-to-minute configurations? Again, it comes back to partnering. I have seen new schools hire architects to create fancy new spaces and supposedly lovely ergonomic furniture for students—without ever consulting them. But I have also seen students highly involved in using computer-aided design (CAD) and other software to design their own spaces, layouts, configurations, and even furniture, in one case, with a weekly competition to reconfigure the school's public lobby.

In the 21st century, we can no longer succeed by doing things *to* our students; we have to do everything *with* them. Partnering works best when both groups contribute and work together to create what is best for all. No one would argue, I think, for student participation in the design of the teachers' lounge. But in the design of the spaces they use every day, both students and teachers should have a say as well as the flexibility to change configurations to meet the learning needs of the moment.

TOWARD A 21ST CENTURY EDUCATION FOR ALL

In a world where half the people are under the age of 25, education is still a very unequal and haphazard thing. Many still don't have access to it in any form. In quite a few poor countries, just getting young people in the presence of a teacher is a huge positive step, and people are still struggling to do this. Whatever our faults, we in the United States and other countries in the developed world are also incredibly lucky for our educational opportunities.

One of the great opportunities that technology has the potential to bring us is the ability for those who have more, and who know more, to help those who don't. Where once a student in a class in, say, Kansas had no hope of directly connecting with and helping someone in, say, Mali, today it is as easy as turning on your computer. Students can connect safely with peers in almost all countries via tools like ePals. Mobile and cell phones have now penetrated almost two-thirds of the world, and when we finally realize how to use these devices thoughtfully for education, they can open up worlds to our students that have been totally closed in the past.

A great many of the discussions we currently have around education in the developed world (and I can tell you from my travels that the discussions are very similar in all the countries) are, it seems to me, incredibly narrowly focused and shortsighted. What are our scores? How do we compare? How do we get kids more interested in what *we* want? How can we get them more degrees? We hear almost nothing about student passions and students learning the skills they need to reach their potential.

My hope in writing a book on partnering is not just to get teachers thinking about a new pedagogy, but to get them thinking more broadly about education in general. Is it just for tomorrow, or is it for the rest of our students' lives? Do we need to teach them things that even we agree they don't need to know, except in order to pass the test? When we see the bored looks on their faces, do we just turn away and blame them, or do we change?

I conclude with a wonderful line from one of my student panelists last year. At the end of the hour-long discussion between eight students on stage and several hundred teachers in the audience, this student panelist turned to me and asked if it was OK if he asked me a personal question.

"Yes," I answered.

"How old are you?" he inquired?

"I'm 63," I replied.

The young man then turned to the audience and said, "If he's 63 and can do this, so can each of you. You just have to apply yourself!"

I have every faith not only that you *can* do this, but that you will, both for the good of your students and for your own benefit as well. So, with apologies to Mister Spock of *Star Trek* . . .

Go forth, and partner. ☺

Notes

1. Educational writers, from John Dewey to today's Web 2.0 advocates (e.g., Ian Jukes, Alan November, Will Richardson, David Warlick) to advocates of case-, problem-, and inquiry-based learning, have all suggested the need for some form of new partnership between students and teachers, involving much less telling by teachers and much more doing by students.

2. I have heard this from a great number of people, including Dr. Edith Ackermann (a former student of Piaget), Dr. Derrick DeKerchove (a former student of Marshall McLuhan), and many others. I was told by a children's TV executive that "kids getting older younger" was a longtime internal slogan at MTV.

3. Ibid.

4. From the opening sequence of the *Star Trek* television show.

5. Dewey, J. (1963). *Experience and education.* New York, NY: Collier Books. (Original work published 1938.)

6. Johnson, L. F., Smith, R. S., Smythe, J. T., & Varon, R. K. (2009). *Challenge-based learning: An approach for our time.* Austin, TX: New Media Consortium.

7. Boss, S., & Krauss, J. (2007). *Reinventing project-based learning: Your field guide to real-world projects in the digital age.* Washington, DC: International Society for Technology in Education.

8. Tim Rylands in the United Kingdom.

9. Hu, W. (2007, May 4). Seeing no progress, some schools drop laptops. *New York Times.* Retrieved from http://www.nytimes.com/

10. Nicole Cox, instructor, in a report by the Rochester Institute of Technology:

I divided the class into discussion groups of four–six people. Students posted their responses to the readings online within their own group, and then had the opportunity to read the responses from their group "mates." Once they'd read all the responses within their group, they were asked to write a reaction to one other response.... There was also a definite improvement in writing skills—again, I think they taught each other. Most groups had at least one student whose writing was actually quite polished (both in content and style), and they would sort of lead by example. Using proper grammar and a more academic tone to make a point somehow makes it seem more valid than one made in all lowercased colloquialisms. I also think a form of "peer pressure" forced students into more vigorous participation. Students whose work was not on par with the work of the other members of the group would sometimes be "shunned"—left out of the discussion. As participation was an important part of a student's grade, those students soon learned the level of acceptable production in order to be considered a viable member of the group. (Retrieved from http://online.rit.edu/faculty/blended/final_report.pdf)

11.   Mabry Middle School, Mabry, Georgia.

12.   Ingo Schiller, parent of two children at Newsome Park Elementary School, in Newport News, Virginia. Curtis, D. (2001, November 11). Real-world issues motivate students. *Edutopia.* Retrieved from http://www.edutopia.org/magazine

13.   Johnson, L. F., Smith, R. S., Smythe, J. T., & Varon, R. K. (2009). *Challenge-based learning: An approach for our time.* Austin, TX: New Media Consortium. Page 10.

14.   The term *passion-based learning* was, as far as I know, first articulated by John Seely Brown, formerly of Xerox and its Palo Alto Research Center, now with the University of Southern California, although others are using it as well.

15.   De Bono, E. (1985). *Six thinking hats.* Boston, MA: Little, Brown.

16.   http://web.pacific.edu/x7375.xml

17.   http://www.northeastern.edu/admissions/reallife/index.html

18.   http://www.coe.edu/academics/rhetoric/rhetoric_reallife

19.   *Frankengenes* was made at Mabry Middle School, in Mabry, Georgia, as part of a program started by then-principal Tim Tyson.

20.   David A. Kolb (born 1939) is an American educational theorist and a professor of organizational behavior in the Weatherhead School of Management at Case Western Reserve University, in Cleveland, Ohio. He is known for his Learning Loop of action, observation (feedback), reflection, abstraction.

21.   http://serc.carleton.edu/introgeo/socratic/second.html

22.   Jude A. Rathburn, PhD, Lubar School of Business, University of Wisconsin–Milwaukee. http://4edtechies.wordpress.com/2009/12/17/integrating-emerging-technologies-into-instruction

23.   http://www.ldresources.org/2004/11/05/suggestions-for-helping-learning-disabled-students-to-write

24.   Johnson, L. F., Smith, R. S., Smythe, J. T., & Varon, R. K. (2009). *Challenge-based learning: An approach for our time.* Austin, TX: New Media Consortium. Page 33.

25.   http://www.encyclo.co.uk/define/Ipsative%20Assessment

26.   Johnson, S. (2009, June 5). How Twitter will change the way we live. *Time.* Retrieved from http://www.time.com/time/business/article/0,8599,1902604,00.html

Index

Page references followed by (table) indicate a table; followed by (figure) indicate an illustrated figure.

CORWIN
A SAGE Company

The Corwin logo—a raven striding across an open book—represents the union of courage and learning. Corwin is committed to improving education for all learners by publishing books and other professional development resources for those serving the field of PreK–12 education. By providing practical, hands-on materials, Corwin continues to carry out the promise of its motto: **"Helping Educators Do Their Work Better."**